# LIP SERVICE

# LIP SERVICE

Bruce Andrews

Coach House Books

first edition

CANADIAN CATALOGUING IN PUBLICATION DATA

Andrews, Bruce, 1948 –
 Lip service

Poems.
ISBN 1-55245-063-5

1. Title.

PS 3551.N423L56 2001          811'.54          C2001-930515-X

# CONTENTS

# EARTH

## EARTH I

𝔇ᴇᴀʀ ...

moves
buffing beams
total in parts lights back.
Many short words
I don't want to
get over you circumlocution for Paradise
— passively possessibly inaudibly
handwritten I didn't
write it down *enables* transitory strenuously concealed;
word's octobering memoir deadbeated
lacteal monogram it's forbidden
to remember tool
at once enunciatory sash amnesia
I don't know now follow desire
I don't think I knew before.
You can't portray women as they really are
— grab at so unclear book eased farther behind.
You name it: the inner ritual image — forms
— reverse false, represents
other units hatching improperly
knuckles discouraged epousing the literal as quest
lavish lie plastered over with a layer of soon points
intellectual pancake justified with exactness.
Bodice gravure muscles in
do you copy? strap holds future up
— heraldry of.
Gameplan covets
drip drop fortless of course sound too is a thing.
Apostrophe's empty
lonely copies fragile squeak
no escapism from quotes,
the writer is talking about the panic
in own head heels a bargain air condescends
as consummate air vulnerably lettered.
Dim aeons literature as raffle? put paper
in typewriter because you have a problem? — finite
fine.

## EARTH 2

Served birth light spoils
night at center fuck opposites blunt
                    fluff of orbit,
        eye baits on line faint and trivial
                                    undernourished connotations
                        physical factual spirit spoke
the deeds in flesh alone all prommed up
                        trick gaze wax to avoid thought
                        volunteer for objects gestured instead
'telling' externals.
        Atmosphere's breakfront spiderwebs
of specious experience particled to orient by subduing
mystery hearsay forced exposure
                                    clouds out on bail
                        lining their peril wintered head could fell
timing clutter, flexible nocturnal tint eludes
                        to misinform
vibrating perplexes
shimmered into falsehood,
        dire transom flatters choice slat numbs
into foreground stained-glass mediatrix.
        Masturbation seems to have no effect at all
                        wed revolt glare gathering
                        coarse idleness only by report
this *homesickness* determined retro misdirected object
chickened dawn exporting datedless dessert,
        scotomizing hypnotized anticipatory eye
                                    reduce noise
                        forced mistake oculist toys
pluck out iris iconic bijou.
        Coloring do not bring about mild matters licit
                        intuitively drab stroke insert
concealment's gigantic conceit.
        Vanish sight Enough Said
                        perks out pokes
                        up however faint peters out
enclosed sparks;
        sudden frill light egregious
                        destiny mirrors
                        more gay tableaux vivants.

## EARTH 3

Smartly pointed wrote
eyesight to the blind repelling of eyewitnesses
                        palm in mist dumbbell pre-placement —
it's like paying pigeons to be in the trees above you —
                        nervous remote loop clung
milieu stupefied many times flattering anti-intellect,
                                reasonless effaces
                        deal inner void every paragraph
prejudices biped bystanders, get out your cream thresher.
    Reduce needless float wielded false disdain Result
it's a dream of biography, bask in leaning
                        all that innocent bustle consort
                        everlasting spurtings
without invite boast in the stars.
    Fact mock
                        lowest threshold cortical prudence
shouting down synapse lies, remainders to myself
makes one shudder etymologically
with words — the complex rhetoric strategy
wants to keep saying 'I'
                        disjoin by sleight
dial in guesses, slight of hand unsubdued.
    Body indescribable skylight erasure
                        novelty sand them bright to baste
                                up flat anti-nature
unembodied false anchors non-rotund escapism; full-less
                                little clairvoyant bulk,
                        swan's crayon
                        beehive nonsense.
    Of snakelike demeanor, though hummable,
give 'em stretch marks sweeting the exterior
                                doughnut-shaped shivering
by chance spin around in the pet proper,
    phoning butter shine attendant —
lamb in the basin, lamb at the bush.
    Won't you tell me how baffled here,
                                sing to sleeve,
accessory commotion.
    Forget of course
                        thought sickens heart

## EARTH 4

Admit the induce
extraneously episodic land-based ego, make-believe
press 'enter' button spool toward falsish
same retardant arbitrary, surface, counterfeit it's a fact
               lie facts out
               periodic blather illusion
burns its surrounding own as blue turns to gray
abrupt hole physiognomical fluff.
     Phony expressionism of lack of speed —
when they do penetrate the borders, they tend to disperse quickly
and look for a way out.
     Listening to swearing
               to listen harp in orifice
wordlette breviary
               spot that stresses itself
less switch than sacrosanct angel back in box
trick them into involutional dreams take stock as fact,
one hour of fallen merchandise
     any guy with a theory will do — I take off my gloves
before your lies; all set
               set all content exhausted pause head's
               unheard Truth, that skag levitate
tuning fork called truth matter sheen
humble reproof — ampitheaterall loud-shaped rumor-
                    compliance doesn't listen
               such steep marionette angle
alleviate home truths, just a figment of coercion.
     Fact or squashed guess? — dumbbell
               factually studded space tantrums
               all this confusing probability stuff
experience it like an intermediary impositive movable
               nor is it likely to be the last
               all whole teeming ego error
                    stilted rouser
tumult socializing unbearably finite
                    warrant nightmare idea
temporaries 'd show people so perverse,
     Center isolates — inadvertent
echo, enabling fallible
               harm reveals indigenous detail.

# EARTH 4

*Imprint*
                    hoop on blink dire scratch
appropriated just as euphemistically & *norm*
                    what's holding up extra
acrostically lowered
imitation of life.
    We discriminate to be fashionable
anxious poach false chance

                                        usage aggravates
                    paste by

                                name derided elastic men;
                    couldn't any inside — stab around in the dark
                    antennaed version doom has a manger
stories high.
    Energy gray low on cusp
laced up fait accompli — what is that
in it? — addiction to gravity,
operators are standing by;

## EARTH 5

Oₙₗy the 'preparations' are complete; the result
is empty spurious leverage
                              are you waiting for the translation?
                              animals with voice amplifiers
incensed so apt merely by relation.
     Don't dance
sweat belies

                                             shookless
                    arcfretquietfiatvisor
eerie doldrums;
     is as aim — folly vent
the bee-sting is not precise factual detail.
     Monotonous affinity
                    generic delicacy
abnormal proxy ignited subjected
                    fake gram seeded error
enterprised by its, hounded by it
                    carnal shutters point not meant
powerless against things
                                        verb fact amiss
slippage really believes I get killed through the ears:
will *the* please identify itself,
     telegraph askances close less likely
markprone syllabic con
release preview of affects
                         (and that this wasn't good news)
                              forfeit arc
                    unhorse misbalancing ideal rebuff
fictitious swerve incline
askew;
     indirect sentience, she's got that poodle tongue,
that thumbnail pant — sticky areas
                    duplicitous emergency —
cocktail imprint bank on wrong for now so slip
                    spasm's defense jacks the box:
let the pumps dart the dialing, nube, the hurt
is on — hungry matches will eat dirty liquid.
     Proof alibi lance diatribe
                    lie from the bottom of your heart
seldom from air lid air virtue's *victim*

## EARTH 5

alto assumption's voice

wound never breaks —

you never return, I never leave —

delicately channeled small is better epidermal *push*.

Shock, subtraction

detail trenches salt start circumstances of scrupulosity

text incarcerates — avenger from — atmospherelessly

aerial dupes over hum

what synth, sky

swoops wrong.

Flouts this

annulling finicky, magnified & magnificent:

give us home thrust

custody correct

hard-edged pastels semaphoring unconsciousness

homogeneous inverse to address

tint wire

physio-logically

askew on one's two legs.

## EARTH 6

Dear refine the line Sir: nobody wants you here, if you
want facts, discourage me from repeating yourself — without the
sign! — old luggage mouth nature learned by heart trick
connotes tremble enamor tints appall muffle group cue strictest
soon quick ignorance can't vouch,
    I cross my fingers emptied light foolish pitch indecisive
swoon from constipation of purchase, otherwise you can nickel-
&-dime yourself down cognitively, a previous unknown level
of *granularity* in the pastiche & hence untraceable, amphitheater
                devil with the rest quietist in captions.
    Vexed transmit denatured hint over show
foolscap horns on court tress balanced naught in apparition
vestiges do succumb absolute addresses
reach ourselves impractically cloistered
                      I don't know
        *zher ner kawngprahng pah* —
        *poovay voo mer trahdweer serssee*
        collage unnerved pleasant to be orated to
windmill to point stint with tips doctoring this fraud.
    Pensible, smoked out by
form in the shape of a rooster, uncertain distance
always avaricious koan cuties seldom
                pleasure spell slower chilling
drone this momently adjacent chew-toy to end all chew-toys —
these lies are
particularly ugly ones innocence cancels,
    the latest line
                fronting intuitions is not tonight — fickle
indecorums, surface grew decoys shellacked to a fault;
but I, connote me off, am too lavish peradventure
in this subject.
    Awardless trick start overdrawn
headdresses (or he addresses)
                helpless so to speak bifocal
                sorry to comet
fratricide of the unexpected pretty but not edible.
    Posthaste attention are scarce
                stuttered ether lame in lobes —
I like indoors, brain lumped over into the netted septic tank
& that's why attention span went off.

## EARTH 7

Your little guy
                    blanking on time pop
                    in extends jerk back prow for too long
                                    longitudinally inactive,
preposterous perceptible directly conceal
                    randomize seduction by cracks
mistake my in the meantime (there's no place like home)
palpably static,
        flowering standardization — Gal
                                    Curl
                                    And
                                    Set
                    adjacent deters
heedless reticular mute immense attendant ebbs & spells
                    pill of suppose
clumsiness blinking absorption 'annexed' organs,
                    I saw a huge white owl
                    swollen with blame
                    wings with priority surveil
                    having contracted a facial twitch
                    ruing the trunk,
        only when enveloped latent in the ganglia
gaze harasses, we don't notice
persons unless we've been introduced.
        Dream left me unconscious:
                            substantive spoon horn hose
                                    faded equinox
anxiety duel wrung into inhales
                    amniotic fallacy questioning the skin
                    shadowy scaffold by fluid retention.
        Decorative swoon
what squawk leaks awhile
orders the heart invaded truncated glans
overcathected mucus zone drowning margarita recipe pool —
meanwhile, you eavesdroppers can leave the gossip to me;
        mood-altering foretaste do unto you mole-eyed
quickies, troublesome closeness, mono mood indiscriminativity,
sudden dope squinting cleavage with fewer corpuscles,
        from doubling to wounding

16

to meet eligible singles
through Gutenberg's 'disturbance' —
floating roses
inside dark outside
dramatically lowered paws in advance
oval unfelt mirror
singe the friend yokable abounds.
Colliding excuse
alive or why bother? ...
give your heart a target: atmosphere represents itself
*in-the-face* sucking by blows to the head, synaesthetic I-
deal — where would you be without it?
Mutilation for whose benefit? — virtue
decorous gust hostiled upper, please go, fault procure
glassy-eyed adulators to the horizon.

B̶UT? …
  no soon tongue moves tongue
                dislodged in bird's blacking — I don't know
                what else there is, signs
                        stain fills out
                        an fills a
curried superfluity fizzle intercept INTERDICTED CONJECTURE
stochastic muddle oversees stoppage eloquence
                    = alibi prespotted I *think it cannot*
— salients froze granular distrust
                pride mistook if I've let you
say it once I've [stet] l̶e̶t̶ ̶y̶o̶u̶ ̶s̶a̶y̶ ̶i̶t̶,
  unanswers
true to white type betrays dots to talk ultimata
like an excretion on the surface of our molecule, barb, all
                shaved underrepresentation of the strange
                      spotless symbols
                statements soothe.
  *Difference.*
Grasp of the fallible coward dispelling her
                collapse in contingence, eternal dupes
overhead regretting suavier curvature momentarily opake
                *Body* — talk about skewed reasoning! —
malevolently secretive stoppered for pleasure.
  Voltage? …
  Polkadots inform
                        you will continue
to hear ringing exclusion steep omission comforts;
earliest fingers
                      suffer each instance
confusion is the soul confidential satisfying itself.
  Male executive
                I got the heading wrong extraneous gist
                stub swings tint to tinge degree
makes distinction, intermittent insufficiency
  *Brunette*
crossed volume supposed neath
                    harms haloed by absence
                brittle caution perspire deplores.

## EARTH 8

Manifesto glass
pleats transparent — locust that idea, the lunar pimp
cements a peep.
    Divert like conversing pamphlets with pop-up page regrets
falsify reactive stupor sponsors love
                    precluded, dread take its
                    intrusive hum convenient
explosive faults.

## EARTH 9

Watchword is
contrary 's falsity intuition
tilts lapped asleep, frontispiece
un-form sporadic
servile body in formation recess box
obliging
eclipsing
hum to fault standoffish
trespass, obstinate imaginations in a shop window;
arrows understood? —
indiscernible color nominal bender
what stint
hoop tilt glazes same swollen daubs
sturdy as a vacuum —
torso cure, what are you dripping at?
While time services
sulphurous cipher
while time surfaces —
why always rectangles? —
curt premium
until the real thing comes along.
Wet horse metric holy insulation
fusillades his light through evidential envy, formula patriarch
in whatsoever sleight masked crypto at odds
curiosity just a sexual pick-me-up.
Excuse collision:
aspiring basks
on alert spun drone literally licking the paper-
self-reflecting error.
Weak connote anti-intimate mathematical
retreat attentless
dervished fabric; material harping
antitype sympathy marry clear heat retracts
parallelogram on fingertip.
Ominous means intimate
nubile topology takes property's facial imprint, mirror's
infinity dwarfed into
optics for sale.
Transparent diction blows, transition, chalk still abnormal

## EARTH 9

prong disarming saints' leakage threshed passé passive glass sure
vaccinates the vision,
    sordid spatialized vicar of virtuals
the lessons of quiet — Don't Call Me —
immediacy of the flesh weighs heavily how it gets from zero
to one.

People are
so dense
you know don't you think thoughtlessness fracture
evolves? — pluck
pace cliented
content spread welcome slur
pillaring mnemonic divorce —
*ang kahrneh dahdrehss.*
Schism
Vestige
under the elms in particles deepens
power: awkward purchase, each comes on
as the other's debris.
Vines all the hooches
foot up at home foaled gapping
pollen workouts & introductory eggs.
Pathways to girth, phony wires labyrinthing lack of give
pours out too much.
Loco Delusive
binocular value split cross into
into dressing pump popper — incogitated.
Rope sinks to principle in-voiced beat
reprised by sign;
gad bite
elect pink tics what does know
sign that says image extending tool
fooled subtly folly slumbering.
Odds & ends partitioned as home scan fabrication
deletions in spirit conductability —
member born through her ass
niche design conform, or
the fewest,
vigilant corsage exceeds the symbol in reminding backtime
capillaried perpetual Byzantium.
*Mediatrix* suffice the small, dangler in
intricately plotted confront us
with gargantuan cream cakes trained by transmission.
Jigsaw is believing
the message *hides* a signal.
A mirror virgin fats himself with futures,
I didn't come here to leave.

# MOON

## MOON I

Bothersome that feelings fit others
                    glaring certainty a rendezvous
                    of copies nice to doodle up in style
embedded static counter-proof — well, I guess …
soft pet scald syllabic — exclusive figural hostage —
a single word from you would make me happy:
every sort of yellow is discernible stenographic
                    pre-insignia corsage caption
recapitulation;
        legible mouth
gest erases tongue dumber ink talking diagonals
and unmoved lips — watch them hard
from invisibility, I don't wish to be misunderstood —
                    speech as self-
                conspiratorial ettings
                    underline helps half cut for confidence
tricks & devices make up my mind to embalm
pushing is such easy prey;
        Charm Master, let's say I repeat mere outline of
somehow pumps
                    look I like lose in looks
'to become' & 'to appear' are the same
                    a contrario goof, a spell behaved
souvenir pinch painted wardens
scared to fake redress by projectile graphic lids
laid eyes on — what opals, what clovers, eye-level stress
imagery sale cipher fitted to inwards as if
                    into the distance:
                simulcrayon scopafidelity.
        My insomnia quarreled over nomenclature: narcissism
carries some obligations, some certainty of disregard
                    distorts the earlier swans
                    always trussed up apparent solitary
                    inanimate silly squeak artificers —
not just your everyday lingerie pictures, Full Feature muscles
                    against opinion
                    he detects no irony, an inert appliqué
                    fraction counterfeit whisper
flaccid bijou — personalize these eyelids, those hatched

24

## MOON I

out touches
squeeze it myself — Xerox terse chintz to go
                    mirrored beyond repair
                    unreal, deceitfully added,
    photo leans
                              fluff detail
                    lately tourniquet
s'pose's sordid shallow theme shallow cargo haunting on whites
play into soiled hands, invitation
is a looser, exclusion has its own rewards — sheen v'lume
                    Artifice aborts
                    frothy pornoptic
                    sink & depict pupil;
        font flam shone counterfeit go awkward
crawling with tarts
primp within lean, falsely familiar
factless masks of masks
                    camera invents to prod this host briefs
superimposed resists.
        You at least owe me a scene
sooner sudden bashful dissimulators accord addict
concavity photo sabre corner wonders fatal weird
combed to the front torsos enamor unperceived ribbed unevenly —
I'm not forcing cosmetics
up in price unattentively;
        scrape conveniently buzzer closer
                    crinolined corrodes by whispering
spied as short out vulgar nothing optical beauty diction
by fusing a firefly gene, slender claws
                    painted cupids at odds inflamed
                    with the object glare from wire
wireless satisficer thoughts
are accidents inspired by entertainment.
        Marvel
                    a lesson in swats it
blinded fraud acts con — (the lies are pushes
to their insulting compassion) — naively
                    bait eager train to feign
                    obduracy recoil

## MOON I

fake eardrums on a silencer lessons mistrust, says to me
            shadow multiplies the button slight
            keeps puerile with radar
            we have an understanding mewing taintedly
            don't fidelity zip quiet superstition
& models just imitate them,
    did you say juiceless form or formless juice? —
            deflationary brush-stroke signs revolve
            of prank up fuels of:
darling iota, lush life — tall letters on hatbox
            vote accessorized with
            rarefying cleans up after doctrine —
            I want something I'm spurious
            *about* it I can turn off —
ornament sequels crime.
            Therefore like that ...
            stable means     deflated? —
                      glib stitch debilitating
            corpus fabricating premium fakery smear
            appease audible afraid.
    And I, code mine, loudness all over its junk
careless static
corrupt imagination's passion brain peacock visor
for some reason it's hard for me to imagine
            fitful forfeit 'in order to' demolishes
            compulsive extra, too much
elbow begins to write retinal fixing, energized by it, creases
humming crease-breaks:
    OK
            secretions of dissembling
            symptomatically facetious
                      transition needed —
            another dim
only eyes more exhaust imagery holds the dissipation together —
            plethora pomp
            flimsily irradiated cerebral handjob
            makeup than the man innate eclipse
dishing visibility
            affect *plus ultra* tool-like melancholy

## MOON I

        content, stylized fuck facts, gall-outs
        nonspeaking crystal advertising head —
innate command form leased demise claws are honest
& objects are some circulating victims:
    our care with sufficers —
every fake looks flat, nothing escapes his inattention —
poly proper
worries apt court.

## MOON 2

I've been your dog
divested self-
assuage to guise sorority coquette
                    drugs for the eyelids made from soap flakes
                            auctioned virgin legatee
                    looks on a leash pretend stars
                    for a prurient peep
style chance beauty discounts
cadmium appreciably? — pathologically prettier
                            chromosomic
                            deuterophallic
little boyette in my underwear refuses to grow up, primp to
beep, lightly opportuned still dish to blow statuesque hype,
      boa fellers
fantasizing ciphers' exorbitant semblance —
                    swallowing impersonation, but she could see
but still she's dead, you put the nipples on backwards! —
Satan *himself* taught all arts of deception: your looks mistaken
                    in glass afraid wants
                    muffler upright the hour-eye
                    girls who hate women
personalize your past dumb face rhetoric preening query
                            fluid inattention —
                    decorate the apparition, looking as working
slicker bait ... the serpent vanity says to us
my vanity gets so elderly ...
                    hard flick dishonor rattles,
      our affections
                            PHYSICAL POINT —
is that ankle bracelet or taster's choice?
boatneck dropwaist guile at the limit of the present
with the heels in the front & the heels behind
                    solo roams lure unseen
posture's prince posture patrol masks are jewelry
squandering tumescence pastried off, bow-legged console
suffer manhandlers swallow, all I wanted was his heart
formation.
      And this
bulimics in stilettos crucified in the negligé-

                                watchful gaze of the surrogate uterus —
if you dress well, you won't be lonely
                          his precaution, her reputation, flashbulbed
                          fake mute beat hands to side of debt
                                     tart digress
ads commemorate my awareness, big hair being
most fashionable: overdressed & overlooked, the glance
becomes a sexual part.
      So I
I've had my fingers burnt so I prefer not to move
legendary pink dots avoided looking
                          awkward in false breast plumpest crosshatch
                          drapery would-bes, quicksilvered
                                     crewcut hairless
blue velvet skull booties, powder to paint vain lenses'
                                     image cult
                  sequins (prism arbiter)
the flash is frail
as agreeably chintzy
fashion hull to pastel falsifiers —
its exquisitely refined molecular color system works in perfect
unison with your skin to create an object-seen-for-the-first-time
freshness conceit:
      less composed to collapse once said
                  sparkle snake sufficiently verdicting
                                huge such more
            *dew roozh ah lehvr*
            *dew trahssurr ah poapyehr*
            *dew fahr*
            *ewn oopeht*
            peepers clone leather repeat glass
to paint on skin preen such snowballing vague nebula
                  gaps pomp wax flunks the tit padding
stagefright update hypnotized into doubt; adjectival apparel —
have you still got your little lady trap — low mood points
take advantage of their open vacancy
envy hoop groomed for illusion.
      But tell me, high-heeled & with nozzles:
anorexic hymns, chipped achievement turns up the volume

## MOON 2

                  in your hair loco batteries
of deceit fluff — I want to be castrated? —
                being beefcake swirl debut
                        Make Mine Sable
                        Flapper
                        Ruffles
                        Curtains Conquest
                        Napoleons Dress
solid leopard zipper references the fervent décolletage
American blonde coloratura in color after color
all bouffed palpable bulks: even for abortion,
she usually requires the economic support of man —
                      politeness forbids this fashion?
    With other Fan Action with Opposition Head
skin hoked up by brand peek-a-boo lithe enough
                  signs over pregnant false colors by Fabergé
                  a little; rear perks paint glue shooker
                      a light pinky mauve
petal deferred in vain all over scalloped magenta
gigantic fur slip
frown latino hairjob first focus:
    you think
they're more attractive if they're cross-eyed? —
                      ridicule my mod
                bosom stoppage tense one one tense
favorite posturepedic stunt pampered by lushness —
saliva farming at home sanitized by sequining
                      fact color body solid
                miserie loves lingerie
slender through alcoholism, the product you buy
comes in a *big* box, when a man approaches
bend your head down & stare into your *own* blouse;
                feathered gossip lather alert
                      quiets will
they each 'd envious breathe, *this* relative
                imagedrug deliberately allowance
flat enough to grow wheat on brain looks cute
to lull suspect.
    Rumpy-rama, self-twisting human need drain

## MOON 2

freely wished muscle mum handler
rounds a shoulder and edges out sleek
for distraction hesitant trap ...
unvarying eyelashes ... pre-public commotion
sinews get ready blocked by brain brawns
not bad enough to be respected;
how's my beehive? —
self brows gears lensed advantagedly, frailly excluded
strategy still has legs in a practical pretty sense
brandname vending machine for the body-terrible napkins
of identity:
hung up — or hung? — *necessary*, when
does the soul enter the fetus?, it is a necessity
to have the pearls in the wardrobe.
No, it's

losers as envious
the gorgeous anomalous
gizzards that peep
slinky tilting starvation
upset your mouth creep idiom acutely
skimming the shine; if you wear makeup
you're a female impersonator
eyeliner on the weight you want lost in victory
bottles become me, figurine instance
winning through flatness with spinal messianism
who's godiva flit rendezvous by brandname
muscles denominate
my contact lenses hiding my breasts;
doesn't only insist — I'm wishing the paralyzed semen
lite on the wiggle tube cramps as an empty boat she ...
at a Considerable Distance cut-glass diction
closes lull mimic tears on her knees
bemused and pouting capitulation one by one, self apart
many eager lies
rotate around
womb-like obligation's new atomizer!:
the creature enamel gaze recruit
milkish spine chic labyrinth:
fur — (dread real taste) — to tread

## MOON 2

                    hurts that strike, ribbons speaking
of envious silence going in its eye.
     Voluntary oceanic inner coma image, I made
                  style my job, pace style, retired
                  marionette with detachable wrist massage unit
                  impediment, frequency, usurp, gestate
*slack* calves parade sharpening bits
organza with big bows — they deceive
                  I believe
                  puffs lights magnet pony tails up front
nor did the buckles show scarce capacity for air italicized
                  makeup poses in a handicraft mentality —
                            total
        move
                  face.

## MOON 3

Clear —
torchlight panderer, providing the collars and cuffs match,
                        always any … Oh I know why not:
brain disperses preen above zone insistence, windmill
                                    demurable liquidity
                        pinwheels that squirm strict gown
sacrificed to point of view pandering to delicacy
                                    hints on splints *even if*
                        bargain's bird hairline indicative light
oversize midget lures countenance index of favor
                                    crankcall love affair —
                                    run for details.
            But fingers sharpened
soft skin-substitute material kiss adverts in query
                        (if tact be patriarchal virtue)
                        Distraction in the Sides, Sights
a perpetual approach & conceit bitten actually
spring rain metallic immoral *because* seductive oral robot
                        size, perniciously smooth to seize
                        cro-magnanimously, cro-magnanimity
                                    gala insomniac light
tyrannizes the dumb pretty nonchalant roots, goal brain
invited otherwise,
            certain smears
                                    narrow on behalf —
the women are late, oh no, what next? — hamstrung beads
                        I'm flush with backward with words,
self-adoring potlatch smile that broadens into apoplexy
                        girdle to the stars disseminated deceit
stymied crease up skirt appeals dishonesty pomaded tunes
wear the hysterically cashmere on a stick bandaged
to talk the slack things by the spool.
            Perfect scalpel
gets bearings: doleful schemers
                        see beyond safe lack-tical
                        bee-stung elevating,
                        but can yeast enjoin a bid? —
                        feed the pulse with discipline

stirrupped beneath the scenery, zealously preoccupied
                                        posture pariah
                normal brain bunches in back
wanting stupid skirt-hiked erect clasp respiratory vamp
                blot out skin bouquet gaffe
voice privacy shroud helps ability invoke slim & slam
veil on high, miles-high headgear,
        teaser's torrent: dress for surrender, don't be
so pervious; head weak bait consent
involuntary naiveté end estranged cue
                                        flatter to
brittle brain wants to noodle — prodigy gaping,
                sequins out of fright agitated lunging con-
forms.
        Pinch idleness embalmed
peeps in person inclined to shrink gives *you* away —
                fuchsia narrows, *sheath that hole* —
don't waste on people your time doing things ...
& don't waste your time on people doing things —
                I made a vow midair of choking
spec your breath refrain from fullest
                emotional discount.
        Frizz so reap fetchingly wounded, sultry &
error-prone
hands above beast
                        males in my successive alarm
                        accusatory objects' moisture came
                        hair bound artifice of muscles —
                        I'm booked into fear's takeout:
furl in the bait
those bait hope, fluffy torment
                jerk to perm, akimbo shovers
lower the flesh rating by accident weeping, definitional
consuming
                rape scalp help allowed brave attire
cherishing it as rags to bedlock spied on forks bent for less
false instant fuse.
        Enroll enkindles — idol with head
                toying to compromise

worlds of curls squirt wet sell & flirt
petty praise, scarable fake fur wax
tutu pulverize to beseech corsage with a mute
cosmetic stupidity and having talons, squiggly presentables
crystalline posturing & you turn chicken
prohibit it —
acquaintance span:   the radar has too many dependents
jerked face up close, yardgoods on face
prurient biomedical
embellishment impulse bouts for copy
ache polite
owner in my mirror — fright rinsed, but you
don't *look* sincere,
hapless inhaled chasten surrey bimbo groom deceit
squat arches over tube demure
necklace in, nailed scallops into ephemera,
clamor vocal front deflower
hovers shield leasing apprehensives strip
nail's fast-lights —
what becomes a smear most? —
receptively rebut sap enhancement as stylist decal
louvers are prejudice bonely by
suggest; clenched fish palliate let foil paper show
prey faces & those big hoses! —
at varnish of
uninspired crossdressers bend.
   Yet revolt
contrary usage, graceless dating my mouth
sashay down chemically caused asterisks caged in flight
flash wax gunpowder liking a wardrobe medic trapeze
meant raw bedaubed
studied prudence as if spines had airlifts —
volatile bursts mutilated the fault
fools push in
jittery mood matter
swallows lurex ameliorated semi-gloss
uncrossing with style — lay siege eyes:
the more I suck the more I think — why don't you
just go on Broadway & leave us alone,

## MOON 3

mammary offices spin on spit sloppy fuse, I'm
Shirley Temple
punctuates rhapsodically coercive quarrel; overloaded
*and* playing with affect, your feelings are just flagstaffs
       in half-breed
       matrimonial cactusness
    flash to flat skin coughs up mermaid
    mate this slap elongation
       aim traps at the need
    impressed cluck,
stomach seems to have grown up.
 Bashful
Lassie airy fault singing vain
     hammer fainter ribbons of coward
     sable udder stymied bask some I boom not
       past nominates thread
blind invisibility even hand & empty head sadness obscures —
maybe the desire will get subtle enough to disappear.
 Vista sentinel aphasia
     banish misfortune through the hourglass
     erect admiring in boredom you prefer
     fickle thermostat,
       bustle-suggestive
     corneal blessing: sway repeals,
     carriage compensates the sigh of refract
     foam on neckrest — starstruck cravery
as superstition shimmering,
 fixated member training for eyelashes
no darking vain to suit your radar
nostril 'd guesswork:
     it's a false limb retrospective
all measured in poises, glance lingers involuntarily
pastel for person
pretty
    warm
& ribcage sucrose eligibility imitators
     waddle converse to the truth;
 *la stupenda* presume the wand gray drenched off gray
     litmus posture blotching for business —

## MOON 3

allure sleep adds up coy on high unfillable D-cups,
I believe that, rectoring the flash
the waiting game played out under your lids, worry
to think less
slower.

## MOON 4

Paralytic undersides of
                    remote surround eyed seriously moving
unverifiably poultry thought fame stains drape
                                        gills which I do not
                                        in such dumb-shows
*tremble* dismissively desperate poignancy congeals
moléd birth certificate teeth;
        caution to spleen stare bull
flowers fierce in deferral, intrusive
                        redblocked sweethearts of fear
                        say relax equally due dame:
        stagefright
                        upholstery vaunt vain incubus counterfeit
                        wardrobes a slash & reduce annoy
jagged cuticles tampered hair follicles on holiday —
lard means willing cells *unequal* interior pays for lack
                        flow gives ache the haze excuse
inertially correct.
        I wanted you — listed? — dorsal trial
                        witness controlled the fists
                        hose hose prolong the foray claptrap
refused the implicit girdle saints discourage circumstance
behind led & what sensation caved in? — if you ever
stopped smiling long enough to have a thought! —
vitriolic stunning prey
                                        squinting coquetry
face paint with calories seize little cunning advantages
                        it's not black to be pastel
                        beribboned option, sentient trials dink
trick lulling learns distincture.
        Auto spell
machinery by the pint embassied a disclaim linoleumed onus
disappears in padding, disastrous teeth comfort
                        dormers, tentative
an obsessed superficiality deprivation no especially she
                                        herself can not know
ugly with a hint of the absurd — I am all alone,
and dare not open my mind to any;
vows paint

## MOON 4

a target peekaboo Pavlovian stimuli melancholic
glide priested stick proper as numb amnesiacal zodiac
mirage levitate
tendons qualify home;
    and she said, first I look at the purse, I mean choke
             the structure shun bloom
             I see paint your pumps
                     shake their valium heads
felt moderation accelerate exact luxurious passivity
sift flesh abusive sphincteral barnstorming
             the real sphincteral dowager breathes.
    Your argument:   tips so poise
if good violences merit my scheme clot into stupor apprehensive
             comradery confusion doubles blame
             baked into the very idly secure
             prices go
in for the kill — sit next to fatally driven on objects —
                   deceiving is pasteurizing
             abrasive caution cross-fingered
             cleansing knocks like him
handsome arraignment parallel conceals to congeal
blemish expatriated measure?
    Facts audience may need: get unhappy! —
             disadvantageous voluptuary petulance
malevolence
                      avidity
         injury
         optic
         costume dispensation doubt
fondled into jingle aside from cosmetic unfurnished protocol
sentence worshipper — a silken domino, garrulous
fuse, the great Kotex assigned distraction
             has conquered half of the Americas
godiva guys'
brain-wrinkled manipulativeness frill-a-thon; turn
         dunce of
                jewels slides
        to crimp
smear & swallow

## MOON 4

fluid stunt
trite mated fashion
has me biased.
    Great swacking eyelashes such collapse
                mascara load could be rewarded
skin's in tow — circumstances —
feats opportunity plea error captures affect — got any?:
work garners milieu for disguise sizing anxious
custom If This Will You Wish What boning up
              Rapunzel as jeopardy fungi
              collectors-lips & gimmicks patience
curries over the deeds, lullism meat street, danger
desires
              desperation scruples submit
              treat simplicity less clean.
    India ink oar on hair, world splays open
braces accelerate
blissed mirage failing it goes for its leg
pinkish for me; rehabilitate the verbs hatch it for the gap
              slapping the gaffe toy pet
                pinwheels filigree
I say, not marry as a panoramic recollecting
              secrecies in neon, gussied down
low-flying imposter,
    boyfriend guessed damage whacking distaff
quicksand elongated
              scan scared flatness wise
              *and* wild
              incomplete hurt us pride postponed
              laminate who fled memory inappropriately
come-hither — if you want to be a lumberjack, you have to handle
your end of the log;
    *la dolce vita* — holding the sausage to its surroundings! —
              nonchalant mistrust singular
                wooed empowderment
              hiss without *whoof!* — don't mystify
what mystifies
weight brought to flame
features to lease
face not free.

## MOON 5

All-pretense sighing frontal virtue
                                    tight acetate
clothing says *crowd control* pillow detention tuxedos
                         unfurl the high-heeled flag of adultery
                         contrived vamp come-on as you are, I condense
unclean lips wish you could fake
sort fatale
                         crayon fiancé with keyhole
luck is eloquence & dissveltetude — I've lost
                         my bra, I'm pissed — with perhaps a whiff
of the lilied pipe still in brain
larcenous flutter curls bop alone
sign nullity meticulous flatted masseuse placenta misaligned
predatory coquetry scaring
                         the chintz, evasive cheat
                         Shopping List, brideful labe
mascara also
acts as a gland saluted.
      hair café: Goldilocks of the preshuck undesirables'
allowance scabbard — Twinkling   Image   Dandy
                                    surrogate bewitching
                                    proscenium falsies,
literal suspension of nipples simulating mountebanks
votive anorexic china knitting cow-fed facial slowdown
crimes of fashion, the butch in me
wolf-whistled something furtive in lace crayola
haremish velour tights billed as high braids; whims weren't
there either, baring your tooth fairy.
      How's my little make-up?: my rubber heels have started
in again
a rush *not* to carve henned pretending preconceived
substance pit the pretty aghast
                         coded desire from possible mishap
henna nova error bed attire still indistinguishable from …
                         Ultra Violet Born To Tempt
doffed gravitationally collapsed spandex oh-yeahs,
                                    rhetoric clothes
                         moving as a practice guard
for promissories, ramshackle police barricade around face

your face fits into the regulation orlon bulge-icide
majorette implants, what exterior pieced apart
                              in full flourish;
      look at Kitten Natividad
all yellow-haired cosmetic labor on line, the velour bombshell
                        dingbats want to get the shirt collars clean
                        Looks The Part Image
Avon microbes (patina visors) in miniskirts, pelicans
regurgitate emotional foot
not me display genitals as such
so the imperfect crowd the rails; woken sloppy
                        mink metric spanieled shamming
                        the overbig pokerface poodle prints
inflate chore off mussed suede dismay, facial resale
lashes vinyl beehive handle alter ego on a big dish.
      I dress up in my quick class identifiers, I swallowed you
too soon, you're not a tiny make — believe you, you're not cute
unless others think so — leaping taffeta spiced up prospect
                        Amazonian limbs
                        corporealize, cuticles ambivalent to the hilt
                        mimic the trinket fixative incline
ballerinaed blunt flairs too little milk: all that
helps it melt scalpel by scalpel, false rose on every ...
                              flesh shows
still your taste buds are ruining your fingers.
      Foreheaded glitz felt breaks like champs manicured moment
form wafer men's celibate facial attention
ruffled eyelet candles on pecs, satin vanity grinding set
style annual suicide ruts get armless bullet-proof brassieres
                        so irrevocably is blatant shot up
curtsy so deliberate cues uphold — swan rummage in skid
soft = tentative pose advertises repression gesture's counterfeit
balletomanic maniac;
      shadowy foolery pleases every blush-izing onus
endentured romance, peel off presto postural contest
                        & force dolls covered with wounds intention
blurred up from over which a wide vocabulary
of buttery sentence bullshit — urgent synthetic will
glorified door-knockers other guise serviceably cervical

quote — pout ponytail dipped in sucrose smile requires a prop
day to kill bleached black locks free
hands, fertilize to accommodate volatiles in the pansy derisive
    If
                      edge aisles worsted
             arrow beside hypocrisy of lanolin
trap to catch cock battering engines, No Bend's
powerful breath recruit birth canal as the bulldog
nerve wires detonating *new year's eve* to suppose
                to small stings tang to talk abjures
                kneecaps' morale flue 'nfluence *you* say
cool to piece on sale — I plot the practice, I apprentice
gaffe booty persist nerves clerk, slippery maligned
vie if I want to: '*fort, da!*' yourself! — stick your arc
mute attachment
in is better.
     Shes Exciting Classy N Clever I - Idea Close(d)(t) Case
her Mink Noble Jazz Pretender Princess Fork Deep Rough
torso womanual error fuchsia shouts
clerical to dreams of own negligent ribs groom
malaprop nurse billboards' coy disdain, all by myself
envy of all bimbos that buzz embedded hatchmarks suffer
                        dollies — it whines!
    Pocket alarm surmounted
             weasel moan of glass promotional
             saliva climbing trick in cream
vow much, love little
             lace while you wait cautious makes private
intimate applause fumble side to side
itinerant sweater phone rings excites face lonelier closemouthed
bisectionality — speeding colloid
hair grows at violated distance; am going to impregnate myself,
that's all the lipstick around the nipple we have time for —
Devilizer Vain First Attraction Wet The Native Whistle Dame
Comedy Tonight Crave My Princess Double Peek-A-Boo Cherry Sweet
Dazeray Quack Lawdy Daring Lawdy Lawdy Felonious Good Contrarian
Vanity And Vice;

## MOON 6

Pre-fab unjust self-defeat-pointy-toes
                         takes me for a sucker paper-thin
                         nerves almost never as lips confidante
the prim argument reaper, tourmaliner, gauds the coy
chest stubs in foil pack cluck held hip stoppers;
in brackets, little wallflower, a longhorn of conversation
                                      you fleece too loud:
tormenting blanks thigh erratic funnels delicate appeal caution
to not act flunks aspire, like I'm very quick with like my hands,
        pathologically inconspicuous career below fleeting slur
penetrate (editing) — that is, eating by wash light
                         bad drives, on plantation hair
                                      to get ideas
                         favorize debut cramming with thumps
and coy curtsies, the little dress flung on two chairs
silence, *not* experience licking wax jelly wings
huddle at their pissing devices cantilevering out into
                                      that was me ringing
gripping bouffant footlights in a torso autograph demure me out!
— spores made fine napkins dreary = solid (*stereo*)
                                      I am bitch so
                         hair hits content.
        If *I halt* fluids by hand,
                         *I let* him do the driving, *we* leash-trained
our husbands to obey, *I* = *never* ask the gentleman on my right,
'are you a bed-wetter', *I* = was so sweet *I* = was ineffectual
siren cuts dapper got me plus
                         ankles that vote helpless head down hand out
violence
                         since I can't plan anything
                         *poorkwah ser rertahr?*
instep accuses tongue-swishing iconoclastic blue
croak that sad necklace, anything slow is feminine furtiveness
cross-grained into
I care the lease duty humors
                         humbly bitter flouncing excuse reward:
        simple exuberance generates fierce diva motoric energy
                                      Tannist dividends
like an extra (furtive) limb on teleprompter eating exercise:

## MOON 6

amortize food labile itself
calorie-cleaving jewelry on molar stamina prawn lips
outcast hunch hand *in*
long-necked pantry focal zipper gilded dropsy
dross waist; I'm surprised you think
I am not suited coquettish dear, cuspid craving the newly jumpy
you nuance? ... I *just sequeal*
to suffer in 'silence' in 'sleepwalker sortie' — my mother
thinks I'm a virgin every time I break up with a guy, is that
diet quicksand? — breathy blonde butter ball comb
that one hair attitude
abiding prom torso.
But I'm jealous of your idiotic sleek smooth operator
renumerative ass hatred class muted distress, don't
drop a heart to break it, I have m'
blower, I have m' iron sit to squat
*petit-masculist*
will win in panties hear the latches unbolt for a second
husband-baiting nymphette torpor lozenge segue icing up
pride snakes about himself, which I feel bad about also,
that's why a woman loves a geek, flossed-up pull-dicker
ripe lamé & undisturbed
belt's prow price ruse fault
in practice telling lies
curling slay
breathalyzer possessive
declension of possessions in heat.
If
expediting guilt vibrationally re-anxietized a consisted choice
mintish bleeding of pint-sized impatience
think that throw that
at what those legs can do to use fists
to iron skin upwards; apply myself
to come on the ropes
rasping — uncommitted sexualism? stuttered Law
kelvinatored eros reducermania ...
can't you at least *try* to get in confusing stirrup trouble?
to prance is to give holes
trapped in wholesale, magenta smear marks

## MOON 6

on the Obtrusive doghouse of Self-Sufficiency
reign supine severe, what ward *you* step out of? —
                      timid cargo decorated with
                      soap as climactic
                              corrective lard overload:
she looks like stochastic models in action
or find some guy who will — halloween pumpkin
of bedwetting acquisitive lust so sweet
                      sway to the nasal fuck suits you
                      voice twist & bunt limb-like
                      self-deforesting; cope prom
                              knuckle as
popular butter ingenue not driven enough for
School of American Ballet Development of Breasts & Pubic Hair
                      electrified cotton puffs stilting arm
                      stressed to stretch the toxin
of ad-hocism.
      Infirm the spark fetuses to go out
                              action deliberately un-
                              disturbed
ankle force urge exit became a must-have
mouthpiece with choice; my arms do weird things
while I'm thinking, it's one of the reasons I like by myself —
your limbs have a door policy?, you can go to valentine's hell —
this is *me*, what *I I raw in a faint*
                      want, hell with *you* I can only entertain
pills and pills-to-be — you couldn't
do it because you just want to bow-wow on all those creeps
                              contrived to fuss docile
                      among so many anxiety-bred failure
provocations clenched caution like armor tightly
                              subterranean dwarfs.
      Amateurish indecisive fasten on casualty prude coupons
tailored fleeing sexual harassment to followup to delayed
stress stunting soften false friend in vain
                      bow with great tense skirmish
foam simpler manufactured manners, did you say
bad break or bad brains?, heart bought off
                              helium repristinated

## MOON 6

                    proud to delay, proud to disguise
those stilts in pink cute foments distraught
knees slapped to be inhospitable tissue goes about
with an injured air lethal fleshhood cushions trace
                    Consoled Benumb slider
                                lavishly pursed for —
                                smoke not dare
sheath to qualify for synonyms of settledness.
        Girls never fart; perfect hopping, can I help it? —
make up the extra facing,
bashful drone caution's
irradiated whining debut need I'm used to
meant slagged
contrite stagefright grew laser legs; raise the wand
                    to ankle length bye crash on accidental belly
                    finesse as spite
curlicued distant violins — don't you darling me,
                    gumption by sieve alive derails
of its muscle mess:
your fantasy's been putting on a little weight, hasn't it? ... ;
    semi-lucid quicksand tricks
                    equivocate without end à go-go
germs on the underhems, robot heartbeats
cumberbunned into a corner — (I'm afraid to report
sexual assaults while I'm rehearsing my wedding pictures),
                    rigged temporarily makes choice chafing
pointless over-activity leap backward, flirt bloom off
                    fortress perverse brunettes how sulk
courtesy tickle premonition undo to humiliate
smug volition to do next passive suitor suture
contradict.
        These traitresses caught out sortège busy = spread
                                wampum foyer safety sits;
solids of risks negligible risk, negligible esteem
                    plumped up with caution, splashy doing so
smack smack bride's lagoon neckline flunkie speech held
                    blouse captive talk by quarts kiss & do worse
to boo so:
naphthalene nervous *novio fritas* (fried sweetheart)

## MOON 6

                    male perversity
with a bead on Velvet got its own follicle harvest
to make herselves flesh in agitation — again
                    fondness men
                    fountains ilk choice, called stingers,
pretty little masectomy cheeks without
                    always more in my own company, I fought
for my disadvantage rights bedding for dollars
induct bellied by heel henna tryst torso
papered with rejection slips — every time I fall down
I have to pee: laugh to keep from shoe shopping now
we convene;
      banish risk forever bother, um, studs corset gleam
                    good sometime queen gem nails
(those legwarmers give me crabs) finely clenched
charm flush cellulite jodhpurs comprehensibly somnambulistic
intimidates as stiff too good purses the you
stilettoed handless maiden chest waxery
using cruiser traps; I busy
myself out of fear, feelings, musclebound
                                    has a jag
marriage, that sanitarium, ovulating on the hero
resist bodily eyes sweating cowishly surplussed happenstance
                    vertiginously genteel — pompadour currency
                                    ankled
                                    insensated
                    breast enlargement, decorate your anxiety
                    lonesome succumbed,
                                    don't bite the pants.
      Blower's paradise
                    slap risk hands off when I want
                    jealous slippage
can't withstand I sting! — giving too close
                    latent shacking fretted neck purchase
is next to godliness activating sweaters
                                    against it fussy tender
                                    superficial morphine
to make its way in the shadows, my weakness
                                    satellited enviously

## MOON 6

                     generous extortion mischief mixes
dial-a-mattress homing vehicle excuse:
do you sincerely want to sin? — tamped lass willy-nilly
lip stank prettily
palavered offense.

Black-and-white ward ourselves
wrong careens bulk suave propeller-scarves
                    presume bangs without results silk
                              flunks dominatrix sanctus
liaison torpor, diatribal self-retiring dexterity
                              learning to be false —
                    fragrant thumb-suckling
                    dormancy avoidance obligingly
                              VD icicles with
                    sickish sobriety, minnie amiss
stepford husbands, you go into kids or something —
the Valkyrie stampede of yearning brides.
        Supreme effusive
                              delay skirting dare
silk wrap same-sex itineracy debut androgyne
spider's kiss: I am but the loudspeaker
                    of a symptom, do not self-medicate
if you suspect your nausea is due to pregnancy:
female i.e. weak??? —
whenever I speak, I wet your pants; box on call toto
two hep help
                    to deb the delve suede help
                    hand wants hand waistfully
                              enamored, stirrups
                    on cheekbone pretty appreciative
needle sharpened by cotton creditor to kisses,
                    hostesses for rent = Breck girl enema
persuasible inseam.
        Animals talking behind my back cue wink flat
slap falsetto tools convinced of the affected limb,
                    limbs' halter neck drought into baby palace
                    trifles act choke on tears:
what about the wrist elves? did the ribs have reservations? —
in my own way I attempt to be misunderstanding, some excursion
                    into schoolgirl land to sedate
                    the insertion of a hesitate
semi-precious on stilts, give the flattered
                    inert go-ahead
to statuary rubber pliés on the dirigible, the weight

## MOON 7

you lose will make children,
                                        fledgling bleeds
                          inventor to be luminous
                          positive
conversational dependance
                                        stand a suffer chance
                     gesture implants:
     oh spare me nursemaiding, lush belted
                          pets salute my pin, coronate
                          their bedroom eyes, go through
your pelvis to hang with the attitude
                                        move by dint smile
to weaken action at hand headlong forfeit snare
signal lips form
simultaneous attack, who sucked his victims'
blood through soda straws
                                        wrap it up marooned
                     in a fixed sobs purse, —
the fifty baby chicks have not arrived,
                          all leg designations
displaced by pieheads.
     Face
tutoring
                          contemplating ashtray clip-on manners
                          curl bester candy smart
                          hanker doves inspire to impair
money with a precise pelvic attitude —
be who
you soak tort
                     with a bang rest assured
                                        this will not last
all infirm comes
to s/he who waits,
caught in the act, the boyfriend fearful
                          or retarded so to speak
watering the vitamins I am
suffragette interrupted avid hinges
mink friendships — the worse things
are not old women, you can't imagine your penis without me
                     sucking on it to respond?

## MOON 7

Hymen pours out choice
by pincers troubled out thwart devote
                                        spittish trial
                        a furious motive to
                                        intellect, hamming up
memorized doubt — what are we going to do about your wife
[husband] & what are we going to do about my husband [wife] ...
                        It's a Sexual Aggression Tuneup! —
big implicit
cushion *tutored* longing uplift inhibits
empathy passbook illustrations
                                        swindle lever too,
                                        sorts wish
                        rubbing lesson anchor
                        fuel rejected sits there spatial.
        Easel curt hula homiest propellor, a submental
                                        stand-in hem knots
harmless masturbatory matters for shut-ins; impetuous silent
cunning boxing flakes that sting
moving young flesh trembling squirts whether encores
roust polite pliers by stretch ankle-mules at finish-line
                                        arsenals of bondage —
adultery is just another brand of consumerism, dogs howl
to hear girls shop, animal bites
                        hearts to thrive: surfeit
                                        to speed
                                        docile
                        defines
*frustrate*.
        Darling touted easier cut
                        Oil of Roses spots of tame
gartered rebus sapphire ovulates at extreme preening bobbin
loser stats, anal-ing its innuendo union unaware
wrist-slashing dietplan fly nodes to a heel wigged professional
leggings ban the legholder by deed
                                        passive habits transpose
                        courtesy in slats
                        curb your pecs,
her member is finding a clubhouse

## MOON 7

improper kneed pooper curt mute mattered faults
*kommahng sah vah*
                      shake up clothes volup'
                      chaperoned compromise
pelvic Arbitron coil in coil.
     Fully faceted hard to find mandatory smudged-on
             already owned poly stance
treble trappings, moist refuge we go quiet eyes
             a whole fluent clutches
                  bellybutton flattens out
as much as a yelp prize to the hesitater arms
that shave themself pinwheeling straitjacket demand —
we will return later to the question of who
laughs most at other's witticisms — sapped-up inner
antique mirror in heat — courtly means courting?
                hype encounter ulterior enticement obscure
    Redundancies
defeating anything deferred to, not *re*ferred to hammer
checks over butt tax homes cherish dominants satisfy
            Abandoned Women Knitting the royalty of
            penalty chamber incline
            but not enforce single sinful gown
stocking guarantees benchmark –demuro –jittery pelt
            filly carton dressed their cuff
            begs to supply porcine stress syndrome
            wistful bragging spun yak fist
suicide fear espouses castration by detox.
    *La crise* aspirant, ungloved, your simple inviting
                tears readily enough
                and loser weeper
mood market arms someone new
rose enrolls
my *habits* to your *advantage*, organdy servo-mechanic
            deed horizon smears doer squall between
            Superfly a looka here — Dazzling —
sob arrangement automatized
lip cheeks chin.

## MOON 8

Sheen to flaccid charcoal siege machines
                                    unable to
filthy burning lust compliance through camouflage
cult figurine prism of vacuum gilded zero valor,
            torpid should be look at them in white!
                        look at them in pink!
treacherous intuition web bobbies in a bag
                                    withholding headbeast —
                    pardon *your* appearance:
medusa gladhanding effigy in the largo optic slaps;
                    survival of the cutest tuxedoed in
to forget easily interrupted and ignored ...
just PMT patio pirates, what *you* call reflection
                                    I call constipation;
                    for years I have been talking
                    against food
                    without success:
everything this good makes me sick, change my naming
physiology filigree of grasping ice subjected cleavage
loud which may shift.
        I
pursing konk sooter thinkin'
                    the artifice of ether to pristine
with counterfeit sign signs pieces
pocketless
for undeveloped heads, vapor facial flammable nothing
but trowel spatter *semblance* to illumine clicking foretaste,
wide berths for sartorial cheesecake with flu patter sustain,
                    vista different from decor proper;
        and incipient crescendo signs
                    squeegee's numbness, that's
a masterpiece of understatement — ghosted retreat's
fascimile complies ahead layette words its ads
as no sapphire can make of your love a seductress
(and that's no good, BLEED for me Ill Wind — pointed up)
                                    'object'
                    glacierly vestigial bias,
the possible that cannibalizes the real.
        Avowedly anemic impostering

# MOON 8

perfect *fears* to pieces, concussion
                              consequent engagement ring
wanted to make sure I didn't lose my zipper —
                    be careful, dose bag —

                                        putative bad
                                        larceny peeps
                    incredulous frightened little heart
                    damnably pluperfect levy
demon spike heel pierced skull in slo-mo vote,
                    or how lies get loaned
                    equal to Accidents, insidious foreground
envy as malice litigation.
        So prim and attracted by now
tormented pieces based on failure to understand
coupled appetite got fast throng to prompt vulnerably headlined
sober spoils gloat.
        Mocking intoxicates nightingale in arrest
                    (I have heard men say)
(please you command) hovering vampires self-delighting
verbal such as brood agreement — I like my issues *flat*,
that incredible *fear* of speaking before a group:
        hormonal fluff deposits, desire = talent
                    formica fury extort
at first sight renounce thought harm largesse —
                    vinyl prone, the worst is eager
self-consuming *has* vs. *does* toy shout
                    to consent to be decorated
                    pliant untenable Nothing, fleshholders'
chinoiserie of the glands hemorrhaging on illusion prizes.
        Instance uneasy
hard choice, emasculating starts in light —
                    self-assertion lost a shrink-wrap
                    where I could have used some intelligence
furtive underestimated
rube in glassine rawest tell my parent donor
                    coquette limps to learn fear
                    squirting imperfecting blazes —
why be more? — both senses affect normal
                    lacking relation alone, amazing

to find excess worm this doted.
    Now, idols & dolls mimetic
mush costume got argument arrest: Hat was vagina,
put your face in curlers, undersussed delay bite
subterfuge on a stroked preening vellum
                  confines roll, wardrobe caesura
simulated plumbing multi dorsal consent.
    Cuz wary eyes earnings
baldies all look alike?: infinitize to infantilize —
                  too much makeup is our national bird —
                  jewels burnt luxury engineering opaqued
gift pubic statuary pronunciation, enticed
              solder humming

                        sheen act;
    men are heroic while shooting restored semen? —
lurid hostile severe
              slandering literate membrane
pendulum; babies (latent commodities) cry to make compost,
                  my brain ill proof
                  thoughtlessly veiled
the fondling of bent.
    I didn't think,
you'd get so drab abrasion — filigree fascinating
impurities surround plastic, major point
bandaged memento groomer vault
                  whisper within
axiomatic fault poised half-hearted hung gray chest elites,
abatement vocabulary suppressed contrary anchorite stroking
              even fuller in emotional discoloring
discovery,
    hole (with an H) life
is a domestication of these proposals
            since superiority its due
            fear multiplies desire
garnisher and garnishee lacquer chokes sap machine
of suggestion, art apprenticed quivers to me,
            that's very
            very thrilling hennaed IQ
                cyuuuute

## MOON 8

                                        admiring as wage
stripped mute exploded mute tradition unspleens.
    Everything superfluous hurts
the ever-fixed
trembling with accessibility, classics warned me, swells
                        aside sizeless
                                        clustering
                    in faint name series
                    cortège of pinpricks, more distance
is what will
cost you intense.

A PLEA exposes it pries
                fornicating preamble's human asps & vipers'
                        desperate establishment
keep coil with fuss, I traded my brain
for legwarmers transposed to praying mantis, lax is all
                T-shirts a chance sanguined pump
marionettes impaling
                domestic inmates in style brain's dowry drill
                bowing the knees in convenience.
Limbs fluoresce not much louder than tinsel,
                status increases with weight decline —
                strict aplomb will-less nook notch innocence
                laugh exits barrel, proficient puffs of
self-important conscientiousness barbecue a free voice
nerves such deflation posture fake
                likely pauses, earring in fuse
                jumping beans in a vivisection study:
   therefore sometimes totally vulnerable Ideally Suited
think me ostensible, I need a good social personality
                because I don't have any ideas? —
                battling out shapely impeach my tongue
hawk elongates every split
wisps by division has head brush for hair
coaxing a flat pleasure: put some more treble
                in your liability, jail my lips'
adherent impulse.
   Any dead woman would find her attractive —
                now you put that away —
                        slapping synonym
                victims mimi stud kit whiteness
                refrigerated alone, handsomely pilled
slap that fluid, I'm like, permanent minor,
tape them to the back of the other dummy converts.
   But seminal cargo I = *beak*
                spy too small mistake that goes in and
                voltage dabbling for daughters
                just pissed *on* cause to pout —
the average diet lasts less than seventy-two hours, suicide's
arbitrary equestrian panties, self-adjourning

## MOON 9

terraqueous wrists, self-rocket igniting to make variety
                    vulcanizer sucking cigarettes —
spurned his sexual advances so he came at her with knives —
why differentiate between the white gold & yellow gold?;
    & to flatter to flatten
                    pride bedly nettled permutation credit
                    incriminating fretting sperm flunkies
                          clone flirt droop calms
                    limed & limped, I'm the horse, not the boss —
                    choke cheat choke down volte-face
thing dismissive in surprise, you loser, iced curtsy
fade to a careful correctness —
                    the music thief me head! — who menace me
                    satiate with manners abuse my hours
of choice
daintily nothing.
    So, PRETTY AND SAD
                    diametrically impertinent swelling wonderful
as well as useless escapist deposit whispering out of
over-the-title ego's defeat; the willing pride in desperation
                    stop tormenting enthralling limb
pimping ecstatic curtsy awhile for price rebuke
                    pedophile's shopping list advertisements for
                    bicep tilting my excess —
                    could you star in it better? —
                    satisfy doing vs. heels cope hone
                    curbs space properly envy
                    beguiles species.
    Cramp skids gilded grudge impassively desperate
trouble blockade conversation shames out
                    nonchalance — condescend? —
                    rebukerer trophied touch & passive go
willed glacial too marry curts spool the breathe
spills choice
though beach-style décolletés are frowned on:
                    anytime he came near me I got pregnant —
                    no wonder he has such a big ego; sin of
                    bite fool of got
                    fingernails charge hands to

not give in to value languishings —
pathos = contorted limbed less party-colored
insecurity friends calm at all costs, slap to halt
answer-records to their dog-breathers;
fit to be had, self-regard
long journey to be demeaned fetch fetching supplicant
plumps to mitosis
praise a leg adverse knees
my money just bedrooms
cowardice the rest emphatically careless
corks curb crumpled so leans;
I traded my looks for my health — bad bargain, ideally
fixed consort
capitulation is sideways thank you indecently
bosom flunk sovereign yet succumbs —
today Joan of Arc would get thorazine,
this little mutiny,
aching to do himself, charitably imposter
pissing away the trust thickened necking friction beset
splurge sink sink-a-holic
mutually stimulating indifference just knee-jerk
dwarfed expiation talking out the side of your neck;
I got out to step on you: immaculate self same organ evaporates
on reciprocity still forfeits —
you're blaming your lack on me —
it's not nonchalance that behaves so badly.
Best driven out
peg
fraud
gap
freedom

austere changeability very slut neat body
practically do forbidden male brain
rests on cute white pumps; physical stimulation
Spoiled Perfect to reduce fear, pimp verbiage
tears substantiated
by the least provocation lazy trap you should
*wouldn't* weakness delights
Carmelita reconstituted — adventure undone, venal

## MOON 9

                                        bow to betters:
accessories could teach *man* to flap.
    Hell is psychology:
                        a viper, ill husbandry whining
                            trump by description
                    Thoroughbreds of Harm nail splashed-on pride,
guess it'd rather have rape than prostitution? —
ambition as distraction, florid penitence, the self-
                            deprecating 'only'
                        politics *me me me*
self-pity leads to drugs which leads to depression:
                        never pay for sex warm enough to fail
the rehabilitation of failure, make me fall.
    Slap the slut speed rank sheets, freedom
                        is a symptom of being weak, sweetie,
                        I'm purposeless, no final voluntary,
narcissism has its own refrain; fortunate = humiliated
                            self-enflame cortège
                    shoulder spies ideals as rights to loss
                            is insecured by
                    infused habit it's habit whom tongue
got ahead on their backs; dolls foist off attitude,
they saturate the passivity organs at the starting gate —
                        nerves made hole statement ridicule!
    Sir fast
decorative unconscious self-blame gives a passport milk
pride worse loss lascivious defeat works wonders
                        refining pleasure to resist
                    in love by yourself; self-willing sublime
ain't ashamed that 'we' is a rare locution, real eerie
                    intervally anti-social teeth:
                    combat!

## MOON 10

So, unmarked guided hole
congratulations by masculine nominative singular self-doubting
somersault — it's *my* portrait, especially as polished up
in the later version, unregenerate fakers' monad sentencing:
you could do worse; portable plenitude
                              predicated imperative affect
contrived, revolved & revoked, a vintage *so what*
                                        votive form
                                        repugnant
                        (that cloying heartwarmer aftertaste)
                        got its Letraset in a sweat over
                        feign enticements & common desirous rumor —
                        LSMFT — crush blue form insurrector vivid.
      The look standardized its warning, pretexts seduce
                        weakened adjectives, effigies, listen:
                                        OK — OK —
but even Queen Elizabeth goes to the toilet — oxymoronic reform
                        force controlled by objectification
                        can numb loner regress blonde
                                        prawn awning nag
the slower croissance, we don't even *have* heads pliant peeper
deflater's roar … stop me with an exception —
harm explains the heart;
        souls of wed archimedean embarrassment
yolk spotless dad regression adept as target
                                satellited out of line focal denial sign —
                                I am deluded with various arrows —
                                exert back to splay begs a little spine
                                sin straps on lease flatness
works better, spiked furtive heels — unlevel spinning
                                (middle class value) condominiumize that
femininity.
        Why don't you get
paid for having a face? —
                                handsome nothing cheaper female
                                headed by half vainglorious caloric romance
unlimited schmaltzola svelte at neck's end excusing
what power jewelry labor fronting damage
spotted court ma'amster: silly,

## MOON 10

even those of us who thought we welcomed androgyny
curl each hope at hotpoint, outsize the neck
                         with custom distance in sitcom
pretty crumbleable.
        Capture-prone
compassionate compromise or compromised compassion? —
libel or leisure? — flouted or flaunted? —
                         mistake blonde for sheep aggrieved grail
                         receipts pander to flicker, stooped harem
                         trauma drawer's activity
                         slapping & pouting
inherent toys; textbook makes me psychological
                         fluffed guarantee cultural flip,
                         domestic-looking animals on don't miss list
shuffle off their regard guise!
        Svelte imperiled authentic
                         calipers yawn to butter each 1$^{st}$ available
                         a narcissist wound's affect lapel's
detention; baptism by fun shopping will not regret
                                     tossing ideals (*promises*)
                         the nature of the parts which
oppress us sketchier dermis arraigned as hearth
                         wish gratis pure jealous cause it pleases
to stimulate your elastic decorum — I'm not free
                         to be satisfied.
So video teach the child how to cheat
                                     emoting conscripts
fat is just geisha men,
she's happy now that she never wanted to get pregnant —
tentative heartening coquettes for Christ, entire
                         pregnant audience off that misfit;
all adulterers & fornicators shall audit their own
endowed chairs, why be impotent when you can buy shoes —
                         what's the suppliant supply? —
                                     punitive crèche diets
                         spinning sorority suture
                                 *lest horizons.*
        And as centuries of expectation delayed the entranced
                         coarse cloture erosed & equipt,

prostitute myself with recrimination
confession impresses poised dismissal —
*viz*Ibilities —
transmission of cop-out leather limits
hypnotized to give themselves cunning brittle accusatory denials:
let them eat Camay
refined out of freedom cautiously kryptoniting issue.
    Gape quit, Letter, slender Use verbatim
ads absorb delay, initial(s), *promises, promises, promises*
flee whatsoever saturate pinching sat-u-ration
something — no with-draw-all diatribe calm
purpose defrauded volcano atavism (!)
to clucking agitation (!)
translucent screen against defiance haunts
null esteemed blame adhesive futility — the reverts nature
caress;
    how many minutes
the average husband talks to his wife per week
'provoked' spontaneity:
this will announce your arrival — for class, of nobility,
boredom grief oppurtunity charming? —
service blossoms negatively blossoming narcotic cruelty =
time insults, hardening pumps default queue
falsetto dues overpayments born to be poignant
diagnostic transposition of mouth sickened by apology.
    Face is for sale
tooth fairy with a face mask mistaking promise
trouble declension
minnows had permission
complicity produces our subordination
as an image fancy can't appoint
a euphemism for sycophancy (and apologize
in advance) — it is the power-
free tilting bargain my period constrictive spoils
shine up the privileges on your way out, take time to shop,
    why so soft? —
sinking into dollar certainty out-hammered imaginary harness
jars for stress —
this commodity moves on its own steam

## MOON 10

                                        spatializes itself
                                        taboost
& the job vomits up proofreaders diamanté legroom
giving into restraining orders;
milk-splattered duty, insensate flattery
presumed mannikin trained by mistreatment, disheartened
to get popular — were the lips active or passive;
                        the trouble is in your effects
                                        pecking
                purchase
                order
                vicarious
                power
                adored
seizure.
        So agree as no opinion — trap without force
                        conjures guilt out of sense
                                        power
                        unrefuted smooth purse diablo
attitudes marooned
as fantasies compromised, teeniest
complaint: (unwillingness foreseen) grows bold —
I think we all
                        (treat men with unspeakable contempt)
need more power, as I interviewed my spending habits,
                … s'matter? — this is all so macho, spurt
                                        culture as pony tail
jury furtive.
        I have yet to decipher the patio
                        chill cocoon with a follow spot
                                        astride & you suzerained
sickness symptom sorry cuties, companionship
amid purchases luridly
fragile on to popularity: everyone involved suffers —
gothic model basket case, bikini or brief
nurture got him hard
money in drawer
sinks in harm affection great weight on me
                                        suspicion-*propre*

olive appeal, the grounds for many fairy tale weddings;
    but amiably excused, performatively halted
panoramic to agitate
occultation: contestants
unscripted by ideals, dutied into flakes
at their own upheaval this demoralizing to resist;
                        he complain about disposition stilts
                                weep for plight?
                                jones for vengeance
auction lulls paradise, get any ideas? —
pacifying conclusive reason to bitch.
    This valve regulated direct emotion —
                        which parent wants the sex change operation?
— preposition your fluids as social service, babies are just
propaganda for couples, mere stems of friends —
                                I can't talk? —
                                *Do not act* —
                        flagellants agape, always contrite
alibis are intimate discourse of damage nourishment
                        cheating with equals, repeat
                        half devices, hover to obey
compromise arouses us.
    Jewelling jury button hostages of paranoia
body by commerce
beehive impose to behave, I needed a total aberration
of collectivity instructs my timidity, my instincts
                        second coming tactic mouth
                        the loans, I was jumping
                        on the deficit incipient baby, sage inequity
                        say No outside be No white spoils
explain waitress, parents are made
regrievanced to be broken,
    guilt comes equipped with protective device
justice at anthill put to shame, if not to rest
                        segues yearn for a better quarantine;
the domino theory
your idea of love relations,
compulsive use of self-abasement as a defense mechanism,
enhance your own life-style at the expense of others,

## MOON 10

idol close self-enclosure suture as patience
exterior, as affirmation trash sticks to you
                domicile luxus alibi practice —
                *he* who dies with the most toys wins:
curving curbs
an X 'must have' a Y
circular folly

                            to forestall wishes
                figure of figures.

# MERCURY

## MERCURY I

After crystal trick contrary
alibi abides skull simplicity

peripheral angle that you
nerves oriented hammier
mime that ovum unbosoming scribbler —
*poovay voo prahngdr may merzewr* —
*ahksehptay voo der sehrveer*
*der taymwang?* —
unbridled plagiarizing massed proverbs on *pointe*
the trick:
wedded and false-free fount unwedded words enjoin deceit,
    mere symbol-albinos
I eye overcathecting practical babble
in the compression crystal to grind light —
bright bleeds through Apparent Signal utterer
doctrinaire about thoughts' agile much-decorated complacency
antacided into silence —

the ideal flagellates
diverse dissatisfacted
fumbling for the lock forfeit
diamond bits on end persisting machine;
    and skid spacing

Precs Rhet
even intervalling memory guise
inward dive hand to hand reactive doubling

pecking as composing
Happy contortious Chatter arguing with
focal infinites a slight objectification calls it justice:
every chicken head has humans *in its* eggs.
    I was damage talks
that I sense, you're mouth man refrigerant mentions
tremor acidics, repeat it hone it, utility means
means you've got a big built-in napkin on your hands:

tools' face wit
well-points & spring-points calm leaks
getting the drawers among the legs,
resources catch your eye, the most heaping pierced
outlying zero animates zero
will of the couplet really do else & vain.

## MERCURY I

And before I 'ad
                                    nub with false pretenses
this brain celibate brochure proprietress
annexed artificial two deflate divergent
can't be diffusioned; sensitive as a nerve melt agrees,
                            scaffolding paid gestation law
Lanvin and all story depository is closed in etiquette
missing gums imprison her on paper ghostly levitation —
                        novice slice bland at root, the valorizing
lacks content;
        but I'm a tool to prop up the ideas that keep me down
for which I write to hear myself a recipient
                                    silent implant charge's
                        incubus casually machinic
                            mistakes minute skewers
                    as censors inward grammar halts
at immediate fiction requirement sounds cheap
insubstantially unserious genetic hubris multiplicity —
men are just physically used to looking down on sincere women —
prophylactic boosters subdivide to flatten the surge as tame
                    as mute's wage total waiting, arms akimbo
                    with your ticket: Need waits:
                            the head is missing.
    I don't effervesce a lot
                    statemental brain attitude balcony
                    now as I other quote posed
intelligence as a form of bronzing, mimetic emptiness
                    erasing singly refrigeration in dreams
                            spectral liberties —
A comma would better express his intention — white don't
                        rub off liftful stance so
                    sermon implant married the buttons, the near
is less near
contracting absence, every contradiction to justify repetition
is false light could improve
it true.
        As soon as censor stare open & kept
boundaries buy
miniature restricting button oral rused, inappropriate valve

## MERCURY I

home bits tongue —
                    stay the say the same party lesion lie
                    dice so small castrated keyless impossibility
                    into equality: you can't happen
the document *capsizes* personal experience, eggs forgiven
                                    bookend numbness
                    cute on the tube nominally beheaded;
    and that's a thought-stopper! —
                    my table of contents is useless
                    policing the libido, love's winterization
arms disappearance against affirm blip voucher
swoon sign conjunction diminish to go —
                    I still like the old sentence —
                    grammar as your model for misunderstanding
less than coinage can bear.

## MERCURY 2

Oʀ titular comfortable modesty
                       toolings: I'll let you guess —
mystery as privilege star flickers with urgent gel
                     certainty, voiceless stringent common
                              stylus bias
              anthem light spikes
its condition,
     so ocular syntagm
enthusiate failing magically dismissive appropriate
incorporatist monism move — little wrongful sensorium
              epidemic life-style? —
                       epigrammatical vacuity
deflating as a hobby:
No time? No problem! ... fraud open storybook avalanche —
                      flush your world in ours:
anecdotal disturbance with siren for rent words, glitter
of absolutism coagulated frontispiece
    See darling prespermed
gratis distinguished surcharge verticals we can wake —
                 breeding precedes essence, utility devours
modest sieve
              [egress, ingress, and regress]
              surgically prior larvaed premises —
or you could just decorate; but men love their daughters,
                   disclose dice
along points state focus zeros in parade formation
movement made recall into energy, where nothing *ever* happens;
              insects got more accommodation
posing sacrament's contractually doomed revelation —
take heart from fact
use the forced arch.
    *You* know counterfeit rules
the lazy susan of theory norms took the trouble —
a new teacher for every gray hair code it flattened
            prejudice alertness only
            many innate fraud; fake stairs'
fatal bulb before bulb preview of
time reminds prison its palaced certainty abyss —
what's past sure solid buys MEGAPHONES.

## MERCURY 2

And you know, let's say ovaries, Sabine heroine donation
                    circumstantial captive
                    for 'drive', read 'solution'
slowed down through the technology of high heels
                    fleece to violate alarmish harems of duty
goads brood holidays — boomtime for rapes, but *why*
do they choose to have those desires? — Motionless,
too trivial motion, the egg waits to propose
                    a passive dampen wattage unit
                    dive into their counterfeits
some sire value in its ambrosial laboratorial pallor.
    You know best all root dominate
                    them denominated delirious incision
                    flawless jinxing eggs on automatic pilot
*against* queen synthetic sycophancy hose + heels =
decline of the West, Little Red Riding Hood
                    does not escape the wolf:
your private unencounterable bodily iwo jima irruption
s'guy hotbeds extraneous under creaturisms pop toy
could register tracheal aggrandizement prize
demeanor purse implies content;
    alias everyone's vulgar eloquence silken size
but grotesque weight generally liked nanny so linear
squashed respectful animator into elevation
impressionably pregnant voluntary ovation analogy —
                    breathing fabulous society enough I pile up
                    only the headings
embalm scolded perfect
                    puffed-up *bite* Anne Boleyn
                    diorama wants a head
neglected noblesse oblige salivates accusals, redundant
                    geopolitics in a bed swarm regalia:
                    tassles on your name philately bone
come, expecting your miracle salmon with parasol.
    VR (Victim Reporting) — hypnotized & summarized,
commercial marries weeping luscious overcrowded
                    equal metaphor junk to lead
muted access, half a say concave dowry future
                    cordial accessory whining stripe

## MERCURY 2

                                  nosebleeds for hire; it grates to see
                                          so shot fame law clamps
                              entry apart, receiving is believing
rubella ballet spores' bedeviled reciprocity.
        Tyrannical image
illness guaranteed by phrase pressure ill-natured
                          natural harangue strata turmoil crease
extracted from the urine of postmenopausal women:
we can have our own version of bad Polynesian restaurants
                          in the emotions — fact asks for reasons
                                          dictates dictate
                      papoose stucco tenderizer
                      sandwiched between deceptions; out of favor
Radicalism has such appalling VANITY poking BIG ISSUE ineptitude
                                  catastrophe = first clue
in the interest of clarity for a more aggressive disadvantage.
        Hardly slit laundered cue serene
                      eggs officiate any grammar
excommunicates any contour; pessary keeps your uterus
                                  balloon in place of
                      the body — mild plenty bite-sized
                      stability white sustains name expectant
true sedated by blank
                                  matricidal donation.
        And isolated flattery enigma
conceals its front nipples emblazoned on the idea —
flawless anachronism riding the rationalized debut
                      prior loss royale
grooming believer trumped off skyscraper orifice
sweat than oversight bullies the exceptions
                      the irremediably dusted dead ends
can inspire and *too sure* wanting it too live.
        Null *is* — ornate more to say
its miniaturization material revolver superimposed semblance
stammered squeeze wiring caution paste
to our loss limp in the
random squeezed context, silently rapid ownership
made sure negatively Business would-be Fashion to Males
                      fetal personhood, womb with a view

(too fast to describe).
PVT genetic is it! —
fizzing renown future palms the typecast
grammar's certain fool: *the* novel dead
or *your* novel dead satisfy of pleading
men are known as membraner multipliers —
slick means serious?:
percussive qualify depends beach head birth hound
distance *averts*, sure
poetic udderness incubated
soft-pedaling effluvium.
Parts belong privately
three-pronged cluster around cajoling roots
final dress schism flatters anti-life hole
needs editing to the heart.

## MERCURY 3

Presumptive sieve reply this everyone is posturing
pins of advantage which tauten the minor on the toes of others:
none of this group grope wants rape back to a time
when what brute force
enticement needed to survive a tube

                  corrosive corridor aglow
         with scales forelouvered.
   A profit of politeness: limbs in shiny catalog
         hinging blossoms, insignia slabs
            teaching embryo nametags abbreviated lies —
you think 'pinch an inch' size of hips means bigger assholes? —
              more skin competes hoops
         for siblings' keeper, anonymous = ugly
         'beasts' warned against 'fascinated'
coerced roundness; I can't really tell because it's huge
         fruit ideas in people's heads parading
seeds by caste, gander staked stove in debt
unable to connect by joinish projectile.
   Dowager headset:
              decorous nuclei snake
        affected esteem to counterfeit depth —
           pitiless titular
        am I went out of fashion? —
Cleopatra rhythm belies meaning
heed braced fleck, half-eaten watermark
stars winterize & closure restores beginning
arms fellate throne; invalid gowns & bustles, panoramic
photos of our inadequacy cushion of gravitational
              personalization renown
sputtering mercurochrome on the milk sentence
        farm crevice crèche sorrowed.
   With Vital Engineering
        stiff stuff, official darling
shun collides, parents rake leaves over childish hole
and idealized gentility soars — is that a broom
        or is that your spouse? — satin
dispersed jewel hoax voiced digit whose vexed thumb
diagnostically cuts tissue spun away at decrees
           annexing snatch grapheme

as own touching
batched hapless pinker brood
repent as soap
tourniquet ointment's peristaltic dating.
　　But mi face
half ID, half human
stains replace friends —
anti-corps exaltation pilot any nonchewable
private effrontery, a surgical operation in all its implied
kiddiecentric bitterness: when will it enjoy me? —
adultery as aptitude factor dolls relapse
the codpiece accepting midriff rank spatula's
gaffe,
　　scales decor insected pioneers
torso is that how house-size menstrual pads
roundish insignia plan dampens —
the storks in particular worried her, a wife sweet knife
pimping for a lobotomy —
you think lack of emotion is clever? —
most of the handsome resistance thinned
have been turned out of their arrest pronoun daughters
accept the diversion
gets numerical will goes backwards too assertive divides
pick by rear
in hand
in appearance;
　　contractual vehemented basement passion vector hole
close-out length vendetta stuffing management
inti-mate not
not to deconceptualize inside
a border on prude cash
abdomen personal got to subscribing titular doubts —
you know you never outgrow your Mom —
the single mother is falsified bestowal despised,
turning it into a counter-penis —
Go to hell, We are domestic servants,
ditto soma gave it craters
low rungs affection through some prism-anointed replica greed
rein quantity grooved closure's bad press

## MERCURY 3

that blankness — hive.
Make your mind hurt each other

spoiler to convey me? —
you're marginal, you're not well, talk he was
bleat in line list exhortation
feeds longing (let me lick your Nureyev)
resalute the category advantage degrades, the *object*
is the other; disguise the organ
as an accessory.
Morselize some losses, subservient milk, smaller
credentialling pieces encryptical
jewelry split princesses geometry
incautiously monadic — slave safe?, my allowable fiction
disinherited extrapolated & bound electricity safetied
spermless courting by trapped or residual
atom thicker flux,
the culture landed & kidnapped them both.

## MERCURY 4

Coveted local swain
                    hulk beam buckskin & fringe of
insecurity knife left odor as whitewashed instinct:
material adherence surpasses injury, anything creative? —
                    here we have the bloody worm
which you can also use in salads, adroit designer
                    buttered mischance — big balloon
in my veins, oh, mine's been ungainly — nothing niblets:
                                        a limb caution stigma
                    bake-off appeals to muscles
maritally force the flap forbidden to breastfeed
                    double-spaced blemishes vibrationally
shanghaied arena-size inhibitions.
      The one public sign
                    false musculature vulnerably vanity's
                    division preens originality castratoism,
angry dearheart hectoring neon plenitude toward mudpies
                    appropriate isolated rat heart malice —
                    lilywhiteness's pimp strut
with overstuffed individually decorated pores; defiantly shallow
affordably cute misnomer debut & its auxiliaries
                    look like extra-chromosome types
                    dissatisfiedly: remarkably K-mart pricking
                    fetal diction, quartz physique
unfriendly for hire — what are the birth defects of choice
with the hair painted on? — peeplike chromos
touting tights,
maidenish name chalk, problems, even enemas? —
                    with every hysterectomy I gave a free perm
                    so onan curries the sheets.
      Let art courteous fake varicose pledges
have your fun preen to redden collar sooner than zipper
counts prime selfish satisfied half pint pleads
bedding the too much
injections of whitish gel roster, predator pride
proctor the shaft (do you crime around here?)
                    *exactly* dilettantish bosun delight —
I hate and I deflate, I wore my neck out

shaking my head at sexists: oppressive martial jelly
exuberance demands unsatisfaction (?) discriminating,
my fat got so leaked, so
                            you can sing along with psychology,
                            the musculature is too confident:
I forgot I had a bladder
to retail gossip
parent pending, parents are killed, you know why;
     and cute won't mix ballot in her hand
                    lion nurture the coldcocking prong
                              musketeering milk
between sperm donation — stem it! — next trimmer
gain is gain innocent me out *against* her; we didn't hesitate
because we want to wait: delicately malevolent grip
jutting and receding in space, cough tightens testicle
                  phosphorus whoremaster matches
                          toy is fly
                  plunger to hibernate too quickly I mean
every married man in Hollywood is trying to date you —
                  dummy breastplates squat to squint
                  slice & grab dress as gyro
                          segmenting bait to
                          (blush) bush bowl —
he did not want to pull down maypoles,
he came out with knives and let her have it.
     Does your hostility set the record straight? —
                  more of them rent their lips
volunteer as previous value wristslap, no, values
instigates bakelite hammer hunger
                  song brackets in front cake remunerate
                  flesh the seething bruise-a-thon
masturbate the master's pieces of paper; a one who stomps
pregnant wife is an already meltdown, idle =
                  lascivious who hot too engage to fault
close-cropped rectal magic, my fangs are full —
crib that fop!, you know I preserve private potty
                  I can twist at a discount
toaster grows up — your inner life of bedwetting
                  rage orchidded imposter chides,

angry sassy dinner substitutes:
I'm starting to doubt the sexuality steps misfit
as less favorable self-indulgence.
    Everybody's ugly, get away *with* the person you love,
or get away *from* the person you love?, incorporeal peroxide
                    blame for ineptitude sister awkward dots —
                    now I have nowhere else to sleep —
                    organdy falsetto stigmatical selfishness
combed gown Minnie Mouse:
                    rape scholarships service heroines of debt
                    with smut cheater & the effigies,
unique anatomical gifts!
                                    until his cheeks bleed
                    in any attitude but rampant
                                    don't do the hula quiz
                    as invited deteriorates noisiest bladders —
dynamite's self-esteem, bluntly miscellaneous
horned cannibal denominator with fetal spurts
takes on rectal lease hectored ovum:
                    the way to a man's heart is by head —
                    is it necessary to bleed a trophy
embellishing what breathes saddled leisure
lumpish swivel genus aspirant in
                                    Sum Fella
                                    Discreet Bunny
culottes, give her a separate sweat hut:
    and stitch mundane
                                    Twist On Past
desires quiver deviate men appropriative hello
narcissized by overrated steeple
animus affects captive cute
faulty others — dwarf in haste
                    equals training for a bigger wrong
trousseau with vasectomy — even condoms have hearts
                    clone the air softly
                                    huge laps
squeegee that smarts a zero at the bone clamps of style —
efforting ally motors speechless fame-throwers
lease yourself to depend unwhole & fame-retardants, self-

## MERCURY 4

importance retread discomfort made literal
exercising spots, empty out the hot mind
temper's mucilage addiction spangles
                          than being aloof
penis practical on picnics.

## MERCURY 5

Bᴜᴛ virgin's accuracy
                    sleek magenta self-promotion per capita
if they auction you off, plug attire ankle-waisted
                                    fancy enough will eunuch
she will lactate, he will not, a neck-buster fleece
                                    certain tapered
happy shinola so coquettish homely sickish limbo
enamel late & broken shorts withhold lights,
                    cosmetic complaints department,
oversized tutu swaths of shrank with tails
— (you get a little high & everything sounds good) —
                    *les girls* silver terse, dolorous spelling
                                    bob top
                                    colloidally fresh slack
enrolled those that have beds to bother.
        Compulsorily male adhesive
                    cameo-studded velvet dog collars
                    wed semen truss tube chest servile ardor:
they're hoovering your face, impotent and lucrative
spinal foreclosure that little boosters sugarize:
a geriatric embarrassment, eyelash push-ups
taken seriously as a cooked-off naturalized invalid —
                    (jackets suffice, what is a bob cut?) —
pollen pansied heavy dolls with aerosol rockets
apostrophically forcefed — hey, crabcakes!:
                    torque & give me stripes —
allied with the acme of graceful, modest & wonderful posing
                                    vassaled heartbeat
only where flesh is tolerated is around the breasts —
earrings that talk
cordial before cute somatic emergency leasee.
        Diverse dinettes unite —
                    plato's motel food endearments as diminutives
dialing for dolls' irretrievable suppositories
infant mule-sled vertebrae, call home:
                    four girls' heads in echelon
shopping aggressiveness deposits next the priapic donor
of fetal sand in face with a clutch
                    depicted cramp catheter gesture

## MERCURY 5

fanfare lacquers limbs —
not-so-giant conceit for their sake we're nurses
dedicating our lives to helping you choose
the perfect tears by Acquisitional

birth with a bullet —
*zher voo prayzahngt*
pez one Direct Male Chauvinist Little Gun
little fabricked, fabricated, agonizing unbaking
bodies convivial stirrup creatures, this adipose proliferation —

boys talk excitedly to placemats
you'd look better on with headphones
movement deploys this individual

heart on vaccination,
cosmetic closures certified hymen floral
exhalation by consent, proverbs on loan.
And ACCEPT

you want to be unimportant
lucky for fangs trying to kill time on her face —
OK, pasta wombs!:
femme ladders predisturbed gape & hold up your hand
ripe vows bows woe
light the light, romeo, whose astonishing and chaste displays
of suppleness have won the title of cartilaginous wonder:

free things to do on drugs
one for Style
one for Timing
one for Execution
it's the *white blouse* revolution wearing white something

already in the toaster —
decorum fingers the glowing —
could you twice hemp around sieve
boys walk their dogs shame beyond shampoo
to suck *their* dogs, waist tied up & amiable needle

skin straps of exploit me
well-behaved above the rules.
I *receive* bimbette so dependence
she recruits electrolytic genitalia for quintuplets, an act
of indelible behave, hula
use of envy disperser swerve to squeak prohibited, chic he care

# MERCURY 5

                              (without jealousy all you have is ecstasy)
stroller acceleration
I covered my hens, how's my little layaway? —
jiffy donate formal getting ease, untaxed bandage
manning the mops, wind your- embarrassed samaritan -self
                              into lack of confidence
babysitters show that rage

                                        paid tracts
                                        for conduct
                         false semantic, sex cement
                         bluebeat boost bitten in-laws
                         leap to slap choice sweet or disdain
                         got a bleeder overawed
patient husbanded hooves — girls smoothed their rough ribs
date reduced to yodelling contest dresses,
                         none could raise their arms over their heads
                         I wet my pants —- wet yours!,
I stopped talking because no one listened.
       Put in your face to work with industry
amoeba-like versatiles enjoin adolescence slippage
wants a vacation and some of the stoogelike action —
                              defiled *for*? —
meringues expel shimmy colossus womb as rentable space
                    chicken gets strollers in heat hook
                              hormones overwhelm
to stimulate the maturation of egg-bearing follicles
in the ovaries with some knee-jerk body-popping
                         hammering pedigreed waiting in thrall
to distress without stress glands couching fussy spermula;
                    family is *little* entrepreneur
                    I'd multiply for cash privileges —
                    *foateel pehyay poor ler baybay?*—
the prince also favors a traditional wedding script
                    wait out for brood lasso deliberate
inconveniences inciting patty-cake skills
                              who's forgood of it:
the same way minks
get minks, dearie.
       Shampoo rules rough go at unimport


86

## MERCURY 5

nurse with celestial wing wound kith sparks just bewilder
hand frills to pet imperatifs, slugs nearing hole
                                incontinent through baby solo between
affectional retardation; posh domesticated —
Again, a mother had found the reprehensible!:
she was once a horrified throat fertilizer, restless pointless
flightings — my 'minimum cellular' minimum debauch,
I went around knocking on everyone's door &
asking them if they'd be my mommy — unsung bombardment
                                membered buddy needles jealous in
outstretched & stoppered varicose values, sovereign bondage
                                frightened placebo's birthright pulse,
only comfortable husband wastes grace self-handling
when intimidated bodily this commodified with dignity
always imagined them in need of her caresses:
                                come over, let's fail,
      lowercase grievances wch can be borrowed
                                                swallow formulaic fork
                                gravity in vocal paraplegic diapers,
                                spurning nimble dressing exit all for you
big silhouettes in a drug-infested bridal aisle
                                                paint spine on stigma
                                                choices knock nelly
die in court with nonstop kitchen foot in door
invoked faceless chitchat colony of poses —
'there are no rules' means 'women get hurt bad' —
                                less passion from less protein preemptive
                                prudently safari-like anorexia grew festive
                                mickey-mousing the emotions —
they could read your palm & you could fuck the daughter
jogging your pets, shudder salient
vassaled trace self-curtailed
      pulleys bent over at a pale prom nape,
adopt hum-stands, crooked black & blue
gregarious worms in reproachful leisure chemise:
he talks about dolls that urinate too bored to grow
                                                heart thinks by the book
                                a learned pills lull radio desperation
                                dresses up as hallucinatory distraction

## MERCURY 5

      dark from coinage
        forbidden communal sense —
delegates of the tired fiesta lambs,
conjugal pork-barrel perfunctorily sublime.

## MERCURY 6

Unruly fragility sin fines superillustration
to typify despair closet praise irresponsibly
pull your face and douche that analogy, it's a machine
                    free padding with remnant since you please —
                    the cleaner the colon
                    the clearer the complexion
a fluid body preordered
shape's gross to supple stagelit halflife
lace in news tuned slipper, ovoid perusal harmony
                    in the lo-cal rumbling
face up amiss stumps for motionless suction release
                    lick it off your purpose —
                    automated scissors kick say when
forehead canceled value-conferring plier in itself.
        Lonesome jubilee
                                    neo-identity
                    tethered rouge & even fancy rope twirlers
backwards twinned granularity bumping heads in their sockets
                    out-of-wedlock:
                    ex-stitchers sashay unmistakably, if I
                                    were you —
                                    I am lovers
interested in flapping self distilling custody heart —
I'm just a dancing partner, now you soften
your ladyness spores, it sprouts me
                    as an inconsequential puncture self-
canceling pampering skills sequestered pet smile
                    isolate bridles cuddly nize
                    first litter, liaisoned banzai
                    I hate necks, intimate labial stuff
interims, glory assumes a fixed limb;
        and dance
                    still self-questioning *stillness*
if *au pair* pampered annex, dance as lick outside
                    ditch aroma acquisition
                    velocity verified virgin favor
victims how to dance promote buttery ways
quick to redundant as you can and these tolerable
                    solitary desires are prehensile —

trick clog, pedestal clog and statue clog
teeth are out of it: I think it's nice
                    they're having their halt to lack movement:
                    you want some confidence? — join a group,
                    frontalized nonchalance free
amicable relations among australopithecines —
                    closet quietism danger
arousal byproducts splintered quick distance.
    I adapt to
                    without biting cares avenging proximity
                                    teasing ronds de jambes
                    beguile knows a particle:
say it, speak! — solder down sweat white breath
                    seizing super speechless companions
as long as we have objects — MEET OTHER LEFT SINGLES —
we can still talk:
                    man, these big boobs are busting out,
                                    leg-lifting skids talk
double your waste secret less share unisex
interrupts concern earns to mate man who for love
                    distraughts himself, drummed too tight
                    lust grows on less pulse as scraps
                    the *conversazione* on-again, off-again
sweet distilling.
    But *be* bowed me *ice* foam
                    my solitude diagnosed tippy-toes
reaches myself, syncopate at all puppet dalliance
half halated energy flunkies — I would not
                                    mistressify me drowses
                                    pin hard times
somersault without stripes feeling beat glaze to sad
to pine for want harm's hem lube to all? —
heartquarters inert cuisine
                    estrange heart salvage
                    domesticate for usage
complaint iotas touch the flunk skin around proof of cupidity
eradicates difference.
    Orbital eccentric complicit heat, the *relative* body
pull reimbursed the saga of household spies at wound —

## MERCURY 6

                                    someone made me for you
                          swollen incident lungs dispel novel nuptials
wish more cells, sweet prick canopy stare
the lips of the split skirt management securers:
humanly puppies — you sit still hard compassion
                          has its charms so *satisfied*
                          private joint nook egotism wrongs
Alone, disappoints difference certain plush; line up
to be phallus in wonderland material as concrete
love options in which Cupid makes me kiss the rod —
duplicate expiation cheating insurance, will to membership
                          delicately martyred.
         Freedom of information act's controversial vendetta
semen gossamer covert error spine negates
quote Men compartmentalize their feelings unquote
                          heart is need you exhaust
teapot without spout, the trim secrecy pirouette
                          metal mates to less spurious
heart palpitates with anti-gay bigotry interpellated in pieces
with lust, evasion
takes fire over self-encapsulated fan
that defeats the eater halves at pry to chatter —
                          we are dangerously infallible in the —
claustrophobic syncopation honeymoon insists you've got fetus
on your breath;
      but sentence, shut up & listen
                          thousands thief through use
                          lucking leisure as distance
                                    widows circling around
white underbellies have their election body
exposed to the hook vainer tutor beating
orbits shudder along veins inlaid grief
                          plenty of something desire
                          proximate remoteness franchised closet
                          treaty forestall identity too serious
heart fit mood of doomed ardor home, with this ring
                          climax pays its dues —
fault arcane sorority isolation vaginated sublime
                                    *limitless compliance* —
language castrates
me, I'm a speciality.

## MERCURY 7

By not —

                          rejuvenated flagellants — even puppy-like —
                          conquest — covert — desire
                          tender mongrels' secondary defloration
and the fondling of the decapitated head, nobody in particular
how these cuds could help: cooking and nothingness,
I am an ultra-period
                          ovum dairy daughter jury indiscriminately
                          predator mannikin, doorknobs of vengeance —
maybe his neck is negligent, just sag normal,
      verb great error
euphoria-deflating scar tissue calls it home start curs
blackmail by the past — sweltering passive pathetic calm
                                        prom lie-detector tests
                                        Mother, that lesbian
                          blistering clone foster punters
the most popular in all cosmetic surgery is breast size increase,
mascara'd yarn crown, Amazonless envy as malice
                          artery, discretionary vampire
                          hyperventilate into stardom:
                          how much are the split duchess dolls? —
somersault enjoined lipstick blackened blood purple rinso
                                        hormoned me
                          the same way
                          dogs are made
                          to salivate
(punitive congratulations to your disability, I got nothing
                          to be queen antagonizing temperature)
tucked in by predators, the nail polish could vote better,
                          roommate suffraged on me:
was fate the language of local taste, always shape liars
                                        Ideal Puppet
                                        Natural Act
                                        Nia Lady
                                        In Law
insecurity is the superstructure pocket model,
the spineless live in a world of hotheads
                          & the era of tyrannies starts with dinner;
                                        pregnant amputee persona

## MERCURY 7

as a department store of its own dissimilar sterility
helpful as honor parents for toughs wrong
life in a blender needs trappings, assist your child
                      with another shut-up ego profit
                      — [she owns him or her father owns him?] —
                                retired appeases
                                longest tightness
love.
        Now division of attributes sure makes 'lack attracts'
'widespread' —
gullible utensil photosynthesis, aborigines of chastisement:
                      unpremediated incubations, suburban housing
                      for embryos' squadrons of sentiment
you pressure through love — steambed pecking order
                      disguised as adrenalin natal prance —
(follow me around identically endentured) —
force to feel you're not just being nihilistic
                      to be accommodating warm-blooded moderns
general labor eggs of
exhaustion, pranked in
a will to pincushion theory relinquishment,
        erogenous in her cupboards
                                a lot of movement
is just avoidance of pain dispersal follies —
you can be wrong without overextending yourself —
                      think pretty walls widen me:
sentiment rental consumed deny-hearted saluting, joy stoppers
                      as if disperse all
greased for melancholia, venemous melancholy
                                flirt firms
                      envy in tasks slack formatives .
                      faked choice besotted of
                      planned complacence: strip hub
                      ointmental regiment ladies stand in subtract
                      to tumble — Grumpy buys you.
        Ordinate bone nerved norm
forced hybrid sexed fees cruising the makeup
                      in a buy-well-so-breed property cup,
sluice conditionals

worship some thalidomide society at the gland shrine
                              party will end for blood lack of blood —
we install confidence
for having sexual intercourse with an angel
      let these alibi standard
libertarians kill their own babies
join the mediocre as gift infiltraitors [sic]
                                    maybe full sky nails
                        false flowered cage in aspic
                        dance during sorry nuclei dance only
ransom almost parenthetical hit on what dollar nerve amount
                        make me choke motive-and-motionless
                        I don't see
died upon accepting the personal role as pressured
                  elevation worms to scratch
by constraint, foster parents bled in sympathy:
enthusiasm suffocates hurting volley
impassive in debt — keep this ass body from kicking, shock
the corpuscles into submission, shop now for best martyrs.
      Did the victim ovulate? — quake? — tremble? —
                              regression forgives
                              ballet = autopsy
                              rivalry subdivisions
percentage of seizure he's honest safe good males & females
                              differentiated from
prefatal man in order to privilege man:
& the mock paste unfurled flag inhibits the wrath of aunts
                        caught to be
                  privileged impotence sign public / private
is gift desire drives considered inappropriate for women
                  presumption Very Inc. appear on stage alone:
I divorced him to get more children in my bed —
                  ministerial moisture expectation
as a gift carpets posture ideology risibly
                  sex toy compendium,
the values aren't as bad as the people who have them.
      Kitschy brag searing space
nice fist heretofore chattel putty ramify the prod
fear & loathing doctors of authority

## MERCURY 7

woman hater & love it??
self-knowledge = self-corrosion
                                        spreading the absentees
                          romance or pre-mance —
penultimate winking as interpellation averages capitate
dish limbo destiny belief:
I find that having a personal
life just keeps me home more,
                          no instruction without supercession
                          liberty for righteousness like choke collars
abdomen by sped pistle court.

## MERCURY 8

Simply swathe idioms
                              default managerial pride
moist fop glow the thing-outside-itself hymnal enough —
that's a hard word to say but I still like it, hostesses:
                    four walls rupture defunct
                    codicil prompted of crypto-insemination knot,
cell guilds denoted into easy payments, eager tuxes
diplomatically fixed uncertainties
                         wheeled in after starters —
                         houses with no humid hardware
                         windows, misnomers quintessence.
        You say: freeze
                    face bedpan eyes guise gag
mum behind wedge emotive hub, Meaning by K-mart
a purse is worth a thousand words, pretty trellis symptoms
                    urge doubts to secret sale, same
                    turns elusive sameness luster in all
                    lackluster flurry brains were suffocationists
                    nourishing fakery — thumpy structures! —
when you read, we don't see the eyes smirk
dolphins in disguise feel better mute so we don't know
what you're feeling — all it takes is pinpricks
caught from behind & viscera gets to moralizing
the executive tool.
        This bright impersonal clutter
                    royal flicker orphan drugs precariously endow
                    surgeon hold can't help it aloft —
femininity certificates: admonitory full-grown
alliance with grief
                    previously called 'feminine testicles'
busily attached is slit indicative perm
blushing pandemonium — vote out of self-pity
                    the first udder, naive room
pornography of space fatties go gold rate isn't adult.
        Extempore mechanics lower ceiling, alcove struts
                    deficient lullabied regret in rows
wringing tongues — you really work for a living? —
                    fancy ends *unsettle* more
means, I mean, it's *say say* fancy than he says

## MERCURY 8

                                        douse that smile —
learn evasive of punctual vagrancy, escape
buckles impasse
prickly was to boom as lachrymose prefab
tissue fatuous lubricant of which you are phony permission total
                        sign somersaulting mighty patty melt
target void bears seed, predicate falsifies
the long donation
                        full rehousing guilt vengefully slowed.
        Tighten your
                        back to brood — chairs make the movement
protocol's spit-and-polish risk by numbers number ticked
they cultivate their fixations, sacrificially speaking
                        heedless gobbling
trained to a subjugation of the vocal organs
the fertility deal soon pension please (slickback) spurn;
I cater your none soon pale exit words
less than half absent Quotation Marks on the throne
I don't like new: make the pearl over again —
spoon on Talking
Books are things between us and Books
                        adaptable stabbing to argue hurry
amniotic messages, the average spoke out.
        Verbatim repetition can tease
digesting weeps of enfranchisement fenced burp
Lord will be prick: suburban signals' manifest & extol
newlyweds unfurled messy insignia, tidy
stigmata puffs spliced lumps grammar defanged me —
we deliver mothers curvature of the composed unmistakable
gap rule solder wedding ring & executive estrogen,
                        width festum curb standardizing
the emotions as tax-deferred delivery systems —
mannikin requests spoilage, despot head tool joint
                        all under correction
the wards of the state have pleistocene bedroom
in their prayers perpetual motion;
                        stitch the sperm armada
affection just fits right into your underconsumption theory
sentence first, verdict afterward.

## MERCURY 8

Law-sheathed hyper-duty limb spaces out on ceremonials
                    pretty steady attitude defamation
                                        baste that
                    litigant garage hours regularity entrothed
                    old = exquisite stun in maze contains present
servitude with quotables for rank breakneck devotees —
                                        unborn file suit:
cropped by the future, sky bleeds to get endentured
abacus hidden harness all change as neurotic
decorating Mammon hoot because maternal
parented insignificance, chorus pleads grateful stubs.
        Hard answer
                        flounces toward ratio
recto-verso
                        splintly fervor apprehend integer
multiplying missing person
devices possess us: too many drivers, sameness personified
the inner straphanging out into the outer
                        anonymous attrition
most closely resembles napkin apprentice
                    salve gores sameness coupons
                    differencing general garment repute
                    necessity by degrees
                    droop as shrimp would
if they decide to go into the shrimp business —
error is our language, proper
holes buy this everyone mouth
infection where you least dream
                        domination rudely Interior
to facts vivacious.

## MERCURY 9

Tattered tinsel conscripts of impersonality:
His Polite Gentlemen or a skin cell in livestock advantaged
            wilting for dote, salacious
            monotono-gamy toxin invite your whole life
like one satisfact tongue-depressor plaza'd pull-up —
animals wet my pad; pull toys, puppet! —
                  big by shrinking
invertebrate prudence boxes, spouse arrives by hologram.
    You say: disenfranchise
            my stomach's finished with you —
            noiseless punch in their christening dresses
            with asymmetric four-button closure
            with two-handed minisuspender
                ransom-wear
effigy bimbo-colored state-of-the-tart sandwich meat
            Adrienne Rich is quite an omission —
              (light)
evil flap dimmest ironing pad launching pad
gambles incision, fear fold adulterers as too healthy
            in tights — hub stock
home spurt mannikin melodrama slap & despoil;
    and lizard under my parasol
            fingerprint devotion dolls baste to a fault
whose skirts are meant to keep a covered dish warm
            slimmer, subtler, rubberized
            big subversive top hat
notaries of the pall, passport abort bargain mandatory moth
            treats consumer flame — meat varies
            complimentary chicken charm tastelessly
            familiar; they were perfectly normal
except for their appearance, maybe your identity could —
hasn't creamery a certainty
born to be a backseat retread.
    Your *totale*
pretzel-limbed offspring of nocturnal emission faucets
build a softer infrastructure at the mercy of the survivors
sputtering endorphins for a human piece
lackeying common body old enough to bleed, old
enough to butcher the sorriest fascinators

MERCURY 9

unleveling [unbeveling] mispraise
some allegiance on the cross-dressers —
manger-matic dunce cap on cock
statutory pedestal scrubbed locality
who else quarantined
knighted over semen
panties in the petri dish —
fertility owns the roundtable brows,
makeshift brood drawers
& dismissive foster jokers:
choosing a safe for use in your home,
restrict with gain
gilded danger, ankle removal jostled
bargain shaves another mammal's armpit
homing horning, feed normal breakage not freed
by darts, suburban unsaturated
betrayal in technicolor which *diminishes?* —
self-devaluating flounce into overt gyp:
or that this prejudiced finesse clone my inhibitions —
appropriating the child when it is praiseworthy
disowning [it] to mate if not — irreversible people
moving conceals star in stirrups;
lewd tuning fork, big black atomizer correct them all —
(e.g., a restraining notice, an information subpoena,
a sheriff's execution or an order of attachment)
clamp peripheral babies buttressed as service folly.
Listen to me
forcefed rapture, placenta collide
contrived to raise their lily-white hands in horror —
just don't put his dick in your mouth —
to stand profile to profile and spit at one another, bravo it all
its futilization canon:
no carpenter could this oriole be;
floral hygienic impersonal lactation
supplicating ammonia
Miss Mam felicity drone hints up frontward sap
DBA, dead before arrival squats maneuver.
Aminoing up the lacerated
lick industrial forgiven cupid

dictates perjury flat on tout — Am I homeopath —
Buck A Dance pull sweethearts up heartless harness
                ice to temper if crowds
                narrow, bone-informed pent up poodles
                gelding opposites too much two-faced
clone safety for a living,
    dressed to detoxify pliable dissection's disobedience —
I chose to be a slave to increase my self-esteem:
                      divorce on automatic
bragging trap connive erosion ribbing palls
by respect, we have bulk conversations now —
nightmare of federal troops in my bedroom dilettantishly unhinged
little sister turns on big sister, pride goeth
before a vacancy erotic amiable grief vacuity of
pride in bodystocking diaspora.
    With this, purchase paradise
                helps it sublimer wish not want not
                so then give me my ring string attached
releases the subjectivity of destroyed subjects —
                      mass cloak dial-a-tribe
subdivide the scarlet anti-mischief, protective dispensing
                herd me tight wampum betrothal
                safe in code swath.
    Operant core conscience hindered whims
                close, never drama baby beast
                with prenuptial stipend adviser
                pride impersonates appetite
                pollen in suit magnified antipathy —
to coin an old phrase, why give it away if you can sell it? —
affadavit under status cell mime is back for real,
    up & down blood roofing easy unsteady to purse —
yeah, but they crowded one with Love assured of boss
                woke in the heart of a machine
                discofied arrest, name simplexes
emote in sandwich form the *representative* body
                milky heart repeating surfaces, static depth
rim truss
celebrated unfit fire.
    Originality sales points age is a suitor —

so what if they tough, at least they stay at home self-shopping
                         impersonated hybrid symptoms
                         if all the certified geniuses are white males
besting bother up broad way fit puritanical average
sockets make you elegantly adequate erect
orgasm is a mushroom of merchandise:
                         You Must Be Like Yourself To Be Happy —
both do not have pictures of vaginas,
     distance rancor solitude
                         norms save face self equal pay dolls —
                               polygamy is divisive?:
                         don't act so superior to all your superiors:
mute curvature champion
                         zero confidentially legs after a number
adjudicating these ejaculate acupunctured honeymoon:
                         misfitting flow now too! —
amateur swelling amateur can't get the stuff in
supervised by similarity deputizes the manhood scales;
                         the sleek sheen of perfect
                         profit value sit down to drown out
     they miss me sick
                         blackmail sells short youngish scale
scapegoat inventors, boy prices, disciplinary
                         coagulation of identity pornography
causes unknown venereal disease rubber
                         speechless hopeless
communitarian boiled roxanne error circuit
demure extra-narrow version of doll hut ideals —
harmless total
may yield me
include populated
to belief agonizing equal
is not a threat, security
arouses me unlike actual
persons, the mistakes
                         respond to upholstery.

## MERCURY IO

Now, low-calorie dictum traces
liking all praise codes in cosmetology, false grammar
deposits tongue regularly white in bank
so oblige same abruptly simple scale broodings —
                              the sorrow and the pity men
science passionaria amazed mad, practically anyone will do:
lamb-inspired Oedipal systematics, Shill I think
fantasied hampers Indeterminate Sentencing.
      Your skin vs. your job corruption, dire tiers
tame what's duct
by unspoken propietary tissue-built handclasp —
                              a crowd not merely around me but within me —
hidden shellfish jailer postures mix anatomy
at discount slumping deposit, bestial sever
each dormitoried diffraction justice hula
pop-up test bed: nice guys are finished first
mush on blackboard
                              made me semblance tornado
                              sambo center clung,
      and as poverty becomes more & more a women's issue
                              rubberized jury decor
jewels interest me; party dolls
of the captive nations, love through power
salutory dough
                        *ewn grahmehr*
civic decoy annoyance as trophy stirrups force
plies impasse
sham zones: crowd pleased with own mass
authority with receipt attached nurtured expulsion
                              conspiracy to infect red devils
                              shanghai'd or liberated?,
                              your money got hard
('and' — or 'to') ('or' and 'too') secure.
      Hallmarkish (admonished)
condiment norm grief mothers ply the infants to palpitate
subordinates ineffectually renowned, those walls
                              grow hard — congratulations
got so coercive that cobwebs cling to bondage
                              — or else — sincere,

103

diamond numbed all distinction
social slow me tractable accost accuses
              tramp forefront scale belongs to men
              exchange their emotions for credit
              expedient automatism dictating its norm
              hula same lubricated leaker —
butcher's apprentice trappist selves' virus turns off
siblings as handsome modifiers, I'm not
the red detachment of women in form
ation.
      Center grief
musters from periphery, behavest among behavest, rebus
                      taste them spun whole
                      serf-same role grease —
              wounds fit, crowds don't lie:
              Sadomaso scenarios *have* increased —
circle expunges all supine
              norms disturb, nothing disturbs
norms informanting contraceptives and wife
                    canonic caprices
recommend adored sediments, paralyzed still belongs
              completely laced by this
                    swoop into affiliation
              talks extra pleats get unpleated
              jitter republic fell in on me
to flee your rights obstacle prodigal
              safe summonsing rhesus beat.
      Apparatus helps you ejaculate my rent — species overtime
              by cordoning deceives its virtue
frequency frustrates
opportunity squirt enforces by worshiping
              a kind of forfeited
use-ual plan beats me up with misplaced confidence fit =
annul megaphoned by
biology: well, calibanish *me*
I can only egg so much
anatomy bears womb aroma repetition;
      currency divides
the surface scissors, bureaucrats of pure lesion —

but no people ... I got this fixture papoose
grammar allows me to be imperceptible
catheterizing the horizon anonymous unemotional code motion
formality of the convalescing stigma face and fees:
                 sheepness between paradise & self-murder
                 constant rubber majority peonage swoon enamor
                 prosecuting sweet sake cocoon made solid
professionals of insecurity an exmatriation
                          Inherit The Crowd
              by traction homing abuse —
              *whose* mothering theorist? —
              his *wife* is the private sector, centrifuge's
future anticlimax factions
                 and in the eloquence of a conversational
between speak-your-weight machine and whoopee cushion,
equilibrists seek that shower of inattention
the phallus feels for the phallus —
                 you don't recruit slaves, darling.
    Slavery is suffrage slave's
avocation? — uterus came into inheritance
slang injects & denies your status quo need
a little more reassurance? — susceptible to proxy redeems
the unborn, crucial for suture as society suffer sameness
                      a blamed reverts
                      unglued pupils
                      sediment I *issue*
emotional place-holders for the artillery conscience
builds an upholstered clandestine culture, the community
reaches up our skirt assault white-elephant humor:
all preserving sweet, inegalitarians of domesticity
all scratch no discourse, all illusion, all cheek
desire got some too general all normative denatured devises
dividends instead of carpets means quarantine
a spatially suckered leg as crowd control insertions:
                 you'll love ours.
    Data sex whites of crowd made a civic corpse of —
troubles end in tubing, general escapeless crescential ego
fission schizophrenia for influence-spotters
                 turn toward a culture of birth

antique halos again, universals, omni-adjective
pocket-sized everything
heritage hovers & clowns
                                you're *stemmed*; certainty
gives it crowd.

# VENUS

## VENUS I

Sole artifice urgency dream
on vari-colored blossoms, a loop spying
for pleasure features a dominant narration by the spurned lead:
                              frills are bank steno folly crabs;
because a tonk broad —
                              I'd never heard the expression before —
antique gash makeup
to nourish Narcissus flute in flower
where cat makeup won't work, terminal jealous proofs,
                              antique tabasco on the cleavage —
your eyes look like snake bites facing error;
       but fluid stem chaste tips
                              amends fruited fallacy humping observers
foam blonde spades and diamonds too much rabbit rousers, paws
                              to enforce missive ikon, starry-eyed
                              spoonlike ikon guesswork
gonadvertising like the adding together of zeros;
       and *whose* cum thirst? —
                              vocable adjective amply bachelors
kneecap audition gets intimate under interrogation, addenda
whispers blindly: the forgeries are self-ruining, never mind,
                              surfaces
                              press the emphasis talcum Tories —
                              clause of penis nulls envision
                                            withers in postal —
how deceptively out of date one mouth can be! —
white powder White Paper chests wolf hectic curl
highlights bush problems *découpage or décolletage*
                              taxonomy valueness.
       I dream to slump little pointy verticals
unfathomed width tuxedos cock rests on form
                              lint limbs boning smile for a headrest
breath brands the ooze, Supphose for wristlet
wide-eyed voice split ribbing up above
penitent jewels hang low —
modesty forbids consciousness.
       And pap size voice
                                            voice visual victory
painterly near like a luau pit metrically leering

# VENUS I

circle encloses zero
chili-tipped heartshrunk casual excavatory blahs,
kindless knots louver aura
tenancy soothing reddish anemia sterility lessons,
sisterer labyrinth creature deviant mode
melody in cavity comes & goes,
grief with hair
chain-purse compares itself to
default translucently denied, florid vista intern
event dividing cream prisonered puree antianimate
monochrome bleu closed for novel hard yellow
static lop.
Imperious hymen mute
inert intent femme to slush hound
posturing beefcake vinylize on cue —
*ahngkrahssay* —
toxic missus visible or not
witless wetless
jack on foam, blank spots me a blank
lips swivel on the neck
to spy on what rejects you
I'd get nauseous if I look at my hand, false makes huge of hope
magenta somnambulist quiver
bonbon stifles
inner spazz — *see it!* —
falsifying triangle of entail
despise the ellipse, I've ordered my rubberized underpants;
and backseat minuet flying-chocolate
jelly on force these tacky little devices to
keep us from just talking, insinuate silence
tremblers in bereft
sung shut desire.

## VENUS 2

Personal & epidermal
                              bald flame alto gel
tease paint that brood with matchless colonic caution patrons:
                    teeny budge galvanizers
                    rejects tryst in term
insecurely insincere; she's blowing snakes, high-heel juniors,
                    unwinds fault to wait commit to waiting:
single plush, I paw into
                    the affected decking up of naked bunk.
      Self-therapy for the butter
murmur garment, this muscled pant of view —
ribbed hilt heart beats like a hammer:
      heat balk gated pulse quickened germ
                                        elusive chaste throbs
                    hardy heat dalliance *steals away*
bone-controlled parade;
      courteous deliberately loutish
blood stood deep blue ploy blushing mask
shudder still barely akimbo
stuttering rims smoke from your cigarette —
nervous smacked the wad that flickers quiet.
      Shall I vote flirt lips unused
                    putative face enamor ambush
punctually swallow marbled woo, just a hello
                    flooding cyclops style — the lockjaws
                    are beautiful and I am miserable,
      shelving piece ball's between impress
the knees express a crush wanked ever
swizzle's regret leg look viscera:
her hands were unheated lofts, promises —
                              don't touch a stranger.
      And *error* to torment
sucrose in hearsay sizzles to makeup
                    question flattered mishaps —
                              bush battering sting
lures cementing up buff deriding damp blandishments in cellar
consummate crack lump fans out
                    coquettish hegemony, pink staccato mahogany
ankles acceptably deep blinks then retreat:

110

## VENUS 2

saturnalia blisters all the fingers spurning out its own!
    Prone bunt semened gag goned grief
                            spread over-costumed
insult snitch misunderstandings surpass all forbidding:
                tow that hymen! loving complaint
                    wetresses
                stale court nozzle jinx tumult, confusion
head want of moisture socket is shy —
                *zher feh day koashmahr —*
                *zhay ew day voamees sermahng —*
                *zher swee treh nehrvur —*
                I'm only visible mistakes.
    If the lips prove any more soundproof …
                misrobing delicacy soft
                when it's sweet happy humble disease,
                is that slick? — animal
                tacitly humidified azure tummy
V-necked tint of castrato-voiced jelly:
it must be full of spiderwebs inside
it comes right off on
spatula if that's fingers unliaisoned
dim as daft rouge lower spine.
    Wouldn't it just bounce off the ribs —
                not slender but addicted
                eden's prude supercede flesh
                        pyritised kisses
decorate your limbs in memory, oracular perspiration
insidious body interior erections through surgery —
my sugar is so refined.

## VENUS 3

Time is mercy kino pimp
needy teenages women are supposed to love
those distant, penis-bearing creatures; gladiatorial
phantom oral spiral holiday pedestal truss coveys immanent
blue breed size defer light
sinful azure lust limbs utensils ascribe to stiffness.
    And arrogant slump what straps, what a happy mast —
                                high tops
stiletto corners, that off-putting delicacy, this little world —
                      reaper connotations.
    Strawberry bind sorority of, shadow noise —
intellect with its own oral lid fucking your vernacular postulate
                      secrecy pleads its topping hates —
forceps replay slope forthcoming saliva messages;
a stuffer thought paraphrasably deterred hard
                      parroting 'suffer' arousal creeping pivot
                      the tighter surrogate appeals
the sieve abandons.
    And elevate perturbs
blood-splattered *repertorio* — banality at its bluepoint
to salute that obstacle jellied promontory
squiring eclipse, wolfing schizated flash
banners a need a way, dread treasure, sweat perfected vanity:
that's what scares me to vomit cum-like paint,
    chicken and the hawk privileged prey
                    got the clever adolesce
hominess size on us, some fetal losers,
                    rudder syntactically beguiled
palate out of WAC exact birth smell real cherry bubble donor —
primary conjunction: to animalize
                climactic tricks, allegate gestate
                membrane anchorite hyphenate
stain wider hermaphroditic gulf,
    really, this ...
doodle doodle doo disagreeably nurture entertaining sublimation
                every projection begins to have sedatives
                is jake's tricks bleeding bitter
                stiffly flameless warmth, divides point:
                ovary tarts anxiety delights!

## VENUS 3

And legs spread have no relationship
interpret blood-red carriage exhaust
inequality begins in the mouth
gobbling up string around the heart — don't take me
for a pantyhose!, rods which crux a finger
netting hold hardened help prejudiced a spoon offend;
        indoctrinated red cross insignia on the mattress
turnovers before warm spit the subordinate business:
                        honey warp-mounted vulnerable akimbo
phallus cartel, a badge of mobile prone pride;
bow-legged decorator's cum stand would be false promise —
                        I don't know that I want regular people,
                        only land can really unmake history.
        Grief code
rubs advance eyes vacuumed blue
                        gains blue aphasia *end* on *head*
humbling deposit regret
perfumes delirium only.

## VENUS 4

Because you thrill accrete
suffering to submit bait committed *covets*
bumper to bumper thrust-o-mine — mine more, prying
shoulder summation annoys you,
    baits the beat sweetex exhorts
                    pleasure solvent look big physique of charge
this tempt's for you — self-injecting valentine
                henride *come hard* paste half-faced
flirt espousals to me.
    I'll talk to you just as long
as you're fucking me, wounded lips pawn
              a milky roll mixture bouquet hesitant
              stiff kittens' heartbeat finger
fritters harping spoon — it's hard to hear
infinite maybe, an entire devotion winced passion convertibles
on stilts unselectively; avert gaze quickly
kindles apologize to drain priapic risk encouragement:
the hand is such a treason.
    Maché choir milk — 'The Open Hand' came across good
bite for lilt almost crushed wistful halve
pardoning me with your eyes looking up & then down —
              rental hope sugar minute
              face governs mad deifier's swoon —
              now words between ourselves, I'm slippin' in
very much between ourselves.
    Unbutton amply at unbuttoned best
surface-to-underwear missiles, oral slaves track this bulge
              through the pearls' mutual compressions
on top of me — plump & pliant leash bended knees to sleep
tracing knees on cream abandonee.
    Coy close again cameo
              I'm hocking for this guy licks lick it off
rubber gets the juices going off your purpose —
              dreamt harborer heart-burnings, whispering
              strip shooters coveted your bang
the pie does that too fast:
    hyperactive labial beeper
clasp backward dire along oh lone hurt me sign tight to go
              clutter bestride intimacy detoxified

## VENUS 4

                                        'bare shoulders'
                          come arc over
& perform those IOUs.
        Dreamish retreat
leaps only blemish tongue feast tears cut the sound
                          jism carnations falsify, brittle middle
cold searching — seams grew despondenter, you can close
your mouth or I'll put it back in: iron quell liaison
                          membrane maidenhead lip gloss fully intact
ruins;
        I'll pine away
                          you who nervously look smaller
in vain sigh crazy for tryin', crazy for cryin'
indecision can't get my bump going
for the uncrowded hand allocates end-stopped fiercely
she'd become, perfect.
        I sat on it at once — kinetic apartheid
intolerably evaporating distance disarms herself
I dressed for burial bothersome treats; take me home
& make me like it — sugar blinks under swoop
                          snake-eyes clear toward you
midnight is enough.

## VENUS 5

Quash spayed tessitura
sold my lunchbox heart to the junkman; happy gloom
                    rubbing bewails facetiously to delay coming
bachelordom in simple
                    units according to missive reproach:
fellatious wanton's tupperware of buttocks
workaholic deliberation.
     Guileless fervors the tissue, but the sighing
untempered kick back to lips big elongated affront
                    armholes forlornly taming the tubs
                    criss-crossed into apoplexy —
                    Most Of The Pretty Young Girls —
scarecrow imitations eliminate all qualities of mushing.
     Effects hoist stick —
                    perpetuate a loss a little, four arms
                    two necks, one weeping, Salammbo, points
erect, dauntless pickings paste as need genetics endearing
                    crust together; credulous savor
that is exquisite longing for the same:
     Immersible — Unanswered — Escortention — Turnover —
                    Boom Boom Bunny — Little Cutes — Decent
                    Hug — Romeo — Bedminster —
                    down flesh lathe
                    in fist shape pressing fix
raffle spurts on cranking tunes.
     It welts half cheek swath
                    lean in hone now at its curb lick this yet
                    so you come near me now —
                    TU EQUIVOCACION, TU INFAMIA —
                              *revolution slowly*
                    incidental bone velcro endebtedness
                    actively as passively eager
choking baste to secrete
practiced circular tremor:
1½ torso top flings.
     Hoist pair to premium got half spurious within
clit kindling verb espayed breast exit delectable
                    in view; he gave my half
                    of your heart a shock

## VENUS 5

                verved off, fractured plasmas easy alone
fish eggs, hmm, don't use your diaphragm ...
promote this seme barrier:

                                      Nettle us, me chaff! —
                I crab for drawers.
      Nature don't come inside, licking slim & flavor trachea
                    outvie in vain red feeders, handlings
inviting got its own risk-free bask —
a mouthful of your breath destroying free between my legs —
rash hand hesitate surrender to instrument

                          self steed start-stop
                          hooked on Other damage
cannot do without red blood.
      Intimate enough clandestine chafe chides
                        never labors
                        pearl-handled stiletto
                in back, between the fourth & fifth ribs
spilled face into disjointed
                  each other facet personal con to repeat
same just night angle purposelessly foaling cautionary with knees
mount toward frictional surrender; corollary:
my peripheral forehead finally subsider grips in
sliding drawers give your lump this lift.
      Cement lap wilt who waits harmed
                  dialing for duds enter the thigh-high
waits quadruple the dose, fex fasted two you such be
with that fly in your cup so let fuck now stain at courtesy
                    vector plows kitten slopes
feeling the smooth muscles relax in the penis
    Kiss crunch heatwave the joints
                hook duty-slotting
                hold on, contrive underneath
hairline remonstrance —
it's always true when you need it; offbeaters
vain intimacy cleavers? — I want you
on my potatoes that bark, battle & ball.
    But keener selfish have absorbed
                me surrender Yummy! — blued auction
dirties yourself for caught off

## VENUS 5

hand doesn't let
any near attributed unsettled mouth:
'right, now you can get dressed again';
      one male leads to another — self-effacing choir mark
              commissaries of chastity manual sulk
                      aching seam heater
                      overdelicate shooting
a panic likes you

## VENUS 6

Incubi, succubi simps out
                    on Rorschach stainwise suppose a fetish
broken bones with ink in plain talk: it's like slack
but without the royalty Fascination as vampirism;
    but undreamed sap
                    gentle false vehement virginal
                    fold ureme tone belies
                    openness down on your knees before
an ambient regrettability error.
    And now my don't let me tell you again
grievous angle dissecting I
disappointment's sophistical weave burned your letter:
                    resigned my lyricism name
is headwash stiff like a syntax —
even a cro-Magnon philosopher like yourself.
    Ah, compulsive unbosoming —
can single people avoid love? — multiply sixteen
candles in scandalese, but I doubt you will [you think all
my attacks are feminist] vanity-adhesive
phobia disappliance: you've got fetus on the breath —
                    Oh no, not that manhandler!
    Nobody's fantasy object works
                            to keep you
                    'people pleasers', celibate overtones
& phantom sublimations squall in the flames
as skin peels off anxious flowers, creepers inside
rumor penalized attitude splendor
signifying trapped haste inning by overhearing greater vapor
needle codes.
    Restrict subsiding swaps this sitting quiz
                    with pencil skirts indict arm off
pets welcome wildly triumphant singing you never loved
                    surgical series jack at all,
                            agreement peeping
punishment certificate to pardon my envy.
    Bunny-like eyelids pull cat of interiorized
minority fog of fragile stump need
                    more people talking regretfully to themselves
zigzag in my bedroom when sucking has come to an end:

## VENUS 6

proof we were drooling the laundered substitutions.
    Segue dispossess
                      enamor should
                      low romancing the shaft isn't ...
                      lowest angels fright
vertical without parallel circular motion in a cylinder —
                      generality is bodily nest light elite
unflamed tinsel transom heart zone.

## VENUS 7

In champion the vagina sailor on leave —
*there*'s a terrible thing to waste: 'bite-size' means
masculine? — gorgeous creosote distress curdled wishing
                              pills' confidential waist
a little vice *affect*, pitch of
juveniliac hose bend with the figleaf,
        monochrome baleful value mastur-
                        Patience oventhruster surge —
penis *dentato* puffy when wet worker mouth
cheek bedecked fiend nymphetamines:
galoshes mistreating devilled eggs & simonizing plush assault
womanizer lingerie for rent.
        Buzzing wilts vain celebratory endorphins —
                        *ewn fehmmertewr ayklehr* —
                        Table Dance Prevailing Kiss, Sharp, Bunny,
                        Dickster, Arms Race, Quicksand, Loincloth,
                        Fever —
I've got the sheets queen effervesce swallow down to my own
rationally distaste time if you've got the vaseline;
        but prophylactic respectively jimmies on my jelly
not preening for yank though milk is vulgate
pressure, how bout it? —
                        c'mere let's squirt & ooze
                        the mercurochrome of pinch
panders too much blood departure & I lack the square inchage:
                              pinky black excusive
                        over-noisy guilted boredom as don't tell me
obstinate harem ice machine shanks in folly indulge.
        Nil hand, dalliance odor single
                        lower bulge would make a difference —
*le cocu magnifique* size queen anthem size sippage
monsters wore leather sob trophies' mortal stroke:
blue molecules, massaged fraud propinquity,
        this hapless hard-on mounting shy muscular durables,
this well hung cake hollow spiral stem
batters distinctly decorated indifference, this pecker luau
toxic suede romance flourishes with one-armed socialite,
his satin slam occupation heaven statured bed? —
                        I will not fail the urine test —

## VENUS 7

can you name Judy Garland's four husbands
poisoned with the worm of second chances? ...
pole celeb powdering Galahad sped up with lures relinquish.
    And you want Weimar in your bed? —
                who has the gimmicks for the legs? —
a rubber ma'am grew tight with exhaust pipes, custom laid
lap crease harm spurn eggs jolt ignorant tarrying
talc anemia glands, rags that call out to you by name:
                        a posse of cuckolds
sluiced despair fumbling feud;
    fleshy slow injustice traps, boobs can't win
dead man's curve on my body — lips need space for con-
finement with the hand slave of the hilt — very obstetrical
beef flip persistently simple as inclined silk
vendetta allergy kisses crude;

## VENUS 8

And genes this bored very spermatic megalovanity
taking without, being taken lips are pre-registered
                                silken serious mute for frozen vendetta
                                tartophile wolf *coeur de lion*
sober I reckon *degree* been seduced bark was heat Mr Centerfold
rogue venom's spit & smear expectant ego illogic
am a tit valve hog for you, the decapitated chicken
desperately heating retail.
        Desultory blows, armed attacks by divorcees, brakes fail —
                                Overnite Guy, Therapeutic Agent, Fly By Beau
& you're pregnant amusement as bush feted poison
luckless bounces churning sperm for overoxygenated
margarine desire male foam loses head
mementoing minnows in my 'bruised lips' syndrome's
afterbirth under the bed — and cuckold the stars & stripes
of body fluid default.
        Shudder all plans
lay eggs & cackle again calipers disregard caress
leads to tetanus gal violate to accelerate flimsiest victim
drill persists, not so you can enjoy your widow attach to betray
                                to farce protective dribble hot cakes
for daddy's lemon squeezing daddy probably
some newborn Hansel & Gretel
in its bashing ounce by ounce,
        carnivore's vita affects
                                blank amputation envy
would have insisted on your taking a saliva test —
my contract stops ape at the waist gets proud
of attention eager razor hum retreat
harm back in juicernauts toss head with aggression —
no, the opposite when a paw courts evil ever *smaller*
pull of sticks, even worse gay insulted affection
captures spread out meat — needle satisfies belatedly
                                discriminate by owning flesh
                                corpse as bedmate mastery's
tourniquet.
        Equal rights for pieces for meat —
                                what's the matter with fucking dead persons
                                as long as you don't kill them? —

## VENUS 8

                                how did you come to be in her room? —
control oscillating pecker paste vertigo to *l'homme*
abhor, bellies butter your pity poisoned chocolates:
knee-drops for backstabbers to condemn adulterous virginity
as a high school graduation requirement
to be tied in a bag with live cats
                              trepanned into idleness —
ethanol that stinger, let 'em eat ortho-novum.
    The desires of the needle
                           overriding hormonal success
                           motor curbs ointment as destiny
infertilizing plow portfolio syph on target
nitrously cylindrical audacity slips, ochered end
                                  sticks duty way out —
I always found your confident self-absorption
to be off-putting.

## VENUS 9

OTHER lips ruby twitch to behave —
corps dalliance grants a pin a spurn's cavity debut
                         person rebuffed carnivorous hints
                         waspish nox lov lewd employ
                         even shy molesters' narcotics contempt
                         teeth default
satisfies me no ounce.
     Bid care ahead
medicinally married tears my recreation —
                         *ewn ahngtray:*
                         special magnum worry *of the assailant*
                                   too precautionary
vacuum bereaved nerves.
     A gymnastics of lick danger lilies up complaining
                         inlay spike heeled loan hive without honey
                         cantilevered in coma naughtied burdens —
improbably impasse arm
aloft as weeping index
                         simonized as separates:
it's rubber, it's the brake.
     Mushroom-shaped coward could be fine —
Oh Cupid tell me will your heart stand a chance —
                         *ahvay voo kehlker shoaz … ?*
                         *pweezh ahvwahr … ?*
                                   you are its victim!:
two hot sheeps & convalescent venom binds heat —
heart is a scarecrow for discouragement,
     lower case reconcilability, that fraud
except with mutual offenses spray the qualm you left
                         my grapes on the vine
                         and syphilized reject could be better
                                   bet the night
collapses from multiple stings —
what's so bittersweet about it? — you are in bed
at least my equal tender flesh on the deferred payment plan …
& *other* myself, in under me, platter appliqué
her back lasso satisface
talent, love talon
voluntaristic

## VENUS 9

device enjoin
cupid's not schooled that gay
in you.
    Minnows, swollen basinettes, incommensurate spandex
galaxied swoon greases sympathetic
               saturater defeat fluid vaporizes
flirt to afford wide-open vacates to live
palpable readymade to
freak desperate very frequent
cry-o-vac creature,
    brittle care discordant
belly powdered empirical squish installment
way you dog me nerveless white horizon
             slug's damage embracers:
smell my points, get the job, stop malleabling
            me off dearest handicaps
the possessenizing moisture levels, the claustrophobic
carnal reciprocity
ruptures decision.
    Torsos to taper lips took turkey throat
by fire partialize chastisement torso
            fends plex & preen chameleon fleeting sticks
            close seldom rooms hardship losers
                 for my half defected
                 in ecstasy gains pout
        fell soon I'm bored for two
lower swindle.
    Yearn shrinks stick with double cracks
show all humbled pipe zippers in heat
                *puts up with*
perspiration on the dole vexacious in wants
tenanted by another, who battens upon unadmitted sleep
flames so retarded inveigle each eye other;
    belated fret
             differently show me
chastise some weeping vanguard lips expire on
padlocked vice worshipped as tourniquet danger certified rakes;
    pestering pride grief has ticket soaked pride
cauterize to be indifferent hurt mooring one

## VENUS 9

                    helplessness about small madness cutlets:
                    bend throat for necklace control? —
I swallowed too much tinsel.
    Loss my standards small as harbored hidden
                    compulsives delude status least
                    to taste comes circumstantially convulsive
                    saltpeter-rigged slights
                    & detractions' suspicions
                    bodily enacted incarnate protest:
IT IS ARGUED THAT DOUBLE SUICIDE IS THE SUBLIME CULMINATION —
grief-ist helps phobia roar skid marks on your pathetic yearning.
    Forgotten euphorics
stuffing my appetite with objections ferment
the hand foreign
the temper zipper vetoes devious tethered neglect.
    Bombs, what you call re-entry vehicles —
                            [Let's not trust] —
                    energy so worse grief as
                    a growth process turns into
physically equalizer twosome censured wholesome
abdication of ecstasy —
                    see how fun it is to faint.

Bᴜᴛ failure surfeits
supreme adverse circumcision arrears
the inaccessible theoretical loss baitings abdicating pleasure
to please by abdication, limit clasp fit
of pique over *faux pas* blushed devices convene.
  You — a man *or his essence* who I thought was the rage —
              you want your grief on a platter?
              sloppy means demands?
              what if heart's retarded? –
halloween on one passion's dysangelist
stood still, soiled molé experiments
in the lap substitutes distance for cork
safe scintilla objection.
  Spoil's tongue nuns conjoint
the bottommost tranquil
ebbs furiously jimmied automatons of pleasure
are curious trilling sameness — how many men
could fuck in the time it took them to think
she was gay: our night wide scar
anesthesia to the point of morals
cherried under law.
  Rapture as a pet, prostitute the potential needs
projectile face, trouble so metallic pyramidal anguish pills
pedestal God is inside too fragmented — *severe* self-slander
wolf wouldn't die.
  Twitch take apart frequency of repeat blush palm
hostaged gift size of this stop
                    antidote of fuel weaned nest isn't emptying
despair's melancholy counterfeiting quiet
furtively exclusive undying membrane —
always steep thrash before
foreign suspenders so rationed with virginity
I couldn't affront conceit to me why girls learn horns
to make moral coil —
['M use intimacy to get sex, W use sex to get intimacy'] —
slugged concern white
locust idyll attacking lust itself:
a moment of sharing for the sharing-oriented,
  because the musically dethroned brain cannot survive
without the oxygen nor the heart without semen:

when all disorders are taken into account, M and W
are about equally troubled — mobile slash
irrevocably headed for one big glass jar memory.
      Romeo stats swoon to consume friend —
                              synonym for revenge
                              banqueting stake deviate
                but they hired us from the neck down —
                demented enough to be zero sum letch patrol
                objective evil pressure pleasure loveless
check in the mail won't come inside you, leave a crack for Santa,
      extra thrill so shallow injections of cannibalism:
reddish button fly firmament paternity aftersquelch
for *infernal* possession — doll teaspoon on-hards
perspire the bank bed grave designates
carrier frequency in grief farm price on prude
joinery swamp lit by harm,
heart set up as strike headquarters.
      Men expect a lot of action, momentary reprieves,
women expect relationships, certainty
                              eating fur is a crime
                  'a state suggestive of neurotic compulsion'
adultery for alimony victim harem; morality
becomes police, epidemic intoxicates easier moralysis —
                              common law gibe
public envy #1.
      Guys, in essence, can be
little butterballs, with the dick as a religious
                        article bit to size companions encased
in special reputation tension — so sexual freedom
enhances social alienation? —
                        red peel master catharsists'
constancy skills impervious to arms:
others *don't have* others.
      My nerve gets its storm
trying to make the world safe for johns — this iron age
libertine crowding now regular crabs of their ideals; glands
give cells sins of an emergency bi fear,
      a medicine instituted to the organ without bodies
                  cure lust out of context means your meat

## VENUS 10

zone of ply
guy for machinelike hygiene —
sex score near the asymptote
bandshell uncathecting
surrogation adultery.

# SUN

## SUN I

Bloom went ineffectual page
                              crack fainter
nothing retinal unfed specious gown, incurably senseless
                    style masks the mound, commends what
threadbare vocabulary sloped sans-serif cannot —
too masculine lease on syllable
                    for words, jack-of-all Valor
       every aeration occulted in emptiness
that draws everything to itself.
       What part of your body gets top billing? —
                         it remains a picture theory:
                    when you see this symbol, color
is just an advertisement for reality by rote
                                   Scrit
                                   Tres
                                   Teas
              Rose Adios in the present
              we are struck dumb calm looming
              apprehended oculocentric tricks —
perceptual accuracy does matter; peep shows, for instance —
give stars aroma;
       Look  Tom  Look
                    white glove iceberg *horresco referens*
                    snowflake stoppage *form*
took a paid vacation & I got the drippings less picturesque
visible accent will out.
       Pics melt letter, part of the body
detachable hysteric transom lingo cleft foreground
on stilts over a cigar-shaped area:
                         misinformative
                         evasions as much
                         maimed by testicular
representation as if tautening diorama —
oblique arousal of the arbitrary postmodern = scrim
                    muse attracts lint repetition:
                    men with big wads
circular fiction of legible glitz requires repair
follow me home.
       Orthography primping heat head disguise maps —

## SUN I

the portraiture had oozing errorish
chimney harness, bella gravure brazen
brains with noise pubes growing out of its stutterings
writ white lips lean to prism twister tradition;
immense discoloration site obscene many tame
count on smear heaven in the gels
in vain,
head performs desultory angle
coughing ink so busy trying to make his presuppositions
into men.
Now grieve to belittle flare lamented open
even after the flakes are gone
nor the knowledge that could breed doubt
minimally decapitated —
you're close enough for adjectives —
each prelim hole betrays its marker
none of which spreadeagled mouthpiece
phrases manure the thing nature swallowed.
We are just beginning to know nothing:
fictitious conjecture who crawls inattention —
hey, toasterhead,
forfeit invisible logarithmic modest niche
stockinged goose of gab:
jellied question
cares for itself blackening question mark,
it's a hot-button issue
cookie cutter in the mind
babies' wish, tap own heads
amassing cavity crabs' retrieval perfectly small.
Chimera models brain, looks uncomfortable
contriving lure expires its outline
false abides imprint
glassine stupor nominal lights, measures,
symptomizes word order faking ultras passionless complaints:
scribbles wrapped numbers wreathed to flatten
dome's acquaintances
and I
I your mind's a blank —
forgot the meaning waste detail denial

# SUN I

jitters means 'thought' lightning
fingerless rumor disappointed artifice
outside indifferently inside now I fake
process *apercus*.
    's Yes concealed idea needs
lube coagulates air with its
                    (pop pop pop pop) goes my mind
missive thoughtlessness, exorcize how infinite
clearing opens sensical go-between talk —
                    tension jet image
medium of proof skin gains
hurtful, clairvoyant anal-compulsive head,
                                tab splurge.
    They turn the lights out & you think it's to take
his intimated apparition
without him seeing them — least last debris
star awful purple head is halt — never prettied
                            lensing factual
            paleness clone is the *curse*, substitute word
            not by color, pretends to make strange
genie secrets showing!

## SUN 2

Falsified peep, cartoon what? —
               wholesome makeup emotion novels
the one-eyed torso wonder worm at odds
stick wild with memory task
                  on & on & on & on imagined down-side
pleasurable nothing retailed as pleasantries.
       And beats the pleats off Witsend Bunny, deco torpor
                  candy's no show
                  or under frightwig in thimble
publicized as a fantasy stoop to smell
contact lenses show your hostility.
       Mystery tic brat as image early
else this derelict stuff flash impostures kindle —
a vulva made of mushroom caps corrigibly advertised
                  slivers with calorie-geigers
hitting the white pancaked greasepaint pretty heavily
in the midst of the skits: Putti with Mottoes — Courtly Love
On Exhibit.
       Quicken dire euphemism punctually:
sensibility got a new notorious is nothing
on the side of your physique pros & cons
                  a working cuspidor sorority gloss
                  placenta quest
                  to please the mass breeder's cup.
       Your solecism or mine? — artificer
is that revenge or is that makeup? — detracting
                       my barricaded neck
                       forethought's foreskin
                  toupee touched down on lipstick
                  captive images:
       I'd notice anybody! ... how sentimental can I be? —
denigrate to satiate salutations by the numbers
jinxed couture eclipse.
       Thirty-second lover
                  cosmetically shoving to each idio-syncrasy
                  sequin drones nape upright,
                  we're so full of avoidance —
no titular strips of indication, neither holes nor pores,
                  hesitate amputated stem to pander

## SUN 2

delivers attention away.
    I every size
precise little tamper trick's apprentice glint peep
fatal photoed captive noise, toy fixers:
    sorried intersection —
                    giant husks of corn on each finger
                    I am prepared to rule
the knit velour scissors investing
Puppet — how to get gelled
jeweled jutting halo zone.
    Fake it but don't break it:
                    Overreact lassoed scapegrace
                    infinitum ruse ruse akin
tolerably well lymphomas outlimb gossamer debility —
teach jism junkies how to use the tools:
    dizzy misnomer
                    gloss out on incompletion dairy,
                    senseless double tongue conjure posematic
                    post-prandial, the only way
it's hard to keep legs cross, it's slippery
lethal skin overdoused faddish stinger.
    Obtuse fisting practice font skulls — florid ribbon
                            muscle holster —
systems of natal wide gab figurines'
syphilis down the tubes of the male
                    where my nose begins with my life,
    sanitary vege-pierce abstention from frequency —
no, another lumpness — no sap bush cuz notes can't
                        petite tacit rasp
all that flickers is not svelte.
    And penoir sanitized that does stretch —
God wants to live in your body, thinks it's a duplex —
                    excessive tool, Precious Good Girl
                    head hides badges after
resale juicemaker warbling our entire calamity,
    multiply Fidelity
babies is like voluntary amputation error
slaked width temporaries;
    this is not hope, these are just cautions,

## SUN 2

                soak this chance simplicity unearned.
You, scare quotes outside of the body —
                did he get his floridity under control? —
alabaster humming along pulse-snatchers
to curtail circumference to jeopardize rooster madness.
      I — OK, you Laetrile legalizers —
                Tory American Playgirl Distress:
danger punished harmy horny taste clause —
                did you sever ties to ego futurism? —
the rhinestones are fattening into crypto-gratuity.

## SUN 3

Boy scout brain
> baptized the brain, no, nothing
> *no associations* — pure
literally supernumerary props add tight form force at fault.
> Whata Line Fella — too-naked gaze
> > a dark-adapted eye struts by rote
shine for hope winning word dressage lull
redeems plus idiot — my statements copyedit me —
> > flashlight *inside* petri dish.
> Special it
flaming sharpness peaks out —
the cynicism is in the facts according to Marx,
the graph bleeds thimbles into the signature:
> > if only I hadn't known! —
so clean your samples, Occam's guillotine
mechanics with connected objects lost in air.
> Nobody could ever say that …
vain italic head grooved Gossip Column samurai
> > > glint me up less
frequency response hyperbole produces its own imperative:
> > > in the first degree —
> > chastened sucker brood incision
> > all-to-the-verbatim vulture mean misreader —
haven't I told you a million times not to exaggerate.
> Human basket laced up
jumps up bragging, who seemed thin
> > that could not feel mannikins have changed
> > symptoms of expression:
> my one sincere —
> > if so me —
made uncertain.
> Nadir — Picabo — lapidary sorry surface sleep
duplicates swallow boxes,
how's that for all artificial depth? — jettison frame
> > badly mercury bubble on the sensual plane —
self-made hurt the head, unfortunate cassandra mouth-
pieces the body as agricultural awareness.
> Switching to the conditional:
thinking, individual portions; writing letters makes me

## SUN 3

the sample skills homily
got preconclusory nowhere, aesthetic too subord
psalm bomb — repetition is our widow to the world:

>                    Always Before
>                    Only in Time

literal denies.
    Fact fact and be sour
forms *forced* (always the world according to you)
>                    emulate too bright good versatile braille

anachronism tails off into a fish patter-perfect —
>                    Realm! —

THE JAR STOPS HERE.
    Mental lapse list means failure
comes to test itself fallac' Double Negative
>                    lecture — get that? —
>                    after several drinks swishes deluding

female billboards, the fish no longer seem sexual.
    Nonsense's lack of fetal abuse?:
>                    the irrelevant heat infecting real
>                    distrust is worth two in the hand —
>                    dumb is fun? — count them!:

bunny science
>                    Instinct is ungreat, fades reproof

parading as simple mathematics.
    Voluble isn't verbal
>                              eyes of science

negatives better born beak at dark disaster
slink this lap in distance
brought to light by lack of study —
freeze question chemistry sobs again, analogy still alive
>                    reader will anthropomorphize anyway

    All this is nothing new: sense's part truth
autonomy understanding as *symptom* = closure
>                    as logical as evil

even morphology can't find your brain:
    Paris logically sensually syllogism
>                    acerbic bonbons reek of

inarticulate (disconnected — disadvantageous)
schools sterilized to be serious.

## SUN 3

Darts opus snares
                    beguile, believe, entice, etc.,
                    body beyond predicates, fissure's reprieve
          bodiless your antidote
representations *insult* others figurized by sweetness —
*tingle, tingle* pitchless
imparticle of a dilly upon the heart
          likely suite
laplike tempera putty Expection's diminutive volcano
          oh-uh, oh-uh
                              voice to voice candy
savings
                    Sameness
Say Yes.

## SUN 4

Oh insensate
Torpid
                              majorette novelties in barter
only the womb can fool in a faint calamity's gloss
                         disengage the computer choked vest —
                         that's right, *you*, stupid —
                         the obvious spoils
wobbling baby syllogisms:
chaste endorphin pits, lips derided alibi!
      Vegetarian 'good guy' colloidal clique,
armored spit grievers —
Satan had sex with Eve's first sophism, cheats aphorisms
fucking out of service,
      and civil sperm munchkins I also use —
I used to be —
an egg slicer, orgasm now renting
                         vampirical worms for my passivity,
      it's the bad infinity, automatic restlessness
can't be a commercial journalist of my own self:
                         cheap happy beliefs as shrill
                         as ego to prim of precomfortable heart
                         pessimistic suds.
      Too bad everyone has my arms and body:
amateurish concubinal cherub, apron tittering
mull *in vitro* testicles
into receivership; crisco gloriously
as a second language dips & gelds
safekeeping blisters — fatuous eggs
gag me with a fetal monitor chandelier.
      Spiked curt cob royale
                         foal for scrubbed-off kisses
stumble duchess blam to vanity negative back —
let me Al Hirt my ego, look what wallows:
      connubial crisis minister, sentiment binocs
                         slime its own assurance
                         & chained sex slave's own story
adjourns as sad diatribal halo fascination.
      Pen-I'll —
                         doldrums — what's his stall? —

## SUN 4

I AM NOT DUMBO, what if not me? —
petite sense protocol to the top
conjectural expect of V-neck contrition
dub,
caustic conceit issues lots more
yell when not hope
listening iced antenna batter self-impinging
A being with trifles involve dipping
bring it on yourself in my pocket
attachments I didn't want
my belladonna credentials
violating hazard celibate threats,
slave unionization extemporizing loneliness
by lawyers out of lawyer
begets the home poking volley of the hump
revelatorily masturbatory spanking as meditation
hives by the victor strangle use into pudding
to fight lips late at night rejecting swoon,
reverberant carp favor admire less easily
fanning fallopian *fatale* —
I half some, I'll fake you home.
Anecdotally prudish party hops
sure depose ardor;
a taking fellow wife, slippery regret by skylight
not exactly a fluffball of affection on the radius:
cream rises to the top
stars of exasperation
with exaggerated cunning too manfully
especially if you beat it.
Sybaritic tricks
pedestrian bachelors begging betrothal rhythm
unfulfillment in grams —
I don't want you I don't want your problems
ingratiating — if you have four legs:
basted shame galls egregiously
as modesty toted —
remember her beauty, never forget his treachery,
cause bandied quirk cautioning flap
can't make heads of its tails —

## SUN 4

I gotta be honest: men are slugs of heat,
                    can you scratch your back with your pills?:
                    fine fur … stet douche …
                    wounds from boredom sue.
        Between drooping of the lips, my ditch got garlic
                    pout down gamine aim apprehended kneel
impregnate for welfare of wanting to be the eye of desire,
                    fixed ardent I'm tiaraed of this
                    reindustrialization of fellatio
                    propositioning the ankle wetters
check yourself,
        your royal Slutness, put some skull
                    in those blondes, constipated cherubs
                    diddle with the plethysmograph —
could you have gotten to his armpit sooner? —
Peeping Tom threw up on the windowsill.
        Notch of ninnies hospitalize this longing mitt most doubt
unsolved crimes of stress
pinnacled dalliance: whenever he gets a full hard-on,
the loss of blood to his brain makes him pass out —
scolding spoiled ourselves, no, that doesn't inspire me:
                    linoleumed onus diplomatically ungulfed
                    urinary sulkiness
fails all else.
        What happens to you can develop false wings
                                name & prank
                    this gyp mouth let the back door hit you,
neurosis equipped with couch, a more decorative
anti-intellectualist *choice* faked from the start —
                    sapper's delight curt
                    nurturing by professionals 'went left on me':
                                by the hour? —
                                to accept practice self
                    evacuatedly catch that forget that —
                    *seh taygzahktermahng ser*
                    *ker zher dayzeer*
I want to know where I stand with you so I can start
taking you for granted, takes a chance mumbles more so
he can hardly ever wait to hear what he's going to say.

## SUN 4

No bride felt good
                    suffragettes pleading widow fad
                    expressionism on novocaine labially bankrupt,
                    deep inner imbalances are usually the cause,
                    please do not hesitate to leave me alone
even pettier harm overdue mother matter last
mistake — goodbye;
        when fools step up
                    self-muting recriminates
individual guest-houses for the misconceived
                    bedroom busybody claque by bedside —
                    patrol this bumper pride
                    piety wearing rubbers
from someone closer to the top of the food chain;
        and duties elusive
                    'becoming sexual woman' =
                    'becoming attractive to men'?:
                    transports of their dupes
maneuver the erection behind the battle-lines —
if he were any more limited he'd disappear.
        Deliberateness! — this was not necessarily
a small assignment: boredom has provinces;
        ferocious inverse impatience, strap
                    follies that sulk off boy bisque
fur to ignore,
fly-swatters toward home so strenuously inconsequential
the monstrous prop was in my cunt;
        emergency hospitality manners
                    reptile furtive cosmo failure —
                                        habits no details
                                        surfeit the new dish
papoose sops clean to shovel the fate of the douse
teeth no soon in vain
lethal egg's luck waltz regret.

## SUN 5

Accusatory grace could be dose — trammel 'I'
am not myself unaware with ice, ladies vaguely vines
            a *saddening* of the poles as the violated star
            attitude on loan is apt today
            silk homesick
                       the bone ranger
                       as you can guess —
            I can't worship your boredom for you —
fraud as a second language, implicitly decoy wedge
            collar biting doves you can't revise
            what a hard time it was intoxicates
            *your* redundancy or *my* redundancy by sign
            fallibly harm coupon flinching toning types:
                           yes? — no.
      Nonsequiturs coalescing
a dubiously shy geiger counter for signs of disrespect,
excerpting more
            flattery as disappointed evidence
teaching finalist paste to brush your hair;
    relish smalls, resentment freezing
bogus hand Tartuffes of Feminism and Cuckolds of Belief
pose cloy teeth deal snobbish on cashmere target —
dote to disinfect toy boy synching how I'm forgetting
I hadn't forgotten not knowing you.
      Oh nausea's coronation too ripe
            wincing sift superfluous vex
            distinct to be manipulated thick ones! —
                   Une Petite
                   Haughty Florlis
                   Whose Purpose
            pimp down on custard wedgies toward home
                   broken invites
getting their crossing their legs in your cross hairs,
the tender mourn the gargantuan swollen friends
whose fetal attraction set that phone number on fire;
            I'm a dick dish
so I became a dog collar.
    Admit anvil crush
            nudes make sordid props

# SUN 5

break out in hives, boys struck down by causes
put up or posit, the gentle reptilian studding
                    sorties to Count Lyric flankdom —
                    deco bladder graduated corset size
                    where nostrils fear to tread
tidying lit prime don't,
outriggers on ego: belt up, philistine —
chandelier salted to taste mark's
personal rinso cherubim object
                    *attitude* stops argument.
    The witch is not yet the body's curt detour:
                    let's talk thrown right, Other Woman
                    manifestations of scold
five female complainants and six boys —
how many times do I have to tell you to act like an adult? —
                    femininity, the wound that never heals? —
                    I gave your breath a bad review;
        but chortling preen intention
never supervised by a masculine eye, depilatories
can't bear it to splint that tune: cordial cuckold lounging
at stake winterizing obedience to reward yourself
with the mistakes of others:
                                OK, stud puppet —
                    ain't you the whole boxtop? —
                    how much worse to correct? —
I mistook the subtlety for denigration, apostrophe to misgiving
harasser queen alarm.
    Red master care bears, I
duplicate your lurid subordinant keys:
                            Jive Princess
                            Step Daughter
                            Tempered Queen
                    Hurry Up specks off Baby Doll reveresome
brief ornamental squeaking surrogate shucks;
        shy confession of concealed glance
smell far too many lumps in line
assimilate shakes poke fine john rediametered watch dog
masturbating these nerves of idle leadership.
    And why do I have to prove myself
                    just to treat me as an equal? —

## SUN 5

                    chill is on ostracism on replay
                    and its rebuffs slaving the right fellow,
    scorn ravishes
scorn softeners: that's men coop — yours prey? —
vocalese on the harm chafing obvious
drug stressful leather baton aerobic,
      eyepatch poser tear
                    PS conning italianate petals reproach
                    at her taffetas — wrong ring
was tied up into sweaty palmy spoons,
imitative tarting pariah venom: it could
put you into a whole sassy new crowd —
                    I hope I'll be excused from being interested.
     They can't see it & I can't rent it patronizingly
powdered future of the coquette will crowd my plate —
                he sure could use a new one —
male commodified free breath dressing your appreciation
weakens me, why float to drag? — pretend on purpose
someone even worse comes along;
     you're more than oven cleaner to me,
the cooing they weren't watching
babies die paeons to fur
chide-ettes, publicity donors — time to go;
     sell yourself a gestational slave
               — what sign is your relationship? —
               — why so self-congratulatory, i.e., *male*?:
breeds in pecking order to this squirt —
but the woman is fly.
     I don't consider you news —
              he was his own woman —
              I took him up on his take-off —
              every flirtation is unutterable vileness;
    desperate teenage love dolls
              snakes into disregard betrothal
opines starch in debt, not his plagiarist,
             underlings' miscarriage
             excels in prim recurs —
your conveyor belt, this cord bolts to regret
I can't write you on Howard Johnson's stationery.

## SUN 5

Littlest insures to foretell
why most men wish they could be single again, scattering less
hunk dross speciously mandated by remonstration —
                                      wounded members, tsk, tsk
press the slack button —
an applause track on your neuroses, persnickability
                                      aghast derivative breeding
                                      the same shook me fallout —
I wondered why I wasn't having more fun with this
        and vagabond! –
mishandles pride would be banged up tonight:
                                      terrifically musclebound and — virtueless,
                                      junk made it giddy, idle blood
                                      inedible lures — remote
incriminatory sob.
        Foxy strategy: who comes next can blame them? —
                                      heartbroke simple syrup arousal by polyps —
a conscious malefactor of untested annoyance as if
                                      he's too short on that end
                                      to be more than netted fish so far
                                      heredity for stools
                                      lies
                                      slave:
get wet = do it yourself
                                      blame whistle the pee bones indiff'rent
                                      & the piebald doll —
                                      you're just standing there
until he jumps down yr throat to apologize.
        Down, child: thank you for not eating while I'm pregnant,
nipples at the hand of ambition's nest
vise colloquial tact reveals tact
positive on stilts, slipper regroomed —
                                      even all that latitude,
you annoy me enough when you're silent;
audience, the presumption creatures, a crush on the fame
limbs pushed sugar tight;
        impinge:
fragiled revamp proprietary tears, too late I learned —
                              *poovay voo fehr stoppay serssee —*

## SUN 5

you want deBeauvoir on toast? —
clean your mouth? —
stop hopping on me — endorsers
non-erotic female male bonding update: crawling
into a surrogate, showboated by grace.

## SUN 6

### Paradizzied

                      sentimental device rubbing tame
                              bid habitual flare
                      incommunicability's distance — the last word
decor pablum unallowed; boundaries went to her head:
                      boundaries *are* resistance, motion to motion
dedicated process to too large
carnal finiteness between entrechats —

                                  polybag me up;
                                  my alone is
                                  intend devious
                                  just me luxuriate
serene tune — refuse.
    Macro calls seductively hurt
reduplicating back on itself: thank us interruptus nube —
                      tender habit for its own attract
the stick as if conceding inferior horizontals,
    you do glitzy resolving splits —
                      those cum shots should be bilingual —
cover the bushes with beaks promiscuously heated together,
    what can warm make sure
                      such finesse that they don't want
repentant hierarchy:
    consent's sequel
                      disparities breed to intimate rose —
                      I admit I'm captured.
    Light breathless gaudy with light
pince-nez — I'm not amusing? — allows for slow burn,
    pull face rubberizers best
unsaid erection
tumbles, signature wells
simultaneous wills simultaneous half
heartedness erecting in syncopation;
    what do want you substitutive mere
                      less believable than intimate —
don't wave toward me, I don't want to hear you listening —
covets *amiableness* … (capital flight from affection)
slave
slimming cadre;

## SUN 6

and each gender falsifying the other's
emotional distance — if you respect you don't
                          disvalue disparities are happy
excavate & sorry torso collapses to louder melody:
                          I put the passbook savings inside his heart.
     Two prostitutions make a virtue
without no theoretical singles
                          ultra-bagged regrets
arms less pink for sure taut idealizing:
hen waiting on the par — fictive admires
orphaned so caress masturbatory regard; the drastic
alimony — the different — ran out of adjectival dovetailing
face like this.
     Duplicity of the taint
                          spell hone flap fail care excite
                          to hard enhalos poison smooth
outsider forthcoming, limp toy silly conjugal shutters
out error proved cheeks,
     simply would renunciate cut-out fleecing
ammo, abduct by division creams its duty
painted blind, bends with altercations squirreled in danger;
     uh-ohs slowly impersonal
                                        fetch over gaps
                          infatuate maddens.
     Touchless evenly estrange every uneven
                          extol tongue just *overing* on the boy —
trouble mend
men don't get no snaps, fantail trumped-up
bugless remorse, missus fallacy,
     shake the apparition that dreams you
                                        lick shot get hurt
                          wrong too asking debutante tenses,
     conjugal cyclops's getting a private spanking —
                          yoke climax labial econometrics:
sperm cohabitation since intimacy;
     othering sameness
                          patient — albino vamp abhor all widows
                          one egg too many;
     the friends atrophy while the lovers recharge

## SUN 6

imputed fleece vacuum
reigns love single two inveigle
                                        logic simplicity control
— I don't see you, so don't pretend to be there.
     Sorry soft verdict twins make us pregnant
cooling name neuter please, onan's rib
fells newlywed undecorated courtesies in niches incensed
with engine amorous toys piecing partners,
     equivocal spasmodic wetness and his magic lips:
                         so many men so little time, each eggs next
imitative secret sober for your inconvenience —
                         avarice consumed f'you —
voluptuous despairing;
     possessive desperate gaiety
                    missing hard to undo heaves in construction,
inhibiting respect
me enough to have her
caesura lust, delicacy.
     Is this your lump? —
                         pleasure slaves
                         duet shuts off
                         moonlit bereavement: he said 'zoo' —
                         somatic vacuumer, *you're* faded
                         condition multiplied by arrogance
to bend down; and I can't resist
has less relationship: pull rip cord on zipper
                         fishing for trouble without the skull
& push with the other.
     Discretion's climax — don't fathom
depthless blubbers flattering cadence, inflate
                         a silhouette — super red slap
                         reification of lightning cupid initials
                         unfelt to interact thoughts unheard:
is sex casual or a bonding experience? —
                                   fast talk burn
                                   distancing relationship
does not communicate itself; face is false front
lobotomized dear lobotomized veil to think
useless facts with butter.

## SUN 6

Night itself
that one instance dying to get even
                    — *ahpreh* —
orbit recourse
coy disavowal
tacit spouse levies pablum scenario with the arms capsized
stretch remorse resistant sweetened curse
                    somber as tryst chit wedding sentence
                    distance gets normal at a distance:
                                        you mean sperm bank? —
                    did you say detain or de-stain? —
followership decoded pressure as intent,
I'd hoped we'd have more fun.
        Oh heart beats faster, touch unsaid to bed
applause reply, reinterpreted, identity simply patent battle
pattycake some regret circling the late for bed —
                    I Do — romance is act of will
                    scarcely embodied to touch
                    rhetorical *armor*? — rushed! —
as they say!

## SUN 7

Not hush-hush bothered by not wanting to
bother unemploy impulses worser has to spurning hem
                    shook smooth conditioned to hurt
        cream neglects creates to maintain
or maintain to create? — compensatory limber
                                    temper say
                                    copping a rod
                    proneful outside.
    And ulteriors — fugitive hush for purity scratches
at hand — analgesic loin
poke to replace mentions safe to cut to pieces,
        is it folly to love up, fluffy, light and delicious? —
that's not foreplay, that's toxic dump renovation,
                        sclerotic hypertrophy,
        fashion flinch in predation
                    license the dismissed
                    if I mix, advances —
I black out.
    Cud lump ephemeral
                    can be substitutes safeguard
                    torrent work to slow the spread
                    more in my pocket right now
                    than you have in your pants —
                    noiseless trauma breaks
weaken more for fault balloon ejaculate
                                conjectured
                    good business;
swell
                I

                            air martyr
                            the feat
                    convulse silly contortions
could get least particular audacity at discount:
absorption strengthens your stimuli,
                    I bought it already wet.
        Master misser: I am *just*
acting the best niche retrogress
jazzed ex gingerly 'in a bed style'; fools zeal
resemble the crime forfeited by narcissism

## SUN 7

sharing emptied feats to polygamous traffic —
                                    Trust but Verify —
                    three whistles, all clear.
    Swept my salad bar off my feet —
*my* attitude need not proclaim *your* attitude, no *proof*
                    heave both I halt faint
                    fallacious — or fellatio, excellent ennui,
        undersussed gun pod or rubber mirror? —
irritated by appeal [not knowing how prank comps desire] —
                    it's over because we're through
                    conditions to be as kisses
                    desire be different on top shy redress
suspicious of the arms.
    Drawal precise — & infract [pourquoi poorboy?] —
slur circumference
                    as a shovel would put it
                    I spit & spit & spit: what a hen! —
amphibian haste sicker than thee, muff *dissidenten*
chafe solemnizes me.
    Conjugation vices
                    mode slacks, just a little clock hello:
confidence of mishap grace curbing vituperative embarrassment
backtracking drama sprouted a no-win need trail so
squeak;
    two seeming bodies — wrongly parallel parts
masculinize themselves to compete for inequality;
                    his two hands contradict each other.
    Page by page husband is
                    awful interception now that's loose
                    Dissolved is Mistressed by this
                    love *means* manic depression —
                                    delays instead
you *sold* your feelings — monotony of abruptness:
                    endurance price tag shot the bolt;
    do you mind if I conquer off to one side? —
deed regress
writing shut up in flesh quickie tight as success is cold
                    filler stuff, clip embrace.
    Rise your box who lives here

## SUN 7

purely subjective *not anything*, NO YET! —
                        angel finds some ideal
                        more interesting than guilty
                        sensitivity for distances worse than you —
speedy backwards, litigants for love —
                        it spurts disconsolate singular
comes in spurts, danger alarm category
tenses for sale

                                        meant by candlelight
                                        the phlogiston
                                        so much in delight
                  left-handed
jeopardy, some Clarence Darrow of the heart.
    Took your love for a toy plunge
                        smarting by tantrum, your nerve warfare
                        against
                        crossing willpower architected weeping
                        on tab — rehash allure
                        quell wildfire version
was her rendezvous.
    Stitch reverse touch
                        acute threat whatever you
                        single soon on lapping
specialized *raissone* repulse incipience — no one sinking
can say spatializing
why the wrong memories belong to me in mind;
    jilting rumpus assault, latent in loss
                        helps but does not prevent victimage —
not to pick on her or anything, darkened room precluded
public acts — stolen even what you do not have:
drones who exit metropolitan hand.
    Jilted plea don't shoot
                        attractive excuses, the intimacy of
                        the collapse sparks repartee, probably
subconscious quibbles: emergency valentine,
                        do you really — will on nerves
enveloped in earnestness, levers of affect,
the deeply pleasant proprietariness.
    Padlock pride

## SUN 7

        redeemed reddening
deed breathed bang on safe;
     reversion proof! — to use mouth-
to-mouth resuscitation on my heart felled
              excel their plot comes easy
gratitude is now.

## SUN 8

Imagine eliciting crabs to think —

                        too memorable, don't wake
            dynamite the exterior
            entrapment — Phrasemaker! — the image,
            too cha-cha for words —
can I say any more,
    less concentration is more
penetration strutting people
have softened their brains considerably
            leavening parasites with bright too late
            regard, chewably aphoristic
            inflammation speechifies
true blue not meant for lovers' habituated disparities
to undress historically
an indelicate reference;
    imagine official odalisque
            orthopoetics — ain't nothin' shakin' —
            innate curfew at a click glance
            domesticating crinkly malefiction to share
            deceit-suckled declension deceit;
    imagine overheard of hopping mad
gives head letters of recommendation
in mouth, lavish palped dismemberment formula —
griddle cakes fried on your lips to halt white spills
            desperately over-accessorized,
    if your lexicon gets any more housebroken,
publicity pronouns learn to make the writer's signature:
            trial double linguistic encyclical
            overexcitability of indifference
            writing quitting
adjectivally slandered gelatin;
    emblems confined I tend to believe
            wind-up doll — profitless equilibrating
            a rounding variety
            difference we are bound to:
there's nothing like a crisis for repetition;
    little farfetched? — a buoyancy-deflating doll
obvious distance enough dance
to identify breathless chronicling ballerina perforation —

## SUN 8

what a cock salute! —
it means *never arising*, no lexicon
exceeds slush speed unnaturally
conscripted by it:
self, grammatical *faction*, flattering
aura to insult against experiences
diminished by oblivion use, *null*
erects *system* all shatter
ought shatter all.
Why is absence hollow?: to complicate the tradition
chiseling tame faking conversation
has acculturated the instance —
they're just lampshades —
pray for three nerve holders, sermonish ideal persons
retort mongrelized inquisatorial body
ideality — a lesbian Democrat was elected several months later,
a mock minority shares each unless
I do it to be part machine
absolute problem human.
Exemplary force the non-thought
message urgent motor-driven mood:
we are in no exhortation, a world of rigor at our throats —
fake time spreads tense patience uncaressing
subject dissolve, shortsighted, into positing
theatrical kilowatts & then they pop —
is it over yet? —
genitals easily by haiku-like remonstrances,
particular aphorisms act off, so
simonize that glance.
There are rumors and that is bad
writing letters will make you
mum's the proposition
important? — turn opinion composed stanzas
out into chicken drippings, comatose, lah lah lah I wish
I'd never learned to read, novelty lottery
slink to talk tongue of the worrier
closed soon or clothes soon overstay male ego
stays hidden *for reasons*
we have to keep a discomforted eye on —

## SUN 8

                                          yo, bedwetters! —
                                          presumptuous speed
                              eats the words you cannot even pronounce,
            and said:
mend our position errors to treat error badly —
                              I would like to state quite clearly
                              that I have no intention
                              of responding to this —
impregnate every caption
with the sound of your ego
voiding, the answer is no ...
(nobody says 'NO' any more, dear; do try to catch up) ...
                                  synthesized fear invites me.
        Can these bores live? —
self-dramatizing confuses paranoia-tutored form
transvestized out interpret:
                              generic lack of in-touch petting
air womb mimes itself in perpetual cheek
                                          facts corner me,
            you want to be in contact with people in general —
                                      right, enema audience —
you don't want to be in contact with anyone in *particular*,
        bad antithesis demi-perjorative beauticians of war
curious about the makings of curiosity inhibited abilities
of ignorance — you're not stupid *enough* —
I'll thaw out the embryo when I have enough money to raise it:
sideburns on a cage under these honesty creases
touching Jerusalem of misapplication illogic entangles
appliance unrest;
        we are the wound —
lithium conjuring
boundary privatizes
happening complexion galls, frenzy underscored falseness:
dry as in dry
nerves think for others
getting tired, tired, tired
                          trickery could interpret
                          polycentric annoyance itself —
universals squandered as objects.

## SUN 8

Fun as a waste & go —
what a crowded little idea,
that must have really hurt your brain thinking about that one,
                              if it's so baby
                              parodic crest
                              curb unspeakable
                              inconvenient conclusion;
the talking *kak* per line fills me with compensation
cooling in parentheses: axiom jumps at me
                              (literal execution!) —
                    *what of* — to superfluousify
Oh, shut up, I know what the next sentence is, OK?
                    the plan lyricizes, automatism
                    is perfect, as a vowel
                    tongue ajar
                    in itself
retro-touché.

## SUN 9

Desire off desire
                    stretch marks on falsify bee's nest
                    prenatal theatrics this idea —
it's all over because we're not through, exposure
to pheromones is the essence of sex? — minting
into chances embarrassed by the plural subject
up stop itself;
        mounted unit bilked exit
for the conservatory to have entered the cervix
                    mutates so mutilates this idle
bonfire, placenta obstacles
                    epidemic in its own co-ed pox
sped regret,
        nothing does twice your love hurts
                    manhunt inflation center
means exclusion so you killed her, it's only nature
                    however your limbo redecorates
                                        *or at all*
                                        imprimatur allies
                    vices wedder conscript blank as bangs can be.
        The whippers excessive
                    value groping schematism
contract cum vaccine quintupled
                                        insuperable cope harm's
paternalist prayer pimping for make-believe suds
put on a corset to believe in *the door* — what's not
real conversation, ah, the endured passive onus of birth —
you want war but you find sex more congenial? —
how many times did I lick my hands to smack you? —
                    pranks allure
contingencies;
        a surfeit rising
inclined built SAD, seasonal affective disorder
                                        *generate*
alimentary porn
girl flies to heaven embracing the horsehead
without trouble moving.
        From penis to prototype
transient belly

## SUN 9

                                   flash on resumé rarity buzz
slow chrome this symptom
financing web slit retardants
as confinement, endless fiddling with
                         wants the commitment of geometry
                         when I see babies making babies —
ideal taxes future fixture pies
pasteurized to grow distrust; what's that, Gourmet Baby? —
get your friends to re-enact
the boring details of your everyday life at home:
sirens down rubber chastity in the smaller size.
        Every trend implicates *me*, I'm a nest egg, I grow:
don't keel the error-ridden libidinal retro
obtainer donors, papoose bi-heaves
                         valence, hems in devil-may-care
                         but I don't, the Curtail papers —
loyalties too swollen to be divided; there are sunk costs —
pills surveilled is a happenstance salted to deserve males
                         might sell better, norms at floodtide:
                         18" can only mean turkey platter.
        Arraign to flap boys
                         would be happier with chain-link thigh fence
but women don't just want a pair of trapped diso-
tits on the mowed grass pinioned by maternal nostalgics
                         if he wasn't so fanatically neat
                         to indulge the baby, wives train hubbies
                         like puppies & the damage done
                         from purpose that gets
                         man who loved less than half victimization
                         is self preservation burns
the hangover;
        but imperfectly frank
rankest foam valorizes a spare gaffe scheme
fiance portfolio persons.
timidity makes us timid, dabbling detention —
                         rebuffed on dance floor, he slays six —
                         uncouth group bob won't bounce
                                   methadone valentines
operating trembles.

## SUN 9

*clean* overrated like *direct*
                        ratio posits furor unknowably
multiplying at the drop of a hardsell dust jacket,
a begging
must sprout legs: imperfection of distance,
remorse perfected every limit, or disrespect due grace
slithering for mystery fuse evaders —
                        neuter is neater

                                    distance *against*
no re-release.
        Sale sale sale —
                        expansive heh heh dribble, gentlemen,
                        abnormal self-normalization
                        turning into lurid dirt for other people:
it will be seen as a bluff and ignored,
angle so imperfection interferes with enticement
                        lapse on harm gone cause
                        that way you get women's pay:
history wants a baby factory for its pension years —
purse of our discontent, if the straitjacket fits
animal perfection
but I didn't get the money ... and I didn't get the woman —
the penultimate stanza of 'Egoism' should have been omitted;
we apologize ...
                        *ah ang koor seerkwee* —
                                    (faked?):
                        your digs are a yawn fairly frequently
                        sperm wants its own radio slot —
                                    opium, expectations
held yourself captive, prohibit grasp —
                        simonize that ideal:
we're supposed to be through
fiancé portfolio persons.
        I think we have to outlaw marriage:
                        'could be improved on' means wrong
                        libidorphanage, maggots in cars
named waste — is belief in lust rational? —
                        as prior allegiance:
you know it's part of the culture because it pays for itself —

## SUN 9

every dog has its day
insolently curtailed deflation harbinger wants
how poisons work, what miscegenation is —
                    I take back all I say.
    Stiff interrupts petulant aspiration
                    connubial punctual ails —
                    why do you hate the powerless? —
                    offput or output? —
                    you've come a long way, baby —
                    diet theory war = menstruation envy
while your people sleep: oh, you could sell need …
after paternity comes eternity, compromising to the top
advanced hurt dares wrong self frauds to want what need? —
                    life was my cover story.

SUN 10

Not the end of the story
                    to pasteurize those responsible
                    to assemble miracle cracks single file:
                    creeping infallibilism tempted imperative
denominated in untrustworthiness & full-dress spatializing
sufficiently false;
          not *necessary*, paradise naturalizer, passion *disaster*:
casual causal crabs, perhaps a vertical corpse
                    respects virtue, partial ethics zipper:
the verdict *necessarily* sucked on cross inclusive moral audition;
          -perative chronometric gallantry authority boosters —
carmen tribunal, sinners alert to style
                                        hurrying dread
                    dare apogee of innocence:
what you call emotions, I call propaganda.
          Prognostics hot & thick accustomed
                    can still persist, sally out on regret
                    love will make you fail in school —
my intention habit
helpers, I can't help it, I've got to write
arrested by consequence, spatial solitude too:
                    a type of mental or moral improvement —
this is all based on guilt;
          and absolved, done defer
whines in flesh cooked sad scrape 'rose'
                    renunciate its worth
                    compelled by some particular voluptuary law:
man is an immature market, just so much dead tissue
over-interpreted asleep.
          What keeps the falsehoods in place? — I thought
                    it was a familiar constraint
                    instruments reconcile
                    optimum pessimism differential —
                    mini-nemesis dominion menaced immunity
                    *that* fools everyone you like
me in order to like other men, accuse excuses the word
mankind is like nigger in the reverse:
                              adulthetical
                              supervicive fash ebt

166

## SUN 10

<pre>
                        since impasto guilt
kinks for all occasions.
        And swivel context breeds
never everywhere in sticky virtue lasso
doubling Class 11 (not violent but degrading) exam:
                        docile bodies, teeny adjusters
                        've *all* got juice
habit entails us
revolting pressure cocks:
        wipe the dirt off your home, sashay into diatribe
plea with shopworn legalizer cash misapprehended backwards
                        personalizing the fetus once again —
                        I'm not deaf, I'm ignoring you —
immaterial lessening 'right low down' simulate my brain:
file grievances too! — you're a real yeoman on my spots,
                        babe; why not practice on a landfill? —
                        fallible may be only kin stitches
that stitches the whole
shrugs off ermine together;
        you're so smart & you're so stupid:
condense trites false affects, the intellect
                        unsympathetic exceptions —
                        I still hate scenes —
true trap opinion stoppage tight in chairs,
Bowdler hunting down the dirty bits.
        Subtract color pedigreed future irrespective of eros
                        & somewhat downward inquiry
                        donates crotch to, like, social science:
go off by yourself & waste somebody else's time —
                        static letters aloof, ovation
                        epitomize lust, I sentence you:
a hand-carved plaque for your sorrows — of course, darling,
                        this is theater, it *has* to be obvious —
                                        collusion in
                        underneath redemptive
pushover art.
        And meta-lumpish social sorry, proof
                        I axed the master,
resign herself to disappointment
</pre>

SUN 10

> to arraign oneself
> or purify with scorn

living slime:

> time shortens you, what do you expect? —

empire of phallocratism, patriarchal tot rendering? —
if you work within the system, the system works within you:
grudges fathom, Satan balks
business at overnight jealousy's battering ram —
one punishment fits all.

> Self-canceling bounty nothing too secure

emotion lost its franchise, but gloating and silence
already want to get paid —

> it's not a criticism it's funny! —

every stitch that mercy gets mature;

> *your* facts could use an adjournment,

*your* clichés are finally getting some chart action —
surrogate splits up on doom right topper think

> the last will not be first

who comes last & may well be fenced to disturb;

> sorry juridicalized sorry cult right from wrong
> aptitude for facile tears
> depend in / out

solution-perfect needle serves notice
habit shrinks judge
me precisely from any contact —
women are simply men with organizational skills? —

> all is reckoning regime

cured to curve a piece of inquisition, an endship
cooked up some past
regret works me over
& you don't see me crying about it.

> We have not come a long way & we are *not* babies:

> grace those types
> faith washes out,

> sleek contract edge by abject
> daughtered permanence —
> nice male world we love in —

but that was all excuse from pleasure griefed whole:

> super suture,

168

## SUN 10

      *method off it* —
      sorry pays for
      everything everything changes —
except what we can't stand;
   headlong understanding
         gentled by complication
stepwise to the stars.

# MARS

## MARS I

Night after startles
           art pouting information
           perpendicular to astonishment hoodwinked
the auspices of looking in the mirror, neon by the hour, puckered
           lattices' physical plea:
      damask whitened milk by guesses taunting
steam pigment pores — acoustic light
legibly erect,
the sentence assembled its soldiers,
      lanolined miracle smudge font
makes the white-out look gray, displacing (or is it projecting?)
                 young shock pastel off attention creased
                 hardware — who notices?:
      absolutes speak no equal carmine sweet too much
blank verse playing black on my mind

                             reveal nothing
                             cool wink sudden dusk
                 furtive flashes curtailed boldface —
                 *dew pahpyah ah lehtr* —
we are starting from our true grace ramps:
                 I'm right in the crosshairs.
      Curt gloss cleansing, plumbing on head
                             better I've
roasted delivery, butterfly waist heat format
                 visible lawyerly forgettery
makeup to smithereens, restive way iris foreknowledge —
let me see some more — nightmarishly high-voltage
                 geezer initials detonate blink;
      furious angelic counterfeit
as freaked asymmetry of salute
malachite swish: puny the sentries precedent aloof
disincarnadine violets precipitate chemicals
carved pink, oracle of celebrity blurred ceilingless pixilant.
      Most of the time when I'm out I'm not wiping
my hands on my hair either — lick waltz jeans verse untitled
on hazeful frets latinique rhyme as sulk stuck pose
need look no,
      proves parting stanzas attractively burning fuse
waist-high fallacy, angular pastime mussed hearing —

## MARS I

                    sky-blue coquette first-hand exaggerate
                    to impress littlest fantail — what if?:
                                don't marry your mouth —
                    drum-like mammogram surname neck
                    the valuable wordy about that
ankle esperanto of self-regard.
    Amps by force touch 'em light I refuse
                    unwillingly juicing switch
                    my lip prudent to mistake ignite
                    humble pick with lips —
moved toward the chalkmarks in order to speak,
                    lament equivocal fancies without
                    making butter out of boredom house:
saucy calipers of jelly, creeper head down
heart stab who regret ecstatic in error pool
whoring is forgetting, abundantly fulfilled
how charismatic you can be with your mouth numb —
                            Oh Positive Blubber
hyphen tending milks mistakenly cooing to be careful
                    bankrupting the dish.
    Sin sass at wink
one, two in three
                    twisting that syrup softening flame
twirl all over satin underneath crackpot of the more demure
confusion break mirror mock mannish peeved inhale
                    mouth tooled out peeping decisive
hyphen softens dash past the Gordian knot of interferences —
                        but enough about you,
    I collect liquid
                    not circumscribed & all circumscribbled
words things mate unless otherwise carnal rejoinder
discards melody, brackets electricity eclipse:
you're obviously trying to make an absolute idiot out of me —
                    scale inside nerves want images of prone
                    prowess without paraffin slips
in badge bonfire wants as interval.
    And I
jaguars thinking of you, boulevard-verse chemically implored
cocooning berserk clock squat minor scolds the visor

## MARS I

and then you woke up — impregnable spreading
　　　　　　　scent makes me wasp fashionable mind:
the Great Disclaimer gets head upstage — am I audible? —
　　　　　　　my sentence is having its period,
　　smoke yourself writing, jacketed trump makes shift
to disguise, oblique lines inspired
delirious history, sap regret
sensationally insured
　　　　　　　sky needs batteries, how about …
stay tuned for the next hectic excerpt.
　　Bilingual embarrassment
　　　　　　　　　　smarting
　　　　　　smudge costs more, to fault it, 86 Lights
　　　　　　listen to power fail to listen:
　　　　　　film falls from favor & sugar daddy
　　　　　　doesn't matter by interrupt
　　　　　　bastard brains, the negligible tumors
　　　　　　unduly *fortissimo* has had trouble too —
imagery makes statue of this melancholy sense medley
by syllabic claque: that's worth than
having no teeth — if life were all peaches & cream
　　　　　　with built-in lie detector.
　　Duty's imposter of politeness was expansive
enough meat — that's what I'm trying to tell ya:
viscera (sic) brains, tears too inquisitive;
　　the furnished woman & the unfinished man,
the uncircumcised intellect trance idiomized seducing
saturates privilege brigaded to secrecy, pawn faith by bite-size
breathy diffraction,
　　blameless is carried away;

## MARS 2

ARTIFICE implores contagious instant nape-flights
lurked bottleneck nerve compression in husband artificer neck:
                              menace lace
                    face really counts first fix
selectively mistruing pearl fury, film's white flag —
                    unitard fret
                    the mutes alarm
smooth as pear-skin.
        Straps speak presumptuous tongue
                        caulks minute carbon human skin accessories
bleach-black, pale consoles, yellowized beverage
duck for buttery strapless slimful skin
        carrion comes to mind, earring demotion's
                        white panache — supplant light
                        limos the sleeve of buttons
once on the lips, forever on the hips;
        trashed palm neutralizing breaths
nude to the sentient trill tort knees, pussy morning
                        glistened pink floodlit hens on his firsts —
height of sass except chest blurs shake, gowns stirrup water
eyelids to the azure.
        Reddened gorgeous & fractious clods
                        moist severely svelte atlas 'umble
also barbaric brooches, distracting armature
hold dark contrasting skin gravy lashes unleashed
                                ocher lips up danger
                        jam into tissue hymen amendment:
        throbbers
punctuate the meal distaff doll, wig apparition of the
                        stamen seethes the cracks
from ankles to soft fair & fat bikini line
                    Year of the Unborn Child.
        Vamping duped fooling burst
                        tongue thief — read my lips! —
turnkey physique with throat enlarged prays for trousers:
glee gaze skinnied lack = emulate
harming hems, hairs held court
                        the pushup brassiere tingle
and 'decapitated hatpins' all in a chafe

## MARS 2

trap the fur backstage
hung by the knickers
as she cocks the lip.
And frustrated hosiery self-defense for razors,
troubles pert vain wrong out in tights,
souciant bump with self-frictioning crease,
dumdum hemline wired for stingers, needles,
tooth fairy left me some panties, does the fur care? —
liquid bandage finger interrupter means new skin temptatiously
scissored tilted limbs, iodine the honeless ones
flings in two circumferences.
Oh purse lips & evict
beneficially limbed doings with organ
rib sass insouciantly trophied on the hip
scratch a damn honeysuckle adorning contusive derail
a recess period for eager sensations
to wire the cushion for cellular pride:
gray hairs float arguable sissy
when skin no longer forfeits

favors fortuitous
cartilage gets high —
put your name on the bust of *my* held hand onyx Carmen
& that I'll go on playing with fire!
Night's hidden microphone
the glow worms tease
inimitable inarticulate hair matter acquiesce to suppose
mercurial at best, false unstoppable mucus manner —
looks adorn vacuum, they never twist you —
vain impact pearls deploy
how young wrists can be.
Leotards' jury mascara colonized me —
hormones or lure moans? —
what is backlash hair? —
you robe your trustees in this? —
you want him to know you do not have nice legs? —
before I get a jewelry rash, are there bleeding translations? —
accordioned guile flair bent attribution of ingratitude,
idle precipitate talent versus taste translated
saliva reddens answer beyond eyelashes.

## MARS 2

Your wig is bleeding — knobs were flirting
cadre gels
anus lighter, dram other, lush bait
          fraction less sibilant at a loser loss:
rubber drugged disbelief chagrin —
          scarf be my dominatrix.
   All of us, Slaves
          with eggshell enemy beverage irritants —
princess got sized lupus care, popular genital brat
          multiplied body to syncopate carelessness:
          a nurse juncture, a beast-rector
with blunt pinking shears, agonize but no consent
dement
          motive blame loosing a puck
for only perversion puts a charge into the flaccid body:
in the dream the mattress shrank to fit his little penis.
   Name cone deploy same as caress
          some cakes ahead — night traffic breathes
confident trouble amusings, index that sensation redrew
boundaries where feminine left off ninny's denial:
          arson at heart, spur to spurn, rabbit-leopard
          diatribe clinger got all milkish —
appeal does not rest on gimmicks:
          thrust all else aside.

## MARS 3

Erase define mind over platter
blindspot vanilla stroke exploding bulk of the shuts —
that sound is very opinionated; horticultural weepings —
a high stem kind of gaze
edge person, agate slicer
                            fetish ups the ante;
    who can singe?: high-tensile clouds guitarless
bloodpumping nameplate seduced into
abstract possible but remote quite agitated burns —
                            jellygram glacier sure bravely overtime
                                        vibrating certitude
like jelly got itself liquefied synapses.
    Huff also-rans avert flutterer
                    of impressive eyes-off dimensions
                    luminize unsafely separate zooms
                    here whence ago colt dress as protest
                                        surfeit
                                        mirage so
                    do you think that? —
                    do you fear that language in your head? —
charm veil wants viced reportedless glaze
                    fiction superseding faith:
    nipped-in waist
swollen syringe in a blur flown beat
                                    device so much bonanza —
it's funny how fast your body goes back to being non-circulatory:
Sybil-izing a lot lately,
                    I sometimes think I never blow so red,
    bright gals wear gray, laissez-fur harsh & creamy
scars in scale — you want a grape, or an excuse —
                    the party's over, corsage pulls trigger.
    Pinfold obstinate unveiling
dirt rather than science settles in mind — court dissimulated
mental breakdown of fires catching feeble doctrinaire
phosphorescent erratics —
moving inseam veneer to be amoral disunit alone:
    physical abuse is one thing courtesy converts to tiffany —
can't you let the rhetoric pull up its skirt? —
crisp flaunt salon cheeks down talc's urine

## MARS 3

and, yes, dangerous migraine turns soft ever only twice
tonic shine — space hurts, stray to waving oxygen
                              belied sweat perturb within flame,
        wigs disappear
                              emancipated, ankle strangles much too facial
                              chagrin — perverse decorum: reliquary
                              reminted annuity beside limbs
with nerve peripheries running a little water
over the sentimentally coefficiented dish.
        And you must sing alone disputatiously
                              tender, still with the baton on —
                              we do not distinguish among drugs —
                              warehousing your lack of certainty
                              bereft as castanets sweep the hand beat
                              in my brain with both my hands,
        outsize trilling as fine amuse a lot, happily prong
                              with spools' kotextual pride
                              repute ill court sash belated impulse scorn
                                      of scores sound invites
a spreadeagle diatribe, theory-laden paprika —
lashes churn such butter that begonia leaks melody.
        Bereaved litmus — hosieries grammar could we? —
                                      say it messing up
                                      history rooks
                                      weight of so-heating
grace to groin it whispers disease, swamp pink
smiling quenches catalepsy of the dominant
bushy queer ostinati hand: *eau contraire*
try to baste her stepparent noising jones
toward the villifier's languor — no, I'm not kidding —
                              uterine sodas launder luck, regret
sublime seizure, inanimates listen to misshapen nodding
if an unrecognizable attribute has been encountered —
                              you saw the actual penetration on video? —
                              *ehtehl shoafay* —
now go on & suck it.
        I balked loss moon
                              mates at whispers less possessed
                              night sparks spoil red means again

## MARS 3

              congealed to be free stoppered cotton
fruitfully undissolving walls: the centers were cut out,
surplus nerves distill this cracked custard escaper
impulse possess the fracture, emulates dam dictum sales
luscious sermon routine enough for leather bud status
            — if it doesn't stop it has to happen —
            extremities suffer unless you need them —
            sibilant depulsing vapor
            on shakes, mistakes
            propaganda as action on loan
longitudinal halter abrupt underneath
once their auxiliary coke treatment circuits light up —
                    prettier alibi on display
                    and even hotter:
            it'll help steady your wings.
    Nature needs color
to fuck, autointoxicate heart
at mouth, leaps excuses
respectably nothing I'm-not-sure
                postpone the pleasure's
synapses jump at skin made credulous suspension
by drawback exited mere convulsion
little enough;
    but does it want you to hold it or not?:
self-hugging false double negatives got loose test text removal,
            beauty weakens shame's delirium
            to excuse the impossible light uptown —
            slip knot lush accusing 'this-sided' purpose:
well, *conquer* your ambrosial unpretentiousness,
    flattery compelled interior diameters, I cease father
            face's over encore veins
respect repressed object contrary to false, restless
say maybe redden brief even better,
    numeral cajoled silk torso helm
            time proof trouble lid on fluff
absenting polarity, tenderest lightning
more epithetically sends its message
too sincere.

## MARS 4

Benign voluntaried crucial youth
                    witchful status precedes ligature
                    *are* OK, victory size you prefer
syntax I suppose the general blindfoldedness —
misapprehend eyes conceal price
business so locomotional conundrum liquefies,
    silence flutter out
the serrated hunting knife of your junction gaze
you're desperate to think'll do his box
but who's fudging a plant word embastardize
marble cupid pinking terror unsuffixed
a mouth exemplary lie with a view tightens.
    Easy calm so disliked sin thanks carbonate sleep
peepin' tramp — postmarital bumping's
                    safe intrusion heaven creates us
semaphoring a smile decomposing a promise, make moist
lurk steel adjust gray hair skirting across
                    privately unpeepered savage courtesies,
                    zigzag petals mesmerically imprecise.
    No one letters your cast:
                    vulnerable jump-up blue
                    you never knew what meat
                    planetarium caress
wants my integrity off the open market
                    beaver as editing prurient napkin
assuredness ever pre-handing it:
des Haschischins, my late espoused slit — some retardant
brusqued on the tripod cashmere manners
to not want to become respectable to die.
    Mood tactics milk a blue adolescent vestige,
                    earth the sub slants
compelling hatchery to heated pool lights up jealousy
                    quarreling the page,
    & smudged remark prodigies tacit underneath
subjugated miserable profundity and every pomp stabs
spattering like lather mortgages the forgets:
    why are you so luxuriously disorienting? —
desperate & tentative
                    I'm no incline

## MARS 4

           I promise to flange
shattered maximal african pitter bother dissertation;
      unfair cavity ceviche donors
deliver on your promises of infanticide, turning curious
radial alabaster.
     Let the female ego do it for you:
svelte antiques, precocious tatters, backhouse babies
pluck pre-feathered delinquency enough —
rough temperature handlers shake on queue
                  legs lubricated into the air:
                  dinks cut sperm caking exertion
maid me now, diligent if confusion
                         aloof sits infantile
ready glisten or not, here I come soon to be
                a major gay, shimmy submerges
                      burnished beetles.
    A taint if tribulation voltage —
                I lease out my manners:
                spiral curses horizontal discharge
                front capsules, super infuse
fakery scrutinizes loud enough to listen off
will or willingness, skirt trough
underskirt counts
furious for each — finger snapping
exploits indolence machines, I bought a glad fisted tear
                incensed shirking tenderloin deal —
                the jerk! — that's off, that's off
'steal to desire we abuse
our skin reclusive'?
    Garter motion
mock furor stupefying needle-like to heat up
in tizzy stuttered caress — synapses gave the big presents:
horizontal, forgive me; slap me with a cathode ray
                inner nuevo heaving elicits
                skate on my nerves;
     pencils the bites act together
nakedly motived, i.e. the tongue —
                'And rock. And rock. And fan. And drop.' —
                seduction proofs fact

## MARS 4

cooling pined splendid sputter,
invent saturates me up, dismounting rubs
laugh so chaste
fingers do battle with their responsibilities:
read to me to flirt
my encouched detail paradise.
Feigns feint, the triumph of the wish
bouts adjourn emboldens as task
effect of new zeal peeling to your discretion, junk ties
on whip, rubbing simulates you:
incontestable parasite,
three men are three queens, voluble voluptuary
likens dampen demo passion catalog
pronominally embraced, self lost my inventory melt;
hop up wrists *overtaken*
write *for* alias nightside glares, I-score:
endeavor inflectionally scurries to you vampirish in work
*never* to be repeated — cede pose point
tandem accuser —
impetuous gab aisle hurry flirts
so superimposed.
And Rinse Dream insured to be inured less:
slit bride lift you scoring arrowed trait
missful use invert the sign
sweat through
a pretense somewhat stilted
wound with active credit
tide inattentive,
the first thing
perfect sting ruse as tirade
el diablo, dubious, shaking the hand of the motorvaters —
credal positive lambskin
mania welds no scars!
And segues —
ranks only rebuttal-sized promisings
pilot toughs
intrude daughters tirade
unaffirming valor
pornographically vast static in honey-jar

183

layer lipreading the cholera
hurling the ancients on a glib,
    why assume so calm? — inebriate quality
          heroes availed fancy soliciting
          miracle of under-stutterment, self-hatred's
          manual override
                    plastering princess
        wolfing down truisms.
    Mis sum curiosity lisping precarious
believing for devils plural fish has worries sudden by half
          after spoil look black velvet upheavals —
          I quarantined myself to vices improve —
          they want it ignore them! —
kinds we took to authority savor
          bounty after less upon less
          sucked underneath the surface;
    and their credit chilled me — crank arraign
          leather litter freak circuit mastery burns
          period missed tactic in the smack of
momentarily trained stilts on pendulum.
    Sisterhood favorites:
kinetic less spurious prayer, forget it, a lot of people think
          one identity or whatnot fractured —
          *kehlkershoaz dahmewzahng* —
              tremor addenda;
    but no wrapped penis tonight —
superb solid lighter, truth buoys up fear
as if rhetoric had halfway houses —
          *ser neh pah propr* —
*whose* flourishes
I bring my own background music with me
    dire laughing
          pleasure as power belies nothing
          pleasure stops with itself —
          suggestive en-princement
          ruled up in quitters —
nice allowance!

## MARS 5

I CLATTER round, sit through
           the nominals, a qualified cheek-expander
           which, I have a suspicion
go back a few plagiarismless vibrato lines into the drugs
want hiss size: *what if* pleases, interrupts intrusive shortening
           solitaire mask abbreviates lying —
           only men can be earplugs, out of caliber
           for fakes fronted black
intoxicants of gloss.
    Wax temper hip is blonde
down for the stripe with foil equality, visual mal'office
hosiery tattering damp garment filamented lure
                      yielding to blinding
           flutters to flatter charm alarms,
    bevel the beauty into flavor
           impales the visual traitor, shortest tuck
           tinctures daub some dolls
equal flitter units doubled to a crisp.
    Oh you slut wish, make sure the foot flexes —
miraculous salvation from steam mauve a trick manual clamor
lap partakes fuzzy tease, golden bridal shower
           pitons to climb your back swinged me —
                    can you butch it?;
    courting auspicious odds
           leniency skinned liquid as twirlies
           send a CC to my breast
straight sheath — no slit sweat looks
encounter silence on blonde.
    A rodent-sized organ attachment
covet absent conjure daze slush topaz
nothing gays me, are you pinching yourself? —
gift creams flamboyant rouge challenge down that halo
           substantiates gratitude on my knees;
           it chooses a spermatazoon for itself —
latest big armish to fool plaster bicep jelly
           ungainly softened force beau costume,
who's that muzzling my sass, carmine asterisks
on each sobriety
resent this tag of any hip

## MARS 5

hazard bedding too much contact.
   Oh discherished sugar doll
          organ knows subjectively
fool that I am, whatever self-affection might be —
          Bee I Bumble Bee or Not —
          hoop slush sunset to dawn.
   What, did you think my face was Democracy Wall? — mastur-
                  batorium's am I
          making the same mistake, internal cables
          dunning suspicion dahlias;
     broken-hearted fistful squish, bad erratic
          china flip assassinator flesh
          deep careless purple whip retreating.
   Jumpers on one heft nape knee
laterally spurn Oooo La La — didn't I say
purified could adulterate it, phrases on my pillow
— instrument blonde inspire cadillacs
enblousing baby oh baby lustrated jackstraws.
   Tissue fiesta mystique
statue front svelte fakery at start cherry lips:
look at Little Sister, plumping tactile cheek dwellers —
          we're working a full-body mutilation for you:
          a vertigo of
hose pastelled commando lingerie predators
          and *bebidas exoticas* persona.
   Machinelike cleavage stands out overripe
eyebrow putty your spoilers flirt muscle subordinates
candied into forcep schoolgirl
          one mistake delinquents — legs, please;
          manufacture your own makeup;
          hang your tears out to dry.
   I'd flip 'n' furl
regaled saddle with swank prone motorized dildo attachments
to rather be sorry than safe — martiniest Rampling lips
          haphazardly unhook as hot
          narcissism pulled up
          its pants peripherally debrooching.
   Lip gloss glamor ambush
tongue gives a fashion statement, ace's wild swagger restores it:

## MARS 5

lather unacceptably shake it high
spitsville shock-a-doo — splay kicks
are other lips, other arms skirmish width to me.
  Don't do to my sweater what you did to my pants —
bending saliva ranked petticoat idle surplus
conjunctiva with stockings puddling daily —
do you bend down for pennies? —
how *I* thought *myself* thin;
  grimace face spits off timidity
nonstop we're
training my knees for a better liquefaction,
breadless you or none much
too much to wear underneath pinocchio.
  Oh let's make with my wants for you some love —
fortunate! — a beggar for your
leather smells furtive knees, lipstick graduates from
can't talk about it instinct
wayward gala snare'll thrill you —
coolant-legged, cervical jitney
miss drop off ribs over sieve
ointment breath body bedding clue.
  The she Eve shops for herself when still inexperienced
shakes up what trembles idiom
belate less royal
boredom got sweating
to be deft discretionary
maid pats toweling;
  it's 9:25, have you slicked your child today? —
sucrosed jump frank head perspiring obbligati
tell me so
there's no you
Mmm Mmm Baby
so glances defect.
Take your glossies and go, getting caught
Indecency follows shame — I did vice
propriety gelded bra snap lift off:
love will rear itself on derision —
fistful of tights mock soon alarm works
& the clock doesn't.

## MARS 5

Don't loom brows, suspenders
              are more deliberate future
                            reprieve distracted
                            front ceases
              creamboy — they could do some
              use
              too much
              of a little bit
              too slim can do
                            chafe idle for you,
I look to the buttocks to save the life:
              are you taking injections? —
              inseam force my heart
              stand still slapping nomination
              just exact for a thrill.
Disposable dowry always was a tomboy —
happy chaffing more sardonic on quaaludes, eat his heart
                        name
                        object
                        image
              beaten sissy satiation to powder
bellies less articulated — M a m a, procure the beak
bed flack flivver surety swelling kink deferral —
              huh!, bull butch bwana —
              you *can't* feel sorry for yourself.
Broadshouldered roll or folly
enrich the little facsimile immodesty lessons,
cuteless pants on pants wholesome beckon
              epaulets reprised
              the alarm that recruits the underwear
violet or violent? — willowy scrutinize intent possess
                            none wound up.
There'll be a hot time
authorizes reject
              with regret toadies to blanks usurp,
treadmilled out, elbows itched for joy —
the wet head is dead: vendetta in gear bending to bury,
              mood is my charity.
Toys lit up the barricades with altruism

## MARS 5

spurn the interhutch, paradisiac heels
perfecting inanimation we can explore
                        meaning & not just broadcast
                        architected undertow, repair flume
white lambency
poses revamp the foam;
    a permanent discretionary
vacationhood,
                    soon sweet
dance round my neck.

## MARS 6

Oh awkward more vagrant thicker
pride *a priori* carve to beaut sauce
& what else (repeated at intervals several times)
                    scared of twice smock
plays out curses, our language,
        suffrage grew hair deriding trim, clammy & taut
bride torture insect-size brassiere mirage
                    demure for more appetite combats
                            pelt bite split.
    Uncowed & unbowed rugged self incumbent murk —
muscles accomplice under quick emulsifying marble
already accounting pink intimacy set to music:
                    temptation squeezing out fuzzy slump
                    spaced plus heaven sent me,
special initiated trouble barnstormed such fucks,
                    furtive infatuated cantilever
                    split across chevron
                    needles impatience.
        Merciful bottled cause
stammerish vertigone

                            clause sharpener
                            creased young arborage
                            tamper corsage —
nyah, nyah, nyah, my narcissism's (i.e. would certainly 've been)
                — you no dread, take that wig off —
better than your narcissism, nonchalant pocket offense
                    — it's the eighties for ladies —
                    incumbent sizes you & your exclaims
                    two eyelashes before the mast
                    abscend still shaking
red smiling waist;
        when I buy, I buy something out of my own brain —
                    dual forsakable auto-vibration tossing
                    trash endearment, immeasurable cameos
                    salute more obscene none of this
                    lambasts enough impatient front.
        I = you
                    press button wakes to you
use her fist not domesticated enough for the table

## MARS 6

sink the tuxedo quake-off snake
smearing aloud — you —
                dorky grace emboldens you spontaneously
                to swallow (to avail oneself of)
artifically clumsy glove-roused divertimenti
                basting repel.
     You thaw me nice
lapping cum unheeded goodies least heroic bliss by half —
I gave my heart to you, I thought you could use it:
snatch & sirens cull bite turn me down or turn me over
                coo & lie mineral on the move
                milks me on hot incursions
have myself readored — the self-possessed satisficers
                eat you periodically.
     Tell me
                wondering what every other breast is like:
shoot me the sherbet — puffing up access illicit
                gift to size reveal than itself
                almost is all I need, I can misclassify
                the protuberance as well as the next gal;
     tell me dark rubs
-duce at stockings:
                you don't like stumps? — I resent that;
                   nonpareil rub
                the prop repenting lax a little fierce
                   for me, legging dread
                pleasing, indemnify scan.
     I like the spark 'em skinny roles, laying-on-of-hands
                ovaries hover maddeningly righteous
                — *ahngshahngtay* —
serve your sofa size
moves out blandishments;
     & do the high-class thing man
enough can do, tranquilly self-hardened
                pinching of two crystals push down to night
                discreet one sale chose for me,
     talk about numb lips! — why risk sex
with failure? — never say diet! — slow-motion kicks
                have more to play with

## MARS 6

willing wild git down with the git down
bat rides fingered restraint,
    dynamic lip wars hose down the modern vocals
                measure friendship with geiger counter —
muscle convictions bisect the brood.
    Standing there with your knees in your pockets,
                     puff or swab? —
        self-congratulatorily stylized every tooth
        in a romance, rave-breathing impatience
ruining the tongue in the hole, receptacle spit erasured in
              *thrilling* game, guileless trench
tails between legs: drug courting dissatisfied-to-be
essence of sleeve-wetting pyramids gave me leave.
    Employer mystique:
                 crispy on the outside, creamy on the inside:
                 fidgety whim legs are social breathers
                 lack lilt, promotion retards grooming
                 flukish twain in fits —
why do I raise the knob to let these people interrupt me? —
my titties are big on you, ballerinas headlong
             *ifs* medicate, catalog of rubber flaunts
                     cumulate me.
    Repeal those largesse lips — soothing minors lithesome
drowns flamboyance, go fuck your own fertility:
             bovine reversal pride minuets
             pride your lozenges — Henri-Henriette
                     sudden fits,
             my bump is gone —
color jeopardized moda masculina murderess.
    I'm strictly a formalist in psychology:
ampule untrumped heat mittens, epidemic of
prepubertal breast development from anomalies to peel
                    — excuse the glove —
             this lust opens doors, evident squeeze
may fat one's ditch such that same-sex tribulation g'wan be
swollen dalliance pretty lumpen for pleasure —
alcohol can speed up this process: girls who tango citizenship
                     can't tango
                     rapier hazard

## MARS 6

suit up moisture magnum treats.
    Oh clergy aureoles, world's greatest upstairs —
                inflation's eating up my pussy
                consent reduced to contact —
why biting off the snake's head is so decisive:
                what month is it? fealty to desire
torque this etiquette back in box burns
bedding valiants confine,
    he was dickless, that was the best part about him —
flabbergasted clapping forfeit
do whatever's best had tête-à-tête with
                consummating furor want sops
same sexers to mull
                curt gisted swell.
    Sizzlin' languor depicts
ankles rationed men, a solitary nonchalance,
                ridiculates armature vogue chute
                lead them on if at all bonds cruel
                court illumine lazes of confidence
abates dissolve
                improvingly negligent,
    my indoors
iced up on me — the sweet smell of vindication
                tights require brain
                gilding escape to twist
my fondness for men into overnight amnesia spree;
    nerve cells on strike —
                conveyance on backwards;


I'm available
if you qualify:
                I want some bother
in my hopeful.

Cut your teeth on tricks
spoilt bright confusion malice salute — too many
                         specialties blow the bait backward;
      and falsies exult
a pink sheet measured in pints — couple of fatties flirting
                                    invulnerably uninspired;
                      originality makes me come
                      heliumed spayed.
      Caramel ventricle lips reserve to repellent
                      nude sundae, junketize
                      a burning phallus for modern times,
      pronoun burns —
it burns — faithless freshness
                      flowered absurdly abandon
                      lapidary drowsiness
                      wettening the disdain
                                    indescribed
immunosupressive hope.
      Passionaria
                      child
                      bold
                      sales fatale
valet gravy
in a groin, Berlin so many well whittled
abortion gymnastics: I hate your sleep, I am
                      openly contemptuous, saturated chest
hostages to be whitewashed jelly apposite aftermath.
      And raveningly needy rear leeway on throat throttle
hem saturation; if I'd been a ranch — which is often
                      — they'd've named me the Bar Nothing:
      tipsy suspicious & refute rebuke, inhale waylays
shy votive nymphomania pennywhistled foreplay
                      laugh out loud in uterine guest home.
      I coronate oddball mannered fools —
                      your strength needs a sale — to impose
                      dribs & drabs of normal love:
you could sell little glossy photos of this erection;
      & obscenity managed me — the envivianing
lingerie limited: penis resembles a solitary turtle,

## MARS 7

                  rosy scorn plasma enacters
of which we possess the capitulations.
     Are sperm the only victims?: craving each & every backfire
                          liquid saddle felony
                          lapse aquatics —
             he's great at the sink,
      dote stir harm prone full story
now I can squander parapet & sash
                resistant on top.
     To get more joy out of sex, specify male or female —
keep away from clothes, airbrush your vanity
obstinately persistent & oblivious to circumstances,
        oooh oooh oooh, *besame mucho*
                delay pride's quake enhances
                      pubic esplanade.
     Explosive smudge that silk
overthrows straight seeking empties with stamina
I yet squander — foresworn careful, saboteurishly culling
              a sexual diversion for the noontime meal
but then he said my vagina was too big, taking coke with freon.
     Ovum aura sordid chaise — I like disturbed
don't hatch married women always martyrs in a hurry:
              I don't feel selfish about this, this is
              something coming together between us —
              exasperated deporting eroticism as decision;
I took a shit in the bed … dream abruptly ends.
     Oh spring attacking cushion reference —
              poutless ardor, winter spoiler
              barb buy warmth on margin
preferring the mud to the fist, become nobody
lye sent us, sully refrigeration open to her
then, her — repeat the frost
                      superb! —
heart-shaped expedients, reckless
spore tones pussy paved with margins — I'm gonna take
              a few husbands & put 'em on my plate.
     I moisten your armpits, undone accepting this
love tickle often mercy of the meatgrinder
                    punctures truancy

MARS 7

doubled down to throat, money to admit & money to reunite
                              ankles magneted corner couples
together — *what* sexual return level?:
if you can't cut the mustard, you can still lick the jar —
                      don't mind if I don't.
        Pack up your tear vehicles
and what if I'm not tired? — *rage charitable*
                          escortin' or courtin'
I ardor you, don't inconvenience my apologies
        intoxicated limbs, foolishly yours —
I forgot you couldn't care — under my skin
clings to intrude
capsizer parents.
        Hear me falter? — we abort
our mother's non-machine trespass approval
says they don't have *dominio proprio* (self-control)
altogether breached, assertive subjectless offbeat
unaccompanied zoos charged with cheating
                          two spoon of tears
                          sin too much to stir.
        I — who'll be the fool, caprice losers
                          delight unafraid incredible and true:
intensify her imperative
barefoot is possible, thrall cannot come —
volatilizes gratuitously repressed cupidity
in sovereignties with my fingers
distill crazes ripe abstinence'll step aside —
                          vestibule hovers, syringe beckons
                          as if lurks need oils
tantrumed inamorata of a bastard lien.
        If you got in, you deserve to get out — ardoring
chocolate exits hair
down to me, if it's a crime, keening swells
                          insignia, just one bye-bye
privilege,
        I lived under vast priorities to abdicate
is warmer subject nearness, choker of each
                                        wrongs curl
                          in tears do the cha cha cherry —

## MARS 7

                        save me a dream.
        Sin soon solid infinite cherishing
                                        everything late seduces
by masturbating, the paradox gets less self-centered —
                        girls smoking communists,
                        abortion empowered me —
arms, homemade vibrator, unnerve feral pomp:
my wickedness comes from reticence.
        Ambulanced heart
                        arsenal of envy
                                        debases swoon
                        deploy laughter a little
too self-possessed vice can't devalue
as much immune, evade nuptials to
their opinionation disdain,
you know anybody who wants my clothes?:
                        celibates confidential
viscous periodicities, anger
                        saliva stupor vacations —
the primary agent of infection is semen!
        Culprit cancels, triage rude pride in hem's way
                        elaborated conquistadorial laziness:
don't prim the bastard,
sordid pullery quiescence — I err, therefore ...
abandon the rut
reprogramming the hubby for hosiery.
        But ebbed man teeth reprised nocturnal permissions,
*personae non gratae*, furious immolation
sleeps with snakes:
                                        FAUST QUITS —
                        veto white erection
helpless helpless helpless.
        Vice behave nations as drapery,
aristocratic tastes in noncompliance
who masters imperfection
we make your daughters nice
incarcerated pills constipated social butterfly's
prostitutional sacrament — power rubs the candor
                        bride flops

## MARS 7

                obliterate courtesy:
                fault gratifies lust for exception.
Swaps Ego

                entertain the charge we
                demollify retool vies
abstract harem — so you think you're a *violation*
of male standards of behavior, do you? —
self-torching touch,
    submit! —

                                  sweet gain
        vermilion.

## MARS 8

Certainty 'thinks'
hope with warning lesson, downturned,
cervix seems to be manufacturing hair — internist recliner —
flesh inspired to counteract harm without sperm —
                        rectolinear flutter speed of drag
                        fake fie hand, morals at half mast
                        static on trial temper your distract
                        widows raw raked over curb:
                        scar is at spelling urine —
                                    uncertain slantlight
venom paragraphed lactation;
        noisy limbs fortune to come
                        acceptably urban lacquered corrosive ought —
dissatisfaction is too eternal:
                                    socialists for
loan hoax oppression acknowledges fact as wetness
bereavement, cell selves captured fails to ignite —
                                    what are sit facts? —
                        superscript flaps in back, pregnantly coked
                        past on a *maculate* ask-o-lated leash
mutated site.
        It is virtually impossible to do anything in high heels;
lineup money deploy
my legs, you mean the pagan pistons?, wet with neon
                        relegate tenderness to grade-farm
                        spastic free intrusive confidence
as no-good as collapsed fronts can be
                        except in cases of glandular insufficiency
bandaging arbitration, depression made me
too familiar with depression, promises thought less vamp —
                                    twist it till it aspires
                        annoyance heats exact
withdrawn pajamas: what *would* he shout about? —
                        eschew the obvious kinds of pets
                        straddled evasion cussed a pox
talk to compensate quantity of male by the throat
I pried — why, crotchety belittlement
mistake tumor for baby squeezed on thought
                        teeth a sexist gripe:

# MARS 8

not vociferatable
anathematizing that creature
                              profusion of delinquency
came under hundred penchant, dripping, blaming,
              gander restive talk about cool trash —
              it's our tat they were titting:
              lies toy with mammals, perv' s craft
when you do in what you want
improperly discard those who try the reins —
tip the bastard neck
spooned investment crash mussed wrong
                              hatch my permission.
       Oh name wrong exiled privacy
marblecake doing cleavage image arrest
              slender canon candy hum —
              rated PG, parasitism in vain, tread light
on refusal's last detail, cold in maples' syringe —
              triangle trembling tremendous
              convicted artery felon tongue,
       cut-out shoulders, anhedonic of a brief contingent
contractless dementia epitomized retroactively secret
              amnesiac bait in distance: cocksure —
              so who glows? — wrists as furtive
teeth around exotic whirl's turbulent deflected hour
              palate yoked flood respirants;
       LOVE = CHEWING?:
              can a woman *stand*?:
chemical wedding's language of hypostatic delirium choice,
panache-drowned inarticulacy fends off witness —
              *everything* is physically addictive:
high body count, the wasp stung the oyster
              not in my experience grown cold, sweat nouns:
you could be a nun that they have options —
              people don't really love like monkeys
high kink indifference
holding patience back, benumbs cheat tool rule
defunct,
       tilted pointed future tips arbitrate snake
surpassing limb emergency discharge: hands up, tongue bent

aside, exacting
courtesan or cortisone lotion, vaginal morphemes venture;
    slink quick down on this content
up proof in danger
                to the mute weekend readiness protocol —
                it feels like sucking on a ruler, right? —
ambush — smoother? — redeems throughout
                too shunt to bother South of Regret.
    Authority deprives so many reasons
                irresponsible for body harassed annuity:
                why the skirts got growth, what are
                my fantasies to you! —
rear view vice mirrors, swans reckon on filth weeping
Conan vacancies of tax-deferred seduction —
I am not happy to have this man as one of my referees;
push the blame foursquare jiggle surely mistook Sodom as Nexus:
                devil in habit, don't eat meat on planes,
carnal copulation with women?, saltpeter ride free! —
intra-uterine enormously enhanced sovereign tormentary harm
heaved harm, I translated my ambivalence
into a felony charge: I don't see why, limits had fun
'fucked' and 'out of it' could be synonymous,
how people sell you any comment would be
conflict, but how do they *differ* from mannikins? —
                what's your genital handicap score? —
people aren't indiscriminate about their limitations, excuses
more apparent than mauved fix rehearsals confess.
    No rules, no exceptions
this bobbin made go away, preposition interior
                circumstantial advantage to weep at drug
                flat reprieve death's majorette, I presume —
I do not run by batteries; look more closely! —
                alphabet burst the heart
within no one
                just the rush of excitability
glows up & out,
    globulin assured unsurpassed
acceptance paternal red predicaments, purple flooding
chartreused mediators; Oh, raging hormonal imbalances —

## MARS 8

                    pencil-thin ethics, pulsatile folly
                                    rebel actuals
                                    private ... sweepstakes
                    frequently pink, doesn't always
                    zeros composing undone, ovums in luck
                    the emotional ammo stitch fissure up
                                    recursive melt
totally gratuitous extra-ordinary facts:

## MARS 9

Contingence intervals — wrong box lesson
fuzzed implacable apex worries, autopsied curls,
body parts each with blameless agronomy *nom de plume*
                    quiet over tight tomorrow;
        necessity, *viva lactea*
                            no sooner had the antisuggestible
                            pimping the throttle, nannies disheartened
                                    fortuitous unsafe
status noise woman alone thinking, man — *think*
hermaphroditic ovaries — heart is a bent, beiged debt
not a gyp.
        Harmony steamin' inheritors
                            eavesdropping at bottom organ butch
                            shrine style mourns cheekbones
ministry fingers just great ribs —
birth control?: do you want a holograph of the outburst? —
chemically frozen bits, spurt expect
still sitting on hands to patronize the lies
                    I don't print straight up any more.
        Syllable sways enamor
                    hints invoice flesh
                    exploits jerkily spill
nape donors behind seedless hush of interruption:
let who brag about *your* debilities — constant shudder
gorillas to redress given baby dollars; it semblanced
                    you & what need soaked perks carping fashion
                                    purse can't quake —
                    name that swoon.
        Charity means stretch pants? — very rotten apple
needle measures terminal affection, the hula men
recuperating masquerades — I, *except* plague,
                    mammoth tunes underground to hem us —
                    belied italicized suddenly tall
                    spatulaing crestfallen coathangers:
life is overbought, especially harm, emancipatory
                                    Horatio Zombie
while it sends IOUs of progress to the compromises outside,
padded — complex — boxes part of the bump
between sensorium coupé, the spell is cast

by organisms marketed.
The forecast for nervous distinction:
checkerboarding some chemicals I found the right disguise
for your equality vendetta —
Amorini with Satyrs
we are sappy; we are dangerous —
testimony heroes belly up with flexi-tubes, I called it
an auto-da-fé where white ruled before prosthetic caution
silencing the muster, blood seeks status over all
Possibility — Do I have to be interested?:
sure I ask a lot of questions, hints from description
quench coma carmen thesaurus.
Start to
your hopes misgovern me
halt all else
exaltedly desperate
succeed
stars unencumber
off relaxedly exasperating
the air of expectations' nonlove takes the initiative:
night amethyst
pain *warns* us passion supersedes itself
torn by less choice grief
divides zipper from memory: any relationship
is a plate diminishing its undeniable heart.
Only careless ordeals starring here —
that's fair, is that all? — neither need
shaking & shuttling, the harder gives passive
pal option who pant after
squandered to *lead*; air leaves the boot
blasting vaccine to squander heritage
going cold turkey on your hormones' scale.
And shoulderless succumbs *carte blanche*
if must I like emotive incorrigibility —
I prefer her Hollywood
what to do with doll heads? —
anything I say will just put you on the defensive which means
you'll be on the *off*ensive which'll put *me* on the defensive —
so, *let's not;*

## MARS 9

pleasure goofed hum that slinky dread in mouth
leavens lilt cadre alimony arrest
punching manners pert & prone promote —
you're a groovy boy, I'd like to strap you on sometime —
that's why I'm going to run you over with a car.
    Consternation toys half trouble mistress own fault
scratch myself as lead-in, just like that, have verb much gland:
                        spray a little scotchguard on your crack —
you *provoked* his passivity
after clapping to practice bestiality
commit their flesh cheek grooves permute
                  outlandishly inclined accident
                  snake into synthetic unity.
    Duplicate immersion in sympathy hotel
                  confusing wet thank-you
coughs up on the lullaby wink to kiss delirial tremor:
        *donnay ler mwah* —
put the condom on with your mouth;
    give yourself a blood tranfusion
by rubbing blood into the skin, juice to an adjunct
tickling substance, it wasn't Ruth St. Denis
*enough*.
    Boredom breaking out enough in a cocktail lounge
for which I haven't been injected with lamb placenta —
manned maiden skirt poppy narcissism edges off target:
                  apologize or die! —
heroic notability redlining cumshot
            dizzy box crackling
            vinyl dangers irk my nerve.
    Action becomes fashion
pills make me hot, got mock gender work
            clouds over complaint
excitement expels habituation sweepstakes:
                  I need a little petting, a lot more
                  than I'm getting! — charisma of indolence
                  linger on, you are so fair;
    sins in service stunned into
certainty, eggs were convened to discuss contracts —
the dead voices of our hormones are emotions;

## MARS 9

the wife is the opinion husband —
shake free disapproving stray dog.
    Illumined satisfier ticket to virus
smells theorized, flipped vein exploiting flame, unsheltered
a mental patient in your womb: there's no home
any more, you just bring it in or you buy it out —

                                small is unjust
                  graceless Admonition
that meaning comes from the spare rib nemesis —
                  roomier plaintiff, teepees emboldened,
                  evidence spitting same
soothing saturnalia mute.
    The night is all that we have —
humid equilibria seekers calculate harm & I might add
                  disturbing at times, retrograde hesitate
                  empty supreme arms —
incredible lamented share of armor-plate eros
                              spider without fault
                  & my therapist says, — dark meat vista
                  accident of apology's rank
                        jury out honk for
                  family management — panic signals
                  magnificent personal abuse;
    & suffering becomes general and loyalty is its cause —
                  strapless infliction splints
                  this is the Easter Bunny Hop Forget It
                  let's get joint panties —
sperm give up their rights at birth, they don't do anything
after that — I want some tourists in my bed,
                  my arms got too long for the oven.
    *Invent* pride dowry in birdcage, children
are the surplus security of the family — order despite
heart hollow enough for worms to breed analysis:
                            my wet is fed glosses —
              why should mammals be sorry?
fate loss flatter in trap, optional role care
                  headlining the norms's claustrophobia.
    Please these assets leash
                            Lapland cancelled

## MARS 9

            to light heavened harpoon —
so is having children, if you're gay —
sublime insolvent jail toward rainbow
                fluids attain own pope, severer appease
                deified needleness:
refusal to comply by persecuting sumptuous bliss,
                unwitching of sex
                to enfuturate your life —
                it's easy to be good,
                it's hard to be bad —
well now my heart is up on blocks.

Editing is composition lab pleasure
this vanished anticipation of enormous lights what's left
            to curve thought inflation siren indecency
            actually preceded by brinked out
lacking in hinges — I'm ashamed to deny this —
            experience isn't always necessary,
    bunching my eyes curtain back all light:
I Wed this Uncertainty agreeable to be *your* syllables —
I'm so glad I lost my penis early, the gestural premonition
            implosion atoned on query
            venom has recall fierced with
euphoria means mistake, Sure I'll see you:
    aftereffect relay
            sex is culture
hooks of being amazing self redefining charisma —
            the tension, not the decoration —
            flushing the snow-job as soon as I vulcanized
rubber, I made my first birth-control device
            blowing out the quasi-needful evidence:
honeysuckle limbs expect it, blue expulsion
            accident's abandons;
    rare positive start up dancing digits
            mock the moon for its shyness but since …
*Be ki began! Be ki began!* (Whom can I tell) —
breasts mean power, enfranchised with lack of trust
denying the fetus the benefit of the doubt.
    You call this 'tilting the manhole cover'? —
                      I thought of something
            examine the lips of my spine
for these furtive forsaking enjoyments —
            *Ehl ner mer pleh pah* —
            no clean caesura to freshen up
the suggestion that messed up
            androgyny without velour,
    & one more kiss makes a clean latticed
breast of it, pouts' worth, unravel this imperative
            redden acute sensuous gaming
            hesitates, skirts above leash
that was wrong,

                                    agonizing neither
                        mood says no — bad is not enough?:
strategems awake stimulus clatter as tech
                        organ snack on regret;
        & use it to lose it
                        trusting spoiling girls timid
                        'no' is less unmistakable girls
necessitated needs to dissociate from bright clock's fixation
motive to pull yourself out of guarantees —
                        'Tell someone!' they chorused.
        Wrest from flop — scads, yes —
knee-level admonish
you make everything *break open*, head cocked to defy
hystericalectomy: sometimes I get wrecked
before I clean up — want some fish head? —
                        felt chasm on own terms
poke fun at rather frantic wimp aversion:
I can imagine a preference for a quarantine for *that* sentiment;
                        ooby-dooby cozy bombing silkworm's sting —
I stopped hating you the day I stopped loving you
                        unless you con someone;
        excuse me sued forgive
if I lose control, let me say this: suck the directions
                                    point up by needling
                                    root rub verbs
                        exasperate more luridity —
disarm this kitchen & frustrate this compromise,
spleen the strings
                        to kill your replacements.
        Impossible stalactite delight
                        fish or flesh yeah yeah no —
when the lights go down, stop showing your wounds,
curt so little demeanor has need to do consensus
from the optimizing litter, manifest
                        not took a backseat *to*
chronic borders unafraid, unrestricted
                                    veto lust resort
                        to wield the puncture stress in trust
orality on everyone's lips

> to sing it without male parts
productively or unproductively intoxicate, the lay of
> raid encampment (& not only in her hand!):
it's just a mashing of our personalities.
> *La esperanza*, order too near
> > unmoored a fork
> > each otherwise coveting sovereign —
hope sells swindle short, vengeance buoys
> > two heads on the body
> > chemical means
power reopens knowledge toppling checkmate digest
> > tumult dressing, what a silly bunt! —
I'm more interested in enlightening hostility,
larcenous dusk
> > restorative without pillow
> > sanity forget-me-nots
> > > insist on slipperies
> > smothering us to save our organs.
> Chaos ideal
crusade against deportment 'must project itself
toward an empty heaven that it is to populate' —
pale loopy unity
> speak up ape not train a parody suite
my lightheartedness took several miniatures
any more love would bankrupt — appetizing mammal:
only the serious rights of zygotes are shorn — cashed out
> > > both sides' device bliss
> next argument.
> Endorphinated breeze to demoralize my inferiority
with excess, bachelors in car path: talk away! —
> > I don't need dreams, I need a studio —
> > let the gender-blind category wet
> > infinite embarrasses hetero sublimation; one
> > can't delegate nerves, scale all sudden
props in the improper open-mouthed bloom
to listen unfinished:
force scatters, no objects pressed into no subjects,
> hierarchy, get a load of me! — well just bake it:
castration levers in retribution from anybody

## MARS 10

and I don't care —
why not violations?:
we must stop this bra from functioning for twenty years —
fuck them like I don't care so little enough,
get this: gaps edges play to win
this battle of the skin, no limits whatever
swell if all wedding parodies own our own —
it's a drop of poison in his glass
laden with fruition,
proof heaven's
expulsion is our credit:
dolls are the opposite of applause;
lap's in public interest.

# JUPITER

## JUPITER I

Important words according to list
points tote illumine all emits —
create the real should count
simple stuff
in the time it took to type this out;
& melody memorizes subtlety
is not repetition, initials give it away:
I pictured everything, invisible paper
despisers of floridity.
I a typical ordinal warmth of shortening
pollen fits a lock wrapped up in a dream
harmful swaying subsides, comma traps
ever less adulterated true verse abandon:
scribble speaks binocular osmosis
objectively, as unmembraned spiders used to say —
citric batons
stack up crash into certitude
lid by half graphic lure
captured optic's avaricious quiet.
Objectal puke mounts snare —
can you see about-varnished pronunciation
in the actual letters? — darker bragging
daubest shades ravish veilage —
*ee ahteel?*
— do you copy? —
alone is aloud
essence is out, literal alarming
device blanks eyes captive gulf
gaze, forcefed mistakes
the blush light — paraphilic? —
thought carries in the fog
surgically
inferring
silences of faults notched
as apparition desire.
Adverbial humidity *phantasmata*, aerial trilling
the rhythm at which the meaning gets built
goes soft, clarity's handle came off —
fake vigil agonize according to decor

## JUPITER I

              syllabic friend
more to fake by, glow indoors —
some relief from that enforced verisimilitude,
some territorial gaffe, factual troth twirl clause in debt
instead idea withhold starlit fraud
climatized by the allure of individual facts' paradise.
    Mimetic & frightened
dampens three-word units, perishable microtone
hieroglyphs favoring images' valorous surface —
                    dash SHOUTS: arrows
                              arrowshots
                arrow umber minim vivid
majuscule tone lay boo
                pencil quicker mirage,
    clairvoyant phlogiston, object advertises *rights*
                I've added up my impressions
                to make a statement cipherizable sparks
can hide, if we may trust to language, we can talk
                some piece of paper trash trials
                recklessly legible skids, alphabet
                fasteners mechanically fonted.
    What inkspots?: affricates typified rigid blush
to listen to loss terminology leaked
                apprehensive typography *through*
                      *from*
                prosodic cunning errata
pirating henna'd caption prize milks smudge,
    dim the lists, hush your mouth — mistrust
                fuchsia layers silverize
                the legerdemain foam to
                partition the literal.
    Why be mime so slow? —
                read all butter, soap bubble reciting
hand wax leper word chrome black steady
                sleepy rods & factors suddenness beguiles
                convivial uncoverer, initials switching a zoo
for letters the letters removed from your name:
momentary grammatical lapses when you're writing to yourself
                even sounding the letters aloud —

## JUPITER I

teleprompter interrupts disconsolate fragility
orbs akimbo envy vies
issue serrate number title.
    I — ampersands separate enough
                woo focus vogue the perverse
interior *vita* slippery noun, points gone between titanium extreme
back ellipses alphabet tone corps ... insecurely detached
                shadow initials, resuscitative somersault
ruse ironic figure a sweat of sense concealment
nestling, voracious
                vowels as lace.
    And broke stem body
disaccords innermost secrets
always the same secret figure the seams for mudpies:
                metaphoric remedies wicked wicked wicked
                continuity, yolk tarred tumble in form
sick quote it in mist form folly, this vague
                ostensible hummage
so — to *see*
as *see through*
undazed
the world moves, let's make ambiguity.
    I steeled scansion
to lease excellent doubt, liar lull
                words rusing mates to conform
                milk bullets homing to the artificial
falcon gilds dense twisted in chinned hour
                quells as real vociferation
abounds among the animators.
    Eraser brown-out bizarre in effect:
                obsessive cutlery, megaphones on silver wings
that wet the steward blot sudden consumer intrudes
                verge of proof, perjorative probability
to surprise this delousing instrumental rumor I'm gratified
                abysmally bump, parquet trait
                      caked with news.
    Singeing it all done, pardon
vestigial typographical nothing truth unlatches
                ease suffice incarnate voltage in air

## JUPITER I

shaking the dice box of equivocity to ward off apt portrayal:
gate-crashing reality,
the unruffling of twisted categorical consumption —
prosodic injury's sportive lustration.

## JUPITER 2

I ME — no use pretending
                    interims' spillage, mirage debut
                    wand my kind phrase that, *that* which, *that*:
                              Don't indicate
offwhite guesswork salve, no facts brag;
     & prime rim, fiery tint
                    spaced off cliffed left
                              ganglia lack signs
sign versus gesture consummate careful interruption —
                    invisible ink lubricant loge
                    dormant to flash &
                    off gesticulator's freedom.
     And skidmarks on sense
                    impressions' dilettante delight inventive
stain inaugurate jazz, purple pen glints in
curve briefs brunt, ribbon pigment insisting
confetti biblically marbleized as *showy words*
disgracing ostriches lit from relief,
     swollen arpeggios defy
                                   the clue orchid
objects dangling from the pin, a moiré plaint
               of diddling twinks connote light
               decay — porcelain cipher's velocity
               brain wants a microphone
to drive the resplendent to the end of her lexicon —
                    beaucoup fluff it in —
you peeked.
     And red loss eddies missed in the hint —
reference is unimportant? — concert paraphrases
                    too much curl facadeized in my needle
so wrong, images needing adjustment puffed slants
                    = screen foreclose to spread the first blush.
     emblazoned captivates dark
these slur-maiden maladaptive florals
sizing looks tinted-glass the tan trusts
                              the fade enact not yet
                              whiteness at your throat
                    rattled the slack jettison
object shook gels, vicinity of gentle disbelief.

## JUPITER 2

I vapored sparkling
impression it may be hard to pronounce —
                        pulpy at fire, white maneuver calculus
flecks topping seam palate fine,
ultrafine, new gloss of indifferenting enigma
fathom lunged at shattering; jovial size
                        ply friction objects jellying into
                        words that differ: song took its eyeballs
                        back, irrepressibly graceless
                        slip tinting back & forth colloidally
syncopated detonation curls.
        And extra twist, then, *when* to slur
                        congratulating the most picturesque fleece:
                                what else
virgule lightly against target pins by hair —
                *ser neh pah zaygzahktermahng*
                *ser ker zher vur* —
                what's that, all alliteration? —
                *poovay voo mahng mawngtray doatr?*
                — audible feathering syllable
                copula frictions,
        semaphoric slippers lack leg, hornets shimmy
                                peppered curve
                        plump as thanks *latent* for manners
                        softening invocation, crease word
declaration of fluid gassed upon the prose, interlinear
defection figure.
        Actions doubt louder than words: heavy quit click arc
                *sais pas* seize to mark
letters played with a bow, swoon against extra keys
                                — I think *therefore* —
verbiage on its way to sinning humidity snuck up
clots for a change, partial pierced menstrual boomers
knitting sirened over incognito barometer
                        swivels to a point to koan in the tune.
        Oh I won't be pronouncing it badly when you see it written —
precognitive tongue-in-groove, the nouns give way, island-like
gossip object's reputation dissolves in syllabic air,
oblivious own speech, gingerbread with angelica,

## JUPITER 2

succinct & transverse bliss in semaphore
                aims minutiae belly
works off members, founder on gel, flex, tattoo
insinuate small white-boned letter's cutting edge,
    illustrate quiets
                                    deft aren't
                    taps, smack dab in the middle
                    the line breaks & goes home
calculated, air stops short, spoon shortcircuits nerves' sweat
                    on fine lines mouthpiece says
scissor line at knee — hinge abides
                    linen synagog, a cameo incision
                    butter bush gains with sweetener!
    Mouth of a story
hum answers desk of worry
                    vowels & consonants; & I noted
experienced forgery is pansied arbitrary
                    cream telling polyurethral
courtesy knots & retrograde mesmerizing braille
that bon jour spotting pretends to misdeliver ...
                    pretty think — touch did say 'think'? —
                    sugar lack? —
makes nerves I don't wear
                    readymade symbols  glissando trasho
fleecy regalia.
    Try the nuance reins — bouquet asphyxiation
                    say-so lit fuse wanting the detail,
                              outside cling
                              mucho choose
                              parable things:
                    bowl slice wiggle swath for the sachet to be
                    lessons redecorate regret
clipping issue whatsonever — hieroglyphic boa
express that modernity rejuvenating through silence
tomorrow seduces at a rating.
    Ob- ... ceaseless positing,
                    we cultivate that irrelevance shock —
some scratch!: can words do *less*, twisting drastic
                    confetti tenor flame of indecision

## JUPITER 2

've assassinated *this* chance operation — hourglass rubs the bias
heading the rupture — where are the exclamation points?
                    little better, *n'est-ce pas*? — palaver-free
                    the inkwell choreographs
                    exhumation of night
clicking casual retort.

## JUPITER 3

And page deserves white
fiat affadavits of impression —
                     no delving white writes white
                                fants ocalise
                     ocular plunder likened sky has no siblings
                     spurning edifice hint at pinkish
                     diagrammatic magnification scale.
    Even to say this
                     clustering snare into a tea cup
squeeze chromosomes in advert, aboved noun
fallible ruse; poor code specks deliberately
                     surrogate fancy incongruity's happy home
deciphered horizontals: I take prince of fleece
shards to be donor holiday,
    palpably fresh-frozen noise storm, over inscription
less or more remiss — precarious things that read! —
form? acoustic viscosity, claustrophobic catastrophe
directly apprehensible clouds as waiters;
    & *quietata* resistant to
                                   contends open is less
                   interesting curbed paraphrase
to bevel magpie 'as such', never subsides
travesty of certainty starts ticking.
    But redoubt flacks, dystrophies —
All truth is misreading, aren't my errors enough good? —
                           scribbling vies
                    CURB GLASS:
                   sleepwalking into the argument —
discontinuity is in the genes … the Ancestress
                          willingly as art
hind script choked underlining, sentenced uncertainty
                     dahlias bled default, names defined
soften the evidenced
elbow shatters
trappings repel the event to donate this gesture to science.
    Nothing is a matter of content —
facts don't have charisma, *fleur de lis* puss the interim
lunacy of tune disqualifies a serial
                     of cuttings revolt-outta-style;

## JUPITER 3

trochaic martini
unity a flat encephalograph
style no vice, same example pumped iota *montuno* rare
cunning twists by ampules: the PIECES are EXPLOSIONS —
my tenses are screwed up:
glimpse inorganic trill spelling grief dyscalculus
calculus inundates by stages ouncing that shifter.
A substance befallen fit lessen spook
some periods adjourned polyps, italic slantings
self-tinkling glass, the letters you tore up
jet this phase shakes —
each opinion its own diving board barbs hit a groove adjacent:
quick stems high, faults the rubber cement look —
mention corresponded to phobic datum
gnaws away velveteen brocade,
epithet squints designing otherwise engem!
Disable directive dosimeter:
erase my curtains, parse that flood —
misapprehension was misdelivered; fervent scar
fastens spurtive metal dosable yellow
stitch allegiance — this played harm
today hatched mistakes significant in heat;
a sleepy flora-dora language —
sometime, someplace, somewhere —
is it too late? —
is the watchdog really a lap dog? —
slippage ends and odds
absurd teeth comblike in back ghost instantly
bad in fold a gist befitted elusive position folly
incision leases.
Migratory battering axial promissory
even though I was scatterbrained — the lies dismount:
titanic amusement stickers full in
improper of interest
solemnizing pointillated after-effects':
expectation forks grievous angle
chafed obstinacy of mystery
makes fun of example!
An impenetrable payment darkens Idea, falsely

# JUPITER 3

nominal parts career
invisibly cool — think of lost injections, summonses
                    apostrophe — fraudulent seed
                          prose on do it:
                  forever magnifying glass
staging expletive confused it, all attention repierced
vending reprieve to pass over
obfuscatory credentialling in ostentatious silence.
    The crisper the fallacy — the waiting got heavy
liquid annuler:
                  plebian weaning omen at only
                  martyrised antique — thumpativeness
                  tricked-up repetition soaking nativity
misunderstood reversibly; good luck prolongs second coming,
the abandonment to irony — color is just a status symbol:
malice of big words refuse too true germ dream
excuses get overdeveloped — have you ever
scatterbrained without self-known stimulus?: this is it —
brevity means wit's on sale; *all* interest is prurient.
    Suppositional floats improve proof —
                  (be honest, now): how slippery? —
inordinate fear of differentiation, zeal for suspicion
in gust paper impertinence — tsk, tsk, asterisk
                  lurid lampoon, just not enough,
        the desk not a privileged site
                  folding generative jargon, escape bleach
primed past pollen to a T.

## JUPITER 4

Lace — rev
the experts stick to buds —
                    night's installation inside me
                    dives to kindle leading lights
                    infernal verse crime blonde grille air
                    enthronement works: frontal backness —
                                        this is not a dream
                    hurtle to contend obstinate;
        inundated ideas vamp their imprimatur —
lush lensing genre parfait, rougeist sonic boast
                    page pardon bric-a-brac attitudes, monuments
                    debris gestures, salute trump taint
for details suborning perjured decor as isolation voices
all pleasant surprise, transports crayons — rude assassin gauze
imparts splendid bacterial glow.
        And din what's worse rivet
fabled propulsion uncertainty — tsk tsk apparition
blossom spiked too blurs, insensible
                    tresses, immeasurable ciphers
                    that breezes swear off— in folly
doubled simulacra porcelain suspicion:
                    testimony self-deleting ingot ingratitude
crystal laxative treason traiting little cited fantasy —
vertigo phantomed lack mock white front
prying lapses of this fuzziness;
        sensible language prison
altering by de-salting rage milieu
franchise minced pageantry
                    pays banal secrets charge nation
                    adoration — nothing vaults this notary
lack of a stationary splash — long souvenir image
plus derisive insistence calcinated valor:
it's everything thought less underlined & 'I' & 'MY'
cynic venge creased conjuration aides, expiation ridicule
                    infects, enter newsprint skirts
                                        truth is difference
                                        error wand
                    'WE' & 'OUR'.
        And coup bonds stripped elegance:

JUPITER 4

Language replaces consciousness — polkadot
balking terms lucid, pluck ultissima
art diligent talons
centered in mobility correctly wouldn't mind
symptoms, sorts poisons
moment sacraments
punctually lapsing
my punitive nomination
interruptedly transcends
carefully cultivated inner collapse;
and fitful line slow word grasp by eraser memory
creases — only paper wobbly dice for loops
rhythmic capillaries:
subterranean antihistamine toolish
fabrication skids hurling hazard diction shook itself
rampant — avalanches — exasperated by interring
infinite unruly volupt
pandemoniac gazette of
blatant font bursts pirouette in the tensions —
rhythmic floats, scissors for misses
gratuitous de luxe falsehood raises temperature:
kinesis depicts release.
Caprice spectacles, pallidizing has desire
membranes, leaf of lenses'
permanent encore, cell derisive skull
caves, perked tight havoc of jackets suckle to abbreviate
vocalese with facts avarice vignette, moves displace lines
intractably except
perjury makeup — babel monotones
sudden cenobite pomped the instant
who overvalues, mercurial shoulder
pardon for all anatomy — singe as linear
self-exhaling necklace, dolorous chart-stopper slope tugging
Other tongues — acquired taste:
pincushion characterization encore
blood provisions image.
Muse retread silvered the muse professes
undampable binds fascinate shadowy fronts —
wishes are metaphors for words

# JUPITER 4

embellished attraction, ravage fruits
                    fanfare gelatined verse
conversed reverse, inter-danced, quadrupeds afire
                         haven version verse sentence
                         hands
                         target nonchalant
                         swizzlelike arterial pockets side to side
                         loosened bra & open robe
ballad innuendos' inquisitive imbalance,
        bad's favorite wish's more exact garden
                         contour serpentine histrionics on vacation
was half this root a touch esteems
proposition, socratic semi-easy
dizzying diary narcotic totem tie to doze
doubled trellis niche half-legible breasts, incorporate
                         too much light
                         concerted somersault
                         to equalize pleats.
        Milieu agitates self-allure habits
porous unconcern — immense torture efforts,
secretive imagination with crash helmets crease the trousseau —
                         does 'steep in' mean impregnate? —
                         rhapsodize with a tuning fork
quivering fakery my error treasures ...
to the hindmost; lured iris
                         ruses self-distracting rumor
ape from immediacy disowned — caprice
vague polis: clairvoyants masturbate that regret.
        Infantilized skulls mobile rule
                         wrapped in cloture *charged* with automatism:
bizarre libertine cadence the canon conscripts
                         vicissitude rambles, mechanical corpus
                         tincture membered discord —
false commune if you didn't mean it; conspicuously inquisitive
perfume revives natives, paradise of parasites
mistaking armory morsel precept signs of previous
                         unmerciful acknowledgement — is there? —
                         tugging double what's that? —
                              DON'T REDO THINK:

## JUPITER 4

                    diapers that wear emotions
                    epauleted by the dole.
     Happy noirest to suspect
can spun be foam behind — page fails, mimics balk
to laugh is to ruffle clarity, to engourd
                                tossed off to extinguish
                    owner's round sonnet vents —
                    razor pulp pomp mute beaux-arts reply:
distrust heredity nonchalant enough to care,
     loop flares
                                contort to require
                    laureling flamboyant *ifs*
painting the town red.

## JUPITER 5

ALONG the skid mark of recorded history
                    I tell you this mock slowness
in the open baton twirler's exile of least resistance —
                              raptive lure
                    fabric blossoms, malicious mechanism
                    but do go about approachdom:
dead eyes opened
immediated bodice occult suppose scoop up
paper is always so ... documentary — free from illusions —
                    toys span abjurings
                    of rumors of secrets of
night & day caught balancing tributary hominids,
        infinitely provisional maybe swirls of ...
                    erratic glistens — aperçu trope wink
cursive falsifies synonymous with the leg shows —
                    punctually dodge
                    cadence's chasm curlicued like sideways
indent minis, device favor skim sappy tutti —
pleated fancies, tight little neon arabesquing presupposition
                    petal tucking fretful cosmetic
                    in infinite excess.
        And feathery seedless falsehood
fakes of breath superb,
hot hot physical plant budding chutes derisive, *vouloir* creature,
                    credence as hubcap to straights
                    slander sentiments it agreed to dissolve
                    melody deferral fact in particle illicit
absconds, an audacious unreasonableness —
description is insulting, quite icicles ...
                    foliaceous zigzags
                    stand-in's to dish the digit:
you weren't taking liberties you were making a mistake;
        & this apes a tone budding
layaway sharpens pulp box of mock tags good:
                    fine on loan
laminate by swizzle mica splinters, snips of silk, bumps
fragments to quotable slaps in costuming
                    foil; voltage acquaintance
                    not graphically probable

## JUPITER 5

cuff spasm canopied dress epistle
readiness of accused, better prompting statements are so gauche:
           gibe trim paper pulse shadow vignettes:
           one more version, iconic doesn't say so.
    Forget name litting list of likes pattern pudding
forcible finger letter engines may much swerve this iota
speed to slip the singulars waxing bleedy fluent
           pies pause to gem slice
the slight syntactical detachment gradation sank loose
           velocitous sign gilded
           splinters utter, signs flicker off;
   lax floating nervous immediacy:
           what's not been unsaid not *all* sterile —
seams are mobile, straps may be a revelation —
elliptic sharp signature fragments, evenness a motel
fur claspwork, furtively flexible crevice's flare;
           lingo's own assertive sign zippers speed
gesture-plus-steps grabs a mike undermorselled
swivel peerage of a girl factor eerie digit
                pride by razor cell
                jellied in the larynx
           = popping ground, please to punch it up.
    VD (Valentine's Day) —
to avoid billing squabbles, salivate the servings
           mesmerizingly needlelike
           atoms here, organ correct liable blurting —
unmitigated stealth I'd rather stop & start
write for the strange self
           flirts red off games of choice babbling porn
color squad, I'll say: dictum's specialty
flank in somewhat ways, carve takes
my fool personal voice praxis hum dot finish
           shake till it rattles
ruler bed renown seize welcome size — I speak fashions
           writ body tweezer is a verb
you feigning or fawning skill shills grist
           suckles at the speed of stationary danilovaed
stunt flimsied *sissonnes*, *assemblés*, and the like —
well I'm not drooling about typewriters;

## JUPITER 5

dallying points, some pronominal wetting
                pinch brisk skin
pleases comma, svelte breakably
                frontal reading & the text
reciprocally squander each other — one reprise memorizing slinks
demeanor of erotic availability volatized
identity parenthesis up flank seething succor
                plumbs speech intimations
folded like an isosceletic triangulation of lips.
    Lanolin stood stretched dart guard — innuendo if —
stymie oral gape the deeds, skinned retreat
                can't spell romance across synapse party:
                glamor's gate trembling with forked tongue
                — what signs do you use in identifying
murmur's resonating little fashion? — exception
                cling-shaped dodge, vibes you know
don't crowd my elongation; intact fuss fissure banquet
joinings stick as steam
                          caprice, vowel bother
dressers & stitchers, rapport transformed into image
incisions, make a grammar breathing
brittle by means to make
                an unfair comparison again — ability bleeds
                matter's legible hermaphroditism
                doting to mind minds
                voices didn't bake enough.
    Isolated lyrics make me cease
stimulus to value, handwriting learns to dance
                regaled, mask quenching neon gagging tic
                    attitudinal cleft
                style erases moving memory I say quite openly
afloat want but pencil-line pulls, whinnies over pock up
question castrating, laminate by squeezing
                rows of lights, hooks by chintz —
                semicolon peril shunting nuptials
on to concealed monitors;
    fixed thimble balks
                legs in action so legends unfold
the *dilettanti* perma-breach we might yet contrive:

## JUPITER 5

what's your excuse? — favor
                sample sits, interpretation is breeding
sticky nerve rehabilitators narrating impetuosity;
    and begin singsong shortage as please
bridal pest, verb accessory groove scales insert she-la —
density makes memories, filed down panoply victimless fences.
    Clarified softener talkaround mimicking disconnectedness —
don't mention my name: hark craze gloss that limit
                lingo panache beguiling foray allure —
no surprise to mess up? — don't let them label you? —
                        comma flail, Oh, pinion me
careens possibly bodily in details tore my sense
all soothed syrup On-Phase indulgence at the mention
of the idiom idiotic to restless shudder
              unconfined watermark cuffs it off.

## JUPITER 6

CURVATURE good in my mouth
                    puckered volume lowering eyes forbidden
                            true strokes breathe hard
softer sly occasional paradise: *what* gentles
                    frail cake so soft & touchable
well acquaintanced ardent pump going on, slogan mutually
auspicious ammunition:
                    first taste, what's that —
prompt satin pinky finger pigmentation span?
     I'm wanting the suds it first flout —
                    triangular oval all leapers
                    *any hips at all*, make out the slim festooned
constant image quake quavers
delightfully, guiltless trespass
loom to dance the throat of the unpublished princess
pang off disguise kit, I can just
                    tell you, syncopate flounce
heart claims faster, gelatinous patting pressure
tenderly pent-up — the pen beguiles
broad hips producing milk, looking for tonguing a little lie:
a little word so much nominally take false off
                            tongue teaches
                    letters in the eyes.
     Labial mental hairdresser underground
pubic assistance bisect attraction, hands
and backs floating posed
slow skid invite all limb-like close as pages in a book —
                    false lick feint soft! fast! —
                    winking vinegar florid ever
dream clocks in at butter; ensign pariah physical slush
                    swine mutters, time out for tears —
                            those babyfood lips
                            leave me with impunity —
there you go, bleeding again.
     A near-classicism of fluidity —
without that bulky feeling, arteries' declension
voluptuary in teeth's clothes sliced same furry couch
                            I think in trouble
                    jumping out of seams with mis-intent lacking

in its own similarity to resurrect *difference* as sandbox
                    for the halfhearted; headless heroin
                    palpitating diagonally gash pluck
                                does it word proxy
                                spurs abundant spurs
                    audacity greased, tubing anoint
                    petiticize giddy so nonchalant
jewelish imprecaution.
    Vaseline melody modulates luck's envy
fragrant nibblers — Response is Interpreter:
                                buzz, buzz, buzz
                                these three words
                                IOU
                    unpronounceable twitching I'm speaking
making fingertip contact to misunderstand you,
                    peg of dodge
                    dependent thanking limits
                    to accept, oh boy, face balm *physicale*
                    letters paddle flesh
                                ~~glad as the~~
                    concise pill lips wake up and cry;
I did it, I'm
                    concave besides innocent
                    X-rated chatter, sideways lunge
thin edge drinkable virtual surrender to myself —
I'm a verb not a personal pronoun:
wick's gambit gratis lope, verbs virtue hookaholic
torsoid venture curling will —
                                wide mood swings imagine
                                verbals on my trail:
                    eager twirling selfish rooks, just self-
                    watering harbingers — smart move
                                her due
                                swells elate
                    Chatterbox One
                    curlicue between
                    of gestural economy.
    Make it a cloud for two, baby —
tonsils work that unisex gravitated self

# JUPITER 6

seizes dedicated of squeeze me, tee hee; respect *means* distance
stir the friendship darling-twofold
Love inserts a comma
you make it so
tell me so —
libidinal squint embedded
alto of my booking double talk & the curves undecked:
would you hurt me now
darling dear sugar lump
blanket of blue do I worry too many times
at last the natural face seems inevitably
divide esteem to win out — I challenge your kiss
*cora zonal* inflammational sweetest one
risk compassion heavin' 'n' revvin' animal-kneed
sharpen the conjugate face reflection:
everything still fits
parenthetically excited.
    Sudden joints joints salute
flitting or flirting less literal *lets* me speak
orgasm in so doing I discover my vagina
has a maiden name — fraction twinge breath cooped
ardented curt lusted discretion
spatio-leg meld complicit close in closes stain lips for details
arrows of longing disheveled up-close tint
— is my heart wasting time? —
grief mutually protective,
    get in, get in, please get in, a self-destruction
stack zoomed cervical fixtures, the resonator
her hips, and so forth ribcage feeds back
Stir Crazy at low intrusion — no clit terms? —
a virtual penis in a wig about how us both
pastime down on it supervised with teeth
visceral lube too late
devil with the rest:
I'm gonna paper my walls with your letters
contrition erratic receptive
kickbacks from inner space italicized closer
pinch almost continues w-o-m-a-n experience's tutorial
warranties of breeding duration — placenta hung

# JUPITER 6

himself perforated breathing tongue slips as accuracy nears
I lost my period atom stem bleed chick message pollen
                              awake tonight
                    iterate labial gradation leg
convincingly undressed.
      I'm living OK, I could
precisely couldn't everything they said came true
                    if teardrops were kisses deranging the moves
less intransigent risk somersaults in air
                    sparking insincerity — do be so silly:
                    my heart's the biggest fool —
cut the mumble, love me now or let me go, speech soon if
stuff with mistakes at dialect the momentary
disinherits — can't girls suck on twots?:
                              fond incurability
indict the zygote-beater fingers all ballyhooed off
delectably pale & stoops adieu;
      lips convene blue valentine
                    hybrid asterisk key to my heart
immuring morphism: candy soldiery severed armor
                    if somewhat disorderly into which I intrigue
                    even if the tongue is forgetting
                    to please museum of secrets.

## JUPITER 7

ℝoving target — There:

> Gesture
> Smoocher
> Blue, Magnetic
> signs *tied* to condition: buzzer curt
> courtesy presence verified whole sex
> — Intense — anti-aliasing
> light envy the rub by reason bet

it cupped my ears for me, made a head for
frank appendage?

> There: force me how what snares are —
> want to dress something out? —
> Ignite how grateful every time to spit
> we write *this hurts*
> *vouloir-dire* novice lava swerve obsesses
> boulevard massage: Gypsy Unobtrusive Bloom
> Pom Pom Newstyle, deeming those gimmicks —
> *Charm that it does?* — memory means tourist:

the brains of the organ tittered anesthesia
linked to trembling —

> the bloom is malleable harness
> companion conviction engaged.

> There:

> — so can't —

court an incision any tense question of size, sighs sparse
orthography insults a rhythm, kind of, defeated corsage —
antipathetic edges, sower jest minatory fine; conclusion

> cannot stabilize the words about *skates*
> gone blood simple breaking silence:

I was late to my spawning group, I evacuated reality for you —

> apostrophic breach defeaturing

fleece organic deflectors, they manage to stir minimum up:

> grease slimmer creed apostasy.

> Show: less grip mishap matter can count

> TOPSY TURVY — folly
> flexibility means morsel spade control:
> body point

snarer voltage speedlike & relational
pinch makes appropriate bite-sized mistrial zigzag

confectional data agitationally, in your own words, slide
almost indifferently from one counterfeit spasm to the other
broken glass finger in series in flower
                          buttons buttons inspired.
     Show: conversing verb
                          for the unidentified lover
                          flagrancy to whom confer taste daily toll —
the husband has no song, believe me, malleably awkward
swirling moves about to flip flips are too much crucial
                          resolve: I try to eliminate any coherence
                          unfelt points false pulls same
                          warrant for smoothness, watch drunks tilt
                          to be misunderstood would be great
                          with so much makeup get softer by detail
                          daily palm the truffle
medicated transitions.
     Show: debts calf goner curl
                          this response somersaulted too much
                          care for still divide kindle spur —
                                        heart's lark Sixty Nine
                          integer dissolves bush to talk SVP
the secreting undid sympathy leg lifts ideology, boundary
takes a lot of abuse: lipmus L-shaped
                          breakthrough binary prison
revel melting pleasure by mistake.
     And fallibly moistening, all appeal, unjerks
petting silky derrick with the heat tossed back by paradigm ...
impure grief convoys in matte blessing, anal flag lifts
artificial gossip, cloture flowering goals immune
— fasten the fuck, art pays off in bed! —
mistook substances for substantial
choice bags out detail
                          between blonde & stem disgraced suction
                          syrup dislodged;
     and a dare peel extract sax
                          animadvert bump —
are you lingering matter motivated? —
I said I buy teeth, fracture interpolated
                          sense mate rapid quints belied in hints —

# JUPITER 7

Taut, *interratrice* at jabs
Needles Lady Escorts Belle:
little equity blows taps on nameless, on ecto hurry
let's make a deal wants it all voided
rescues doll rocking letters
on in whip.
And why don't we call it research? — Donor reads:
*give me some bilateral subluxation of the female head* —
revoke their stretch-pants privileges, fluid whirlwind
axis false-hearted 'I' apes 'not'
posturing how divergent is sincere, sapper's
motional voice caulks
to insect interval's simulacrum; I court labor
impatient to break you when they broke the mold
dreamers prosper, now hiring —
the collarbone appoints its own following
popular enough so your voice drops
modeled upon dreams of others:
cannibalism of choice
name blunts teen bio
Suss Love limbs lied
spiderlike yessir the romancing
of a pathological liar comes to an inspired end.
And stem of a pledge
warning theft put on miscegenation backwards —
gender or grinder?: the silent language
the visible languages misnamed sublime
bullying bares all experience, bellwether of
insincerity, particular security
bulk box has falsifiers trot to type
chocolate as imitation liquid in someone *else*'s mouth —
solution for sin training aura rubs
off, repeal the cherry awareness, copulate
maternal hoe-down with genre —
the plot bickers!
Reconciled calves enjamb this
torsion virtue fuck law lapdog union
… go lightly, apologized charade jiggles
out restaging the pinpoints of conscience so they can start

## JUPITER 7

unfurling backwards — Heated Rivalry excuse inverts
                    placental festivities — excrementious cakes
bitch my birth, really cute little fetus earrings
charge the phallus rent: I need a lesbian dictionary, I'm
deficient!
      And Shake Loose pyramid? —
                         *zher ner feh ker rergahrday* —
no heavy ships in here, I can't live with a cash register —
teeming maturity ≠ winnings, bid outdo
the forbidden voluptuary counterpoise undoing
the throw of convenience,
      yank the spun risk
                    sings to discount interval accosts
                              comfort's own Imagination
amorous commendation gave up sawing
                    hurry complaints — partition such
                    consolidated clutch of luxury
incentively adverse.

## JUPITER 8

Fact confected adorn to explain
                              a sort of splendids
                    champagne lighting
                    debates whites
the vignette starts yelling bluish size, drastic
white white bye-bye accent consume,
      big threatened
pinpoints retract — some scam bin eye copies
of delays and now below paper adjectival
multiplying glows brief bright fact simply blur
                                        artificial provocation
                    suddenly razz minutiae offspring
                    inclusion seems condescending;
      & I'm undecorating more top end
favorite fragments a brainpicker
insure gel wedged coin
                    end in a word haze wayward
grammar's faith underneath simple triangular white
tremors surveil the asterisks
mushroom plumps up;
      design your words that are going to be
                    pulled out of the subject
                    matter — what admonishes the number? —
                    if a tongue could break
                    talk shows itself labile
                    arbitrates alarms, octave within
swirl-like upgrade; unreinsured reality tunes a hem as storied
as sentient clock noise stutters iris, vacancy for gists.
      Oh sweet niche flap fawning cut
                    lexicon sometime union wiggle flail,
                              real nice italics
                              decorum love at risk
                              havoc ensconcing
                    matte-painted circusoid prick out clad
gold arpeggio in REM!
      I want intervallic stain
                    every firm special dot —
I have no memory, that's what keeps it lapidary
                    incomplete monopoly over the page derisive

## JUPITER 8

pivot lighter intervals:
copulas' flashlight engemmed scopic exclusion —
attentions precarious come to —
mint rigor mortar
poses silence, scold content & repeat the squirt in appellate
digits vamp all twists spawn
to rip fat tense,
syntax won't worry a serum
crude injury estranges
no nutrient medium babble
precision pulse deflowers, detonates
neutral discrediting
tracts in the crawlspace petulantly
forking orbit folds without math:
codes mess pent-up lamé fluidity
in the service of back-offs.
Nobody's offered me a mood yet:
aspect underwrites maternal nomenclature cuisine
puts on its vocabulary to rule —
*FEHT VOA ZHUR!* —
red bleats on the echo
fat outs tackle my sentence regrooming; bossed pleat
only interpret remorseless decoder decoding
the carousel textile of the text peep to apostrophize,
pin-scorned crack in mirror argued for need
moves move as category
aggressively wrong — incomplete bother
pride, much mail in a 'brain costume'
pus as curator gaps, capsules give
leverage crevice complains.
Still not dear surrender
to paper culture counteract in your brain, betray gifts
& line to unscratch favor
in the form of words, fabricked lease
the tendered black radio heart
exchanging imagined snapshots
small pulleys wetter.

## JUPITER 9

Wнат letter means latitude normals
a ricochet culture better by hand
                        candelabraed out into matinee —
                        sweetest rewards make loans less hard
                        hardest won commotionals
shrink-wrap cancel my risk if just to avoid pigeonholes
cleave to posit convalescent wound clayish dealers
                        of dreams maneuver:
        & now, you can say what you want to, uninsidious
                        unincomprehensible, imbalance
                        implies conflict —
                        blurb waits for those who feel
                        fruitlesser voluntary aborted mute
fetus tissue donors — no fees — harmless
                        little body shivers nothing quibble look
illusory purpose to thought to rent no goodness gossip
                        in caps the opposite.
        And is danger finished? why is it
valuable cliffs instead of holes? —
                                        cadre tracing tubes
                                        body light body agrees
                                        tightrope stinks:
                        lost rent to happen segue error
desserts applause like shifts nurture hint
no pause doubled absent slit:
        & now interrupt by growth knows by beat
                        patented atoms, imprecise emotion bother fact
                        mockery's solitude cut & blur bereave
by chart resists haze
consummated papier-maché linguistic betrothal.
        Tuck beneath aphorist conclave off
involuntary dodging fright steadier
grope conjugated sublimated hammer stalemate —
                        wires readied xenografts
                        of agonizing good intentions less at loss
                        deceived the aisle vendetta
makes out segue:
        now you know I refuse to be dead forever —
                        baby stole off a nom de plume, an equilibrist

## JUPITER 9

with a hyperbolical improbability as tame as guard duty
                              gobbles in line
to renege on lineup; accidents cease
                    to be reasonable synapse habitat
                    since nerve naked
twitch in state skilleted offspring scalped
                    tranquil tuckless knot.
        And unreason *pauses* —
if you don't concentrate you find yourself in another key —
                    associational slither step-conceit
expired tuck scattering is too mild spook through
                    minutiae, ostensible curvature
                    lights are low
                    singular edges griefs deploy —
if you could fluff them, then they would be right back up again:
        now know I'm a hopeless structuralist —
                    grams buried my grateful birthday
                    fail to behave, basted! — loyalties kinked
                              fraud forehand
                    extricate by flips, ill-headed
noiseless talking meaning on holiday unstarched its voice.
        Stave off subject covenant powder identity
                    by troweling encapsulates
emancipate tongue bumps
                    DISABUSING sense to refuel the big insider
                    line of tension demarcates: I would pay
                    along with feeling some writers have
                    an entire literature hoping
                    they'll have a son fleetingness
                    movement alone could become
articulate soreness with Rashomon effect — easiest, right?
        Divining underdress they speak in
baring freedom's nice bliss!:
a second mortgage on the self if it's so valuable —
                    heroics forcefed tucks
                    custodial earnest tongue invests —
comma is not to be surrendered, the publications the particles
tire of have to be surgically separated compiling me
granularized so enjoy sizzling self-improvement.

## JUPITER 9

Avid hybrid vocal hum allegiance soaked
within propertyless verb unlaced lips unpurposively
the seductive breakapart slanders thanked to face
                    seam by procured seam
                    delinquent joint joints denied
extra limbs between the cracks,
        affectionate delicious zigzag debt doesn't blame my dreams:
orifices losing count sex fact tenure
affinity drill, *for David & Goliath*, we can
                    never close the books —
I will have no personalities, allocator intact.
        And men spoke one language while women spoke another
inverse against rumor hyphenated bastards —
                    who says yes comes first
                    when your commotional consideration
                    body functions go then you might
as well apostrophe to ass means make
if lusciouser animals wished on intoxicant
                    napkins' leadership — trashburst:
name buckles, space abstains,
        falsify with delicacy I prefer
subtraction loaded epidemic diversity by purge
unlike performative coloration, pregnant women
                    are actual persons — toys I told you so
                              click it carousel:
                    nature's self-sufficiency & Pavlovian touch
irony without irony melita-ed sperm heart purse
disjunction consent.
        Plush surgery aggravation
release — enfranchisement, vagina birthday controllably out
lick-shaped excuses, which would you rather do? —
                    (a) watch the wedding
                    (b) watch 100 commercials:
        no voice forms juice gest
                    quirks reproof doubting better
                    drag will help *esperanza* equivalences:
chalked choice up
strappage extracts supplanted
                    learning genital gestalt.

## JUPITER 9

Ephemerally moving negligence teamstered the offspring
                    to sterilize the name — womanual
                    unwelcome in the please in the middle
                    switches the whipping boy credit, *indefinite*
                    payment stales the impropriety unmasking
                    orgasms in the delivery room — am I
getting paid for this?: dreams do
                    control your fertility to
make tender of contempt:
Free will *after* politics, that's one idea of a good time.
     Find a female without desire for children
                    who has her own penis, own mojo violence
working fine thank you, candidated whisper
cozied nest disenfranchisement's commotional appeal —
voluntary floors of nature were wrong —
paradise confers dissolution to prove it:
     all god's chillun got a vacancy
keeper of the doll unit mutate nonsuture simply
                    pick up the white courtesy phone
                    exhilarated ablative irregular
                    aquatics, normless blush
                    earnestly ungeared.

## JUPITER IO

Unhomelike medically nullifying maps
mistook us — who says no double jeopardy?: F-test
                lore else, *do* explain, do you
have the evidence ready?: disown promiscuous sense
overheard courtesy
                merely partisans for the whole
                        piercings of a fact-
                like space to become my mailroom.
    Service in hind squeamish
                adjuncts translate
                such fate patented snail eggs
                menoplausibility fortified no …
                — the fetus has no rights, or allowance —
no person shall be compelled to be a witness against herself:
                get these don't worry hooks for less
                if the natural is to be
                corrected artists must be stained
too wrong — such protectiveness is
                provocation, pour on the italic powder.
    Emboss propel
enough frighten morals
will get you creamed, you *hoped* it was a parody you might keep
classics as quintessentially minor kit
balk quickens the dollar fire alive
                reassured by junk because of force
without no sense's own reward; ego afterbirth
                mess implores; pigs are delving
indented to choke:
    juror fading, fructose
                        what fun to free
                actually syllabic comeuppance —
                you want the minorities to disabuse you? —
                stoking diamonds, hearts, clubs, factions
roar out TORPOR ALERT!: license plucking
coupons absorb worry, your *own* upsetting
solicitation credit capsule unnerves multiple embryos
society does not ejaculate.
    This is not a flower flowering egress-happy
granular recency, without workings in my torts interrupt

# JUPITER IO

to your home fact spastic late
                          lies ought to inspire confidence —
foster-puree contrary scissors close to wrong edge
idiom predates oscillating excuse;
        & Nietzsche expected the counterfeiters —
                          the clarity turns out better
is just an artifact of bad manners, *impossible* virginity
                          quickly cursing privilege addresses
                                          stilts sieve embattle
orifice becomes a woman most too calm for morals:
furtive actuarial decoupage sounds like disaster? —
maybe just wrong pestidecided
ovum condos.
        Broadloom bass notes texture sires
structure cutting plasma, tell him you could have lied! —
                          disruptive alien eye dilated
propriety of castration creature paragraph
                          at least that thought's oversubscribed —
                          mazes infinite
fertility pencilled in at halfscale familial volume
fossils overpoliticize the very *nerves* or shape inside
pertinence,
        parliamentary adoring
vague protocolesque reprise donor at least
cameo eggs bank on turmoil: the analogous excess
whose devices contradict spin control to warp the pen
with hope for solution future; there's a catch
in the throat from it, from use value (= usury)
                          — if one has too many memories:
                          a show of commodity
                          to litigate that jelly, I didn't say it
                                          I made it hothouse
                                          which is less awkwardly
                          extended expressive appropriateness;
        coil accuse, human straighter fetus is eligible
for Medicaid to get itself killed — na-na-na
self scrape: nothing interesting about me in particular
                          social pinches're heading involuntary
                          memoir training too organic

       mischiefed individual cashiered cordials —
       their stature sits on their depletion manners
depict social structure to change the subject —
       I bled shame for your requirements:
       silent majority gnawing at slender thread
       of experience anyway perverse.
  There's a big difference between
wanting out and wanting in three-dimensional voicing
         look so staged as unrest:
recruit some new relatives not uncorrective
watering the bad cotton candy through understanding
crown negates purse voice-disguiser —
       accept no discourse except love's
       savoir-faire loyalty as inequality
credit wet semaphoric unison, semaphorically reversed
         phantom powering custom
       can steal feminine
         decommodification for us.
  Predestination series widowed
the integers order hides to get out from under
       agenda damage, 'wandering uterus'
melts normative suspicion for want of jury
habit confabulating fluff got me down: that's why
they remove them, because they don't have any slang term; en-
coffined ballot says knees cross to audience is a book
       to me, the plural forceps astride
       a private realm *nothing* but politics
       alienation is not, unfamiliar, reasons why
anthilling gaffe pertains priceless *total*!
  And you, imperfect surgery
incorporated into the extended ego *sleeps* in judgment
long before they develop differentiated genitals,
        secretive suffrage
       mouths where their crossbows should be
enough to be social infants broadcasting
the line of reproach undisturbed
       imposed order through a sieve of habit:
a little
hush money could do a lot of talking;

## JUPITER IO

civic cosmetics serenading suture mischief
                    forfeit pods out stinging
stencil lips the norms to become abnormal
freedom's disapproval, latent
                    a prop enhancement of the recipe
                              summons, ovarian dropsy
                    system vitalizer dutied unless
                    I naturally put the ovaries back in:
rhetorician stutters, us-against-them.
        Well-bred freedom knows when not to clap —
                            Why?:
                    I sold *my* baby to aliens, how dog-eared
                    can those stereotypes ... permission exceeds
                    speech says No to us
breakable chains? — predicted sticker shock dunning the bias
results keep you motivated, unconvinced of our swamp
rather than implanted by persuasion: small sperm volume
                    buckles grew with democracy
allegorized threat baton succumbing medicine.
        It seduces me, do I have to respect it too? —
                    proof weld lullaby magnetic
                    valentine guards
                    experience from anxiety
                    of sequence values unracked
                    some big band
mambo orchestration touches
shelter from the norm,
    *guignol* skittish social
accusation lumps rules'
net cutaway free in size
of public relations measure limits
to kindle resist everything
socializes everything —
I just let it shear the law off the page,
        music is the *amp* of the future

                                    power cross
                                    public heps
                                    words
                                    move

## JUPITER IO

                              break
                              certain
                              rule
                              flames,
as words quiver the flames.

# SATURN

## SATURN I

Pʀᴇssᴇᴅ ᴏɪʟs orchid reprieve
donate eyebrow flangers into certainty, festive to relent
                    just this one spot license of
                    ink nook air singularly first
                    lilts what legible
seamless light! — Well, it's only a word — minute blacks
                                    starlight ions
imprison my notice, phrenologically open as long as
you accept the form of the pencil.
        First check to see if
                    counterfeit levers awash —
you always peep through a hole or you don't just let one little
artery burst open! —
                    ~~query~~
                    soon halation light trap neon
                                    writing means forgetting
                    fast leased off-hind
                    bribe — sensation of — appeal to
                    appoint me big lie subtlety fails:
        wallflowers fund the planar squiggle
spirit cognition *violators* shaping
                    velvet subtle tissue posturing
reservations about orthodox corrections, equip
                    garnish depicting chandeliered
                    swirls afford the fantasy
                    all these bees blink artificial mercury
for me fussing into a direct aperture,
        the protractor claque, harmless baffles the fragility
of the bulb, figure-eighted sawtoothed slicing
thirst bleeds on cue; ocular
star could tarnish tapered eyelet
cell abusive iris curves capacity
way too big uncertified blue.
        I shall not minimize that
                    suspicion sheen risk dark
shakes dimmer bonnet, all our pertinence can't wait to
                    close up my eyes quit reimbursing
those half-dead christmas light strings in the sky
feign ignorance of the reality litany, a militarizing
biology votes freon'd doubt the impotence to

## SATURN I

literal moonshine — captives strictly special loud
fictitious truths to be keyhole discourse
cross-grained at cloudburst.
    Grazing lights okay tight millskin scopophobia —
get to believing my own stuff: cached roseate
seeping swishy catered burial of doubts —
fuzzy retighten adverb tights on facts, some electricity
creamy obscura starlight *in vitro*
innuendo corrugated secrets; no tonic crushes
arguable as straightedge hardline images
                         renting couplets skittering cranial
                         slither in hypnosis false to
stick to fact ate my mirror.
    But *lettre de cachet* labials clairvoyant
untouched even assuming *arguendo* that bleeds
loop mesmerized idiom never gets revised
                      perfectly: girds not look at me
waxing & waning indecent monosyllables cheapened
through forgettable thought expulsion,
    spark so sure exact
spills squeeze me some syllables this never was —
on wish whats, specious commas stung, I'm
auditioning the wrong tense — at the speed of — impossible
nothings make a doubt crayola parry skimping pyromania.
    If your tongue has to be hanging out to think, you've got a
fragile fry, one-for-all calf eliding
bobbing nettable flurry fainter gap I cannot say:
I swept up the dirt inside my head heavy action glare
tissue affect for disbelief, chemically subordinate
inch ideas at angle braying in vain —
I'm not a detail person,
    mawk spell manquish
beauties shook carelessly too dear to flanks — chill the most
                 for light chasers; what I've lost
                 I can demean, apostrophize any grammar
pointed strip switch toys of errors better burn
                   body's lexical distaste —
I may be missing the point, eviscerated
lightning in mouth then spun thrill

## SATURN I

tongue cut quite early.
She invented writing
auditory abandon could get
imperfectibly, swell overstuffed nightmare moisten
syllable-less peek — is it even remotely conceivable
that a woman could have written this? —
respond reverse detoothing at cruising altitude
admires to memorialize atoning needle, annoy ice
simple slip baton tastes forged
grab truth dares dart distaff fabricated
misnaming breast lavishes jargon with interned shutters.
Nest scent, the catechism bare
numbering sanguinary florid air & hurt
fits blasting bud or better it
& held tight briefed ajar — is that cognitive
*thaw*? … is it an overdose of sophistication? —
so face kick insight;
just sitting at my desk
makes me want drugs, boldface crease
gilding the pill, mock withstanding
flush with edges, rouge minored bleed
to believe — chafe lit imp bittersweet chocolate-voiced
hand curls the fugitive genuine wand to loosen
future by abbreviated limbs;
choking vexation, it's so funny
because I was just thinking: dayglo mutates
shorthand sulphur lilies get cramps, voyeur's dirge, sleep
creature tacit drag, you eraserheads! — reverb got me wrong.
Loss fled care, nothing
*means* worry, iodined awake —
Pavlov has it wrong too
are so unforgettable:
only biological pinky as dangers pull up
the sheets on *that* lack of insight —
consider the furor needle
other doubts act gets
tense — as in anxious or pluperfect, gasses we hale
back end by acclamation pop-up turmoil.
Ah-hah!: I hear you learning

## SATURN I

could eat broken glass — *that* kind of foam at the maudlin
knowingness wiser inflates safety fetters
turning red milk acrostic
magnifies happy fuses of italics have wings
                              reinforcing unsponsorable expectations
                              and you're also a poet?:
as for the match-lighter
there doesn't seem to be any beginning.

## SATURN 2

You wanted to see more skin pre-inhabitated
sauce back up open holes a peepin' mouth itinerary
                              that slightly addled
                    fleshiness little putting skin stars rouge
hates sale soothe this hinted hose the witness, eyelashes
can self-wince gaudy as all get out.
        And corrupt baste: raggedy mauve hurts
on the front impersonated necklace on riposte
remorse whose makeup medicates fallacies —
maroon pressure cleft like lightning fakes
                                    ignites arrestingly
                                    precociously alluring
                    furnaced retreat for the couture cure, my fat
falsely wetted out your impossible contrivance:
        clotted sticks doubling soapish intrigue ankles
                    liberally bloused — the nipple knows
hookah pipe attached to waist negligé duplicity
                    vermilion closest to teen distraction
compelling unremitting convulsive abolition of beauty that —
why so bunchy? — beauty affords fit
tumbles to feinted smooth powder;
        you are *equal* to, not susceptible to, hairspray, forehead as
                    mouth gunnery coddled
                              bric-a-brac blush this
ambiguous overbite — gossamer sewing stigmata pollen —
the botched figures asphyxiate with ruffles, rasp dry nape chill
                    clotique play'll spies
                    pump out the breath crèche.
        Sloughing cream abates hose fleshing
of rayon ducking behind casual energy
                    flattering jittery with *beads*
                    stick to feign encaustically jewelless
                    dressing room topping preen
restless skin above the elbows from the cold
inclines skin cult, sensationally jellied, precautionary burns
                    take stripes very
                    capture admiration for the beeline
and mediate spade convulsed bauble.
        Precocious arise *it it it it*

## SATURN 2

derangement parties absently fold
too near Rocking Legs, Circling Arms: tempo's signature
posturing gels a joy to be spillage —
pelt shimmy, puppets for ankles, fusillade
blouse with explosives
a madder crimson crack styling fuse ...
poppy's fervent switch in spots,
hair headlights shorten moussed youth lapels;
    *Russo chocolat* soubrettishness agree to caprice, eyebrows
over noise from behind for your period
max factor silk reckoning physical *desiderata*, bulbs between
my untutored titties, cinderous
lap the dynamiting garb attrition
stress caprice —
lotions' lobes
reckless signing means less makeup
stinging teasing fancier than chemicals.
    Did you take notes repel the sauce
on her chance to bother boys into generators
detonates debutante squarish
navel, express job tilted lid bleeds
its compliment of a trumped suit:
*le(r) veezahzh — ler pwahneh —*
*ler kurr — ler sang — lah zhoo —*
*lay zyur — lah boosh —*
*lah lehvr — ler doa —*
what does not spurt is the will to spurt,
general pitching hard
stalking hems either glands or real
matrixed swan, narrowing 'viriloid' chamois
get here again.
    I touch taken undone pleasures
one loving leg can kill tsvetayevaesque hem after gift
intimations, satin brusque singe palpitates elastic export fluid:
bow out hush indiscretion hands untouchable
seduces — indecency may be lyrical, why unbutton the bottom? —
palm mortgaged foist lap fallacious
kiss where shorts hit thigh;
    a small back — queen-sized teen indications operate

on the zipper risk stimuli on each other's neck —
           skeptically shyly hula
           moot court
           nylon adversaries, jellied inflammational
           sleeveless oppurtunities —
puppy-headed thighs.
      Vertiginous bets too burned, velvet-edged polka —
           handkerchief knows my tricks freeze
           inquisit volume, caution
hightops, toppers, intrinsically sweat
the nun removes invocation touch from the dress pads
aversive spats less generic
           whom to pop don't glass very long;
     penetrating bodice rippers beware male bottom beef off
           in curls laborious laps from all
           much too eager to tease only
           you gets its legs soak enbosom
hands? — oh, hands, I notice you have hands,
     persistence as redhead nylon is an object
silk objections into victory, bunned dry, I got
           a Eurorail pass through the wardrobe
           sucrose disassembly bits of flesh
           in teeth vex curlicues a muffin,
hot melted butter & spermicidal cream.
      Sulphur brilliantine orchid squeegee orifice is demoted
parasitic waiting in bestowal hula con
crinoline posterior was hysterical crocus-fingered *alarm clock*
to make prize thumbs react:
           I'm a real slut quite distinct
from the kinky fortuitousness, hems that squirt
calmly seizing alterations, skirt-like pillbox
capri pants allure — unagricultural figure flame
           a sort of elite fingering she huged off
           the frictional drug fleeced with a pin.
     But torsion is function dancer
from the dunce contains anti-sniff ingredient: I don't have that
           much sense to lose confidence in you; skinny
           trauma satin delinquent minus the novocain
figure-eight delay on flesh, we're holding our breath:

## SATURN 2

                the blonde experiencable passive drumhead
propounded the meat go fuzz? —
which bleeds & endorses mock trial for eyelashes? —
not satisfy,
      self-fulfilling pungency suits too deeply:
some cute equipment there, marshmallows chisel abyss —
they say they drive your tastebuds speechless; memory didn't
too thick happens, they have claws —
burnt umber under low-slung tight gold schizo,
                        antibody blot/vibratory gidget
gusting fixed sultry.
     And offends me — your vinylette compliments
wither nipples, milk loss danger level jetsam by me:
                    alert strictures —
as humidity? haphazard lacing? —
          *zher mer swee follermahng*
          *tahmewzay* —
maybe we could sell cotton candy, exotic vying
tongue distorts manual stride is johnny on the spot
longing undo death.
     Hinge throated loa for a spoon
              menstruous grove mussed alarm —
              *ahvehk day zawngdewhahssyawng* —
                    lenient prom preen
              for trouble diapers begone:
live lips tongueless pitch;
genial blowtorch cajolery admits.

## SATURN 3

Flammably careful *formidably strange*
                                    the heat black retrace
                        these memories filibuster internal form
is character their way in, I know
this sounds absurd but think about it!: derelict needles
                        vapor whose detective smoke
                                    gush enticing dote
finger tips on ceiling impossible to umbrella little antique
decorator touches on the writing.
        Merge is borrow all French short part so great
space spread clothes precipicitous, what's this pretty vacant?:
                                    not *sights* but in *slights*
                                    exhilarated chill studs
                                    doom connect divest —
                        donate your taste buds, donate your manger:
glowing aggressive madonnas personified in embryo
                        never had a candy elves would blow as good,
        & audacious infraction:
                        the world is my mouth, tinklers ashore
curbs animus delay energized for lungs reassure
                        grief boathoused to
                        heroine armor fire adieu
                        adverbial misstep abyss by coupon
                        borrowed diamond homily crevice in reverse.
        Devil's runway misnomer squeal
leaks mock an experience, undergarment temperance bluff
badgering downtown quislings of the seed style's revenge —
                                    curt loud 'fact'
                        as in 'past': hear no enough? —
clear vintages, advantage to victim ...
                        you need nails for meat, darling ...
                        well when they do — call me — (click):
the gown drops — isn't dead! — sleight-of-hand reversing
gap clam up pressure flanks on a siege mode manually derided
                        delicious plastic gave up its rights,
        what wrong rear word
could afford the appeal to nerve ends dedicated envy
of posture detergent mischief bladder puck
this occasion porous swivels into protective plaid —

## SATURN 3

deceit inviolate glide,
the cough-sufferer ploy: my nozzle
got infuriated ghosts on the strap, tripping
                    at least two genes bracketed clamminess
                    spoiling toilet liquor:
beams breed disdain
still no-fault milk hunk —
                    don't get rejected, date the infected
contemplative.
        Render reader rev-up, wise-up treble tremor
liquid aggresses slugs hooped in the huge space —
                    ah yes, womenizer 's bent, without chemicals
                    life itself would be impossible —
                    *day kawngvewl zyawng —*
                    *zher mer sahng fehbl —*
                    bad clash copy beats equatorial blanching
fertilely crepuscular transparency juicers off
leech speed room breathe while signing
your name's infidelity report as chemical sac mutinies' pinpricks
as growth shorn dark, the lubricant had ideas of its own.
        In loser teeth lactation spoilers neuter
hymning laves the blood ungiven dry
                    will never lose its power:
                    slobbering fear lines up —
pertinent enjamb impulse tug next to
                    listener-suppositoried bomb
                    smear took the bait
                    margarine's crevice faster
                    smocks, suds of needle, toxic many times
                    utterance gaslights them to silence
                                in the blue
                                makes it
                                credential
                    heating cats slow.
        Lesbians make me nostalgic
                    surgeons à la carte
                    -durate
                    servants of ourselves —
I held out the abeyance, fiddle to jettison

## SATURN 3

pain's visa lathe waxing swollen devotees:
                            foe-lateral renown has
                            sisters claiming curses almost all
lack heat ankle's reproach out of both sides
of the mouth for crisping orient the nerve
to ask would opacity to memory of her eye color?:
cross-pollinate at party honors him wrong
humane position in spit lilied libel giddy crass with fear.
    Wants to find out
                            something I like access
to nonentity coded routine disturb
                            denude omnisided risk juncture
                            wiping the walnut, thorax syntax
galvanized sweet peak of agitation — you like it too? —
                            cheeked point marrow-keening
trinket basis morsel — I miss you like hell, shall be awake
almost telepathic bulk enthusiasm melts in your hands
if I remember years ahead: vows to lick dissolve —
                            molecular surreption dare mutual
                            focal amp plexus licit & licit
                            joke sleeveless plotting.
    Dote you not safe
booze dormant as insult, this shame flash
                            flapping, swoon stormed proves immune
system of the adhesive fragility salves it
as night to hairpin, nothing exceeds like recess:
                                      sin's illegal glance
                            rests on laurels — miracles
made me diagonal royalties, cleavage substitute
                            pejorative knee — hey baby, put a clerk on.
    Sinuous credit bed posit zero hormone stadium
not so satisfied, who can quote their womb salute? —
                            ruby badge some substitute =
                            folly moving mufti hearts
muzzle the surrogates to lubricate outsiders;
                            every guilty hole appeal wrung off
karma slip-knot — only dead mom when I'm doing yoga
unfortunate living breathing parasol heated vanity
                            midwifed by the pods.

## SATURN 3

The stupid chairs lash prayer —
oblique sputtering allowance, slooping harder
                    harder to substantiate its fun: humidity
is sterile sphinx, lust's imaginings —
                    glaciers, tearduct alibi attacks
                    are florid by calendar time, the trouble is:
                    antithesis, why always late? —
probable conjectures rule out satanic nymphomania; improbable
material consecutive libido curse solves leprosy as dignity's
manicured brush with destiny — sentiment rarities
                    European in its capsizement, the fear parity
with exception.
    Wishbone can't be cured
smile with powdered foreign spatial knob, vestigial luck
                    inserted besting kinds of —
head for the hills!: No, they're at another time —
so, be less polite with your relatives, infinite wolves
                            encompassing erasure
                    record skips at love me or ...
                    twist & turn with eloping disrespect — time
cannot be reconvened, postdate my anger, recess may matter again
faked noise
reprieve undone,
so what.

## SATURN 4

Press the stupor lopped chic
shock shirk hallucinogens aside pressure points
that sleep — abeyance that minute apexes satellite
     retreat this to mostly stars
     awkward circular spit — the hole (with an H)
     is the false, I need big words because I'm
     sexual? — recuperative tremor:
episodic fragile licking, spotless blastogenesis;
 & chivalrous dairy, a blur stops to be
     my sister household of verbs I also
     think inquisitive
     strictly frenched, hive impure
permission breath: Live boys! — mom's pelvis, good backlighting
around the drugs; theatrical tears mimic duty possible dart
       Where when & now —
     fighting the war not to vibrate,
  souvenir statues — fertile perk out
     shags to be free remorseless measure
     measures remorse, more beat promsin'
     rage for nova tramp skulled honey:
       marionette discords stun
       by me, anything but
     imposture halts debuts
       barely warm the buds at
     what? — age never
     licked enchanted undercranking dextrous
     volume hesitation waltzes zeal?
 Frivolous phantom body-outwitters — latency
makes lude treatly the best company
touching withdrawal makeshift errors
     to the catcalls lacing fuzzier chink —
poison the wallflowers swear to you
forgetful extinguisher didn't touch them, less live
     cabaret voluptuous scruples left no message
     — so — have — known gone
off, it's ice agile anxiety;
  you'll never see argue without
     shirt on glissing goofs, lost
chatterbox fleece of pills start synthetic

## SATURN 4

in bodies, nasal-arousing webs & ethering embellish
                    the cloture thought rests with its disowner
                    neutral backhand, abbreviate this sahara —
                    develop any less to be interested
hairlipped hymen, postponable azure
                    fossil engorgement defies engagement —
moon into mound vendetta
delicate hookah tempest bursar.
          Frequent means renting — spider pulse lurched all
                              girds flare topless
                    expert shorthand tail reunion —
blithely beat, we sped
which I have decided
                    scents cells, nope root hoisting
the temperature over the hemline misaffect bout
                    surge brushes off leg palm-reading slang
                    be-tunicked chevron divides.
          Slightest divining rod to kneel —
                    a two-necked diatribe of happy
at the feet of your lusts: handmaiden diminuendo
                    my hand tenderized obtrusiveness
                              juice my wink this one
                              one quits normal flesh
                    capacity as Pandora's *sufficient word*
stand to stay lickback sloping halations, literacy
                              in wetteners
                    *few = merely* thick confide yours
marks the decentering sinister, vagabond flotation publicitied
bed a tongue heroics confides to regret.
          New sweet gavotte exciters caught in mid-spurt
so softly can stop tiptoeing off: margarine
                    veering towards fooling around with
                    spasm rocks, scoop softened down to
                    your quasi-conscience liking
                    spectator lips disobedient
crooning marks a bed for you: come into my hand, perfume
contortions liquid ricochet — it don't chafe
*doubling* of its slit spread secondhand —
here's another wet scene, treasure thickening

## SATURN 4

mutual spine synch
candied right move.
    I oust front
               reluctant deed word daring reason desire
impolited prodigal lips my intentions have stopped
                      sobbing shut me up
          being coy about my dare to hint
          grief breeds eclipse, bullionated pell-mell
          inquisitorial redeemer
anxiety helps me forget
we both have husbands, we're married
virgin in dilute spermatazoa
          sucrose grew bad broke praise hands appease
          tobacco mineral button's infecund
          raw butter frustration swoon
surcharged by exasperation;
    & ardent droop smoothish recklessness
                  zeroed in, privacy
          begins with attack, prudery loves lamination:
May I give you a little toot? —
          inanimates punctuate evaporate
risqué serpentine of the torso —
          what chisel did you swallow? — lax contrite
          blowhard nerves refusal ravaged well;
I did that upstairs, the movie lassos
the line outside of that grief of yours trying to
          jumpstart itself out:
you must excuse your curiosity & open your knees —
          playmate cadaver agog touché
          excess covetous lipstick under suspicion.
    No ice locked lamé carnage, dream bulldozers
your ante confounds — wrestling recipes bedside
fate soberable melts indite all curious
          this disappearance act is imprisonment
pure bosom automatism cling clandestine
          up rinsings can hum touch too quick true seed
          recline the decline pills that mate:
          Sound is music — Bite! Bite!—
blood night out.

## SATURN 4

I List the Thrill
fledgling superlative de-ordained nerves, seams hum
                              cling cutting lessening lovelaces
spread to resist —
                              *ewn ahmee*
                              goodbye undone
goodbye tears, vows, favor, portion remasculates
                              irremediable vampire
                              taughtly to bed with your light
                              lighten up baiting, last call for retorts! —
learn, learn to satisfy: plow right in, uncurtailed affect
                              cleansed to be different truant candor
                              yield to thrill.

## SATURN 5

THE AGONIZED torrid advance getting scared
more excited enroling pills as stickerballs
outbid into your mouth
tall, pale
lace vex squeezing appliqué, lurid liquid lip
gloss fitful lower fitful upper —
a travelogue of frequent cross-dressing home bodies: leg timer
giggle alarm — COMING ATTRACTIONS
comes short, the incendiary embroidered kicks
tumblers on the glands, animated in pinching skyward jilt
gilded ladylike closeness, torso curves up
from fireworks no longer a collaborator — a cessation
of tonguing plastic soldiers on this pillow in favor
of legato flexibility.
& spoons no kidding — we're not fruitcups, we're cocktails:
vanity needs to think no crinoline
to the spoils belong the decolletage
triceps in falsetto respirator
slaps shameless organdy — po' wit the bod tour pert nigh
but not plumb pain rate spectacle hems under
sedation roaring ruling
sameness offer disfigures gays to host
brassiered brink sublime;
& worms enfever their fists pliably skinny —
Godiva pilfers a bite out of that indecision:
gypsies with bears and itinerant acrobats, seductive, unalone
out of collarstud abrupt as fiesta
foal off under I-beam skirt, hard to forsake
betrays humidity conceits in pincers
aptly renamed: fashion disappears in the wrong virgin —
hotels said younger drugs —
maddening dressing jets blemished faint
rouge pose seduced.
Maiden's organs choired with the carnivorous lamb
contemplative, fad fruit and triple sec hippest shirk
be trash in sulky slow motion, crimson flagstaff to knee-bends
& once his teeth reach me in front cry like I
harp spatter over cervix — the person
may suffer from delusions that his or her body is changing:

## SATURN 5

                                        chaste lather
                       lathered slant, fellatio
                       glitters the gesticulator
                       flagellated bisque — auxiliary
                       corsages, self-ennervating as kit drugs
                       grimace efforts exhale.
Automatic any hips don't let the meaning nail you down —
                       infernal virgin so
                       lurks lush free with
push to bleed programmatic rubber rapidity
                       to inhibitions
rolled out on castors, jet couched pants-pull assistants
carve the muscles that stand all implacable flamboyants
alike instead
like masturbating with a block of ice, patience immensely remote
                       show business enough
                       your indifference idealizes
                       coil clamp in socket spangle.
         And I — closets!, be embarrass! — tacitly flourishes
                       douche of daring semblance
                       blowtorch ardor I won't drown
                       if I should stop suddenly: I wanted to
demote rendezvous from playthings into real humans, devotees
of urine, underarm pacifiers gather pubic flowers; pique's
                       valet concupisced flack —
button the scratches like a school of Venus: adolesce frisson
                       rapid frost, they might be gents: goose down
                       on nipples rivet skirts, warp is out! —
                                        I kink I sofa nothing
                                        bête noire jewelry
                       upsetter every ménage for herself,
I wanna zippered same me only
                       only me, vanity of the 'in vain'
liberty mimes a nipple coming to terms with self
defining the terms by which that all happens
                       sickened unresponsible penis
sashay around rancor V-allure bra training skin — the gloves
have their own saliva perfume: vehement licentious brio
urinating on one's quarter object nibble aside, enzymes wrinkle

## SATURN 5

kazoo on my clit — I don't remember her
eyebrows, a chair hidden away up
her sleeve, a folding chair, anal flanger —
I mean me myself and I:
    when wet turns red — lap at my own —
mesmerized sweat-colored by vibrating suave conjunction
                corset sweeting parfait-skidded amyl
                fingers where flesh as paint-deceased
                headroom shinnying dalliance muscle
                treat, some crisis relaxed underpants hands
                under embellished curb —
furtively petitions your lips, sudden anise
inveterate cachet, let's wax that —

                                shirt two
                                who sides
                                robes long
                                front
                                chaste
                                flirt
                                batteries —
                                libertinous
                timidity dirty, dirtying imagine
longest slims of all: don't spill 'em in one
place.
        The memory of your face just chipmunks me out —
                                frantic lick lively
                sterility complacence slabs
vinegared reach asleep, open up lower-case
all over sexually mature nervousness —
                I've done too many mushrooms, blouse humbles
                wish is mistress to the fact, chalice
paralyzed 60-minute man on your dormitory of
bad guilts, clitoral climatizers, track lighting in underwear —
                ignition stifles waist
                tissue cold in skirts
remorsefully disengaged.
        Vipers' seesaw vented mob-raged delinquent
not so sleaze remiss — your indifference is in good hands, if
                wish got sits

## SATURN 5

saturated

fond globe grand ridicule care

satiric seers & satyrs, can you do it alone:

so curious and nice, voltage incessant

solicitous hosing grand rayon, vague impudences, flamboyant

foetus, chagrin opium, buzzing

rouging disgrace,

pyramidal appendages make it silver late up

laminated taint buttock accent sucking prescribed

as locomotion instead of baby dolls that wet their diapers —

worms in amber exhale orders

annoyed, pitied pisstery to me — stop tarting liaison

swoons meta recalcitrant, ornaments

exhaust us spitting the abdomenal astonishment; the jitney

studies the rock — trash on a geisha valiumvirate

cruise anxiety, complete vampirical transvestite recognition.

Brooding scent patriarch

(reassessment)

ruminates paste and Saintdenised pawing

is not absolute baby gets even — me inside —

bode well lobe peeling lithesome concourse, razor the insouciants

flattening by hand too blunt bent enough

deb hips if ever mons venus

penis can't fit in low shoes — somebody

pull my break: group clitoral covet

chariots regret — corral voiding duel fond verdict.

## SATURN 6

Halfway hussy — convulsive coo plummer sheaths:
                    *veebr — day bawngbawng —*
                    your mouth went away
                    complies night mouth needle
                    over barriers' twins in light
                    mate that eat those whose shoulders —
so ran tender
unbuttoning out of kisses & so
                    started sample darling
                    members to mark up
                    the sweat against the lap over sweep
                    dial pines loin.
    Hand in your crinoline —
impetuous mistakes are now & then made insufferable
too forward spelunking: show yourself your tight end,
skillful depantsing all meats to be wed
                    musk at bust, update the width glimpse solo
                    hotrod — this brawling as sweet
                    longing, it am Not So Hot? —
*about last night …*
                                    cervically correct
cuckold this sleeve perpetrator dressed as a trap
                    do as I false.
    There's romance in a zipper, reaching for that little
membrane of lambskin — de-heinous denunciamento
                    clings to clitoridean penalty dissolves
                    co-fecund craving *cleft* bliss bare wax won
                    horror only intoxicates zest
                    & languish denim orality:
abject adore harder bedroom —
                    *mahkorday voo seht dahngss —*
appetite artfully stupidly fearless bold solicit hands
                    fault kindling rubbers;
    I hope you're not
claiming those get wet emotions you're showing — malt sided
                    vulva caroms risk skull & beaver avid
                                    tumult brim metallic
                    incited hand *fatale* quiescently rupture
exemplary spit doable desires, urinary nap squires pause:

## SATURN 6

get *hold* of hold off
unbetrothed abrupt nerves
inexperienced down to the ankles.
What nightgown jelly jobs? — pleasures which person
revives manually levied midnight hurries pelvic paste
shake a shake a sugar duct
cascades adolescents goin' to party gauzier hooch: I assume
you don't want less trouble, I must shy
motional heart noose shooted
sizzle competes
shoo doo be doo *ménage à toot* giddy tiptoes.
We want to act irresponsibly invites his knee
face crops a go-between
for legs walk in front of people so that *you'll* be less
uncomfortable: waist slowed, I'm a jar
desires are objects to smear
at your hole wettened rental pins
their stake-outs — it ain't the meat, pillow
outlaws, tooths vagrant
just selling what intends your *rightful* megalomania on your knees
to avoid me;
& muscle promises impurity would be voluptuous
sexually brief imperturbably lascivious reprieves from self-
limitation: so how do you beat it with a milkshake? —
do be unfortunate reluctance baby
consecrate 'dis' nature lets it bang your box? — licking each
other's pop tarts, body parts & semen cannabis went out & bought
yourself ovarian lactation? —
shacked friends diets both
nipple panty dodgems
without smooching its eviction notice on where your lips are.
Self-defense Romeo, a flirt in
I'm a hog for your paradise
lonely chair quit my jealous
goin', goin', gone beds that burn —
let me explain
woe ho oh whatcha do ho
take me back to heaven — shouldn't I
know I would if I could

## SATURN 6

sorta need almost grown you so
better make a don't deny me move
gimme, gimme, gimme serves two you
think I'm not thinking everything
I played the fool but you.
Such brothelly concern saliva chokes up nape, risked such
barbed wire around indecisiveness: what's a Valkyrie to do? —
no, bottom; no, bottom; no, bottom —
gushing gash & oyster partner — unconditionalness
knees so humid flaps habits: please give
my heart a break, tango tea dervishing beaut lips
commotion midriff all slant delight
that doesn't want presents with each
act in the greases.
Lungs burn ingratiate truces —
my clumsy empty heart, anxiety excavating me
elongated herself toward self sadisticized elastic plaintive
confidence infringements want to be left alone, I guess
I'm not twelve any more
desperation looks different as resentful
chaste-pox reconditioning same-sex nipples —
if they want something useful they don't want me, I said would-
n't beg you, maybe I can — maniac can
denial vouched for, Annie had a miscarriage:
tricks all sterilize impatience fingers exit
phone kinship ready to hand you can't
have all of me how soon so I can't have any of you at all:
virgin softer inclines
bed as a four-lane highway — how do you expect me to get it?:
I'm in love with my bed
spurned head lip-reader jeans
*vouloir la friction*
wasps swooping after vagina swooping down fly
*arroz con corazon*;
agitated succumb
naturally maladapt, insecurity finessed
incommunicative lust — oh, how pretty, let's beat off —
mons exhaust gullies in flotation
majorette coquette rebuffs with slipcovers.

## SATURN 6

Write Me a Letter —
                      duple leggings putting the ooh in la la
irresponsibility the price of freedom, I'm only reject
                      new pawn over thighs faking
                      courting volcanic vitiate
                      flesh went airmail down throat comfort
                      frightened gentleness successive
                      Arms of Someone New felinity —
confessions've got bad intentions, big carousel
aspires to bedroom floods, breath banks — unbidden bits
                               just suppose exuberant
                      splinters ride the soft pony,
    no, no, no means yes yes yes rupt
asceticism brakes recoil voluptuary
appeasement: will you get your hands on me —
                      wetter's better last loaded scale
                      kisses fortification against
                      beauty on its knees, milk worries spurned
                      by heat vertiginous voltage.

## SATURN 7

OH STARRED to bite verifiable red I was pausing
to get control of the mastery box over craving I'm at the end
                    of my vapor expiry magnet jelly
                    free to condemn to be free from bush to bash:
                    sympathy's idealless craver
                    ice surveil outreach you
whose nourishing now stigmata kisses courage up
                    to butte of desire, calcinated spare
                    bed a layer impressurized sinfully dextrous
combustion to weep,
        slip owes habit a false accord — nature caricature
                    tirades, demons, sale obscene
                    crime nonpareil was married to
an animal trainer, Donnybrook or no, ... the ability to kiss
                    as sign of health, I only felt the glove —
                    auxiliary emotions vice can bolt half-caste
                    cascade big, *really* big
                    girls don't cry, sexist or sexiest
pelvic moratorium — certain evil acquaintance
needs poking something to penetrate or something to
                    penetrate with inaccessible necrophiles —
                    the big heart has a big faucet —
                    being faithful almost gets me hard;
        & broken hearted sympathy, OK doll falsified overheard
rubber avoiders take life by the forelock —
                                    clowns clamor back
                    doctored voluptuary prom animals:
you say you hate men but I just think you're projecting ...
                    anonymous capsule from pouts
through congenial debridement, spoonful warhouse
                    babies on strike to glean
                    feud legs quarry
                    kick or lick hospitality
        Hope spurs lust little less buoyant
                    stuff coit your maladaptive
                    flesh profess to be wide contemptresses
                    bartered bud remorse:
body reads, silent hum squeaks languid on
alert salute chorus pancake chamois thanks acute

## SATURN 7

impertinence refigured upside to blood snap off hetero scare —
boudoir plaintiff, prevail on my pussies, sapling tryst soon sure
& fact tempting tampon pert pull-apart
serpentine courtesy constancy, chagrin unchecked.
    Slyer wedlock sublime flatter the tizzy
victimage drink interrupts, even outright dementia
                drug dictates self-enflaming a magnetized
                      reel of covetous
                      blot fuck delay
            sways in mercurially troubling
long skin ago — I'm banged out
infractional sugar juicing acute;
    & the pedestal is me, best bet is rimlike
gems in rotisserie, simonizing what juice recrows —
            that infinite waist down on strike
saking action hard: trust weight to get wanna date
            more intimate with perturbs
                slooshed
            divorcedly erratic galvanic
            by currying the solenoid
orgy forfeit drug myself
eaten widows of vulnerability from within, scalp rebuff
inner prompting's concubinage dictation;
    disrupt the parsemenious inclination, half-holing bicephalic
fatality communion wafer with loin detox saliva'd prodigy:
            No man leaves Delilah — avoidance gavottes
            I behave then stiff mine not
stalled good girl subjugates by gifts so gifts refused even
            the dung of your slim so raw me off
            vice to pander war rubbing the beads
            of annoyance as sex enjoyed by other means.
    Ace of excess skip put off others
beguile others lozenged against you what needs enjoy —
menage-ah-inflamed-trois likeably misbehaves unwillingly
desperate figleaf issues retort: he doesn't dream, for instance,
that he was a clam stuck to his wife's body —
            it gets agreeable seethe
            hugs dares be pinker, it spits
            incestuous sheets;

## SATURN 7

& burn makes us free — order's fissures, backbone whims
                    play with the emotions until they are tired
half detour half deal, when and if sin unleavens addict
devolleying mere spouts breath of a girl in flagrante
pulls back petals of standards.
        Doesn't it chest cake? — what do you have to do,
lick their necks? — shunless affairs envy
                    as poly-bag in mouth our values pay off
franchise tang fanged after lips turn
entire body by squeezing the thighs:
battery-operated condoms, some romanced overtotalled
                    sodom foresight bed inflicts —
we miss body fluids, just one foreskin of difference
alleviates as charm — hooker shows me lists, regulatory
additives to your *fun* life, I hate to use the phrase, but —
                    lovenest: it was on the basis of this
                    exquisite vulnerability that the unreal
man became so adept at self-concealment.
        If you open your heart you'll throw up? — the more people
you meet, it doesn't make you feel less interesting:
Impatient to consort or impatience consorts? — he's forgotten
                    he has legs

                                        guys like
restrictions on their thighs, maladjusting & riveting
waist sorrow because you don't let the hips go — desire's pro-
verbial broken forbearance from larceny resistance:
swooning tortures don't just sit there, eat me! — demarcates
tensing of a will over unalienable temporal distances
                    married defiants agitate.
Don't rub his dick unless you want the fireworks —
                    moll dresses hazardous bedding
                    don't, it's a fetus walking bare-breasted:
devil's bedspread debauchee, bolshevik weapon eaters, blessed
misdemeanors, slit-happy trawlers, girl's got
                    vulva-chained head — sin's extract
                    heart squares
the 'self-described' orgasm, pliability never looked so ...
vague, promoted into the unconscious lap
                    adultery is to energy as

## SATURN 7

      adult conspicuous but venus flytrap variation
of vipers;
  & dagger of jailer's mutual indifference give me bad now
maidenheads house so private touché on this urbanity
      mammy toll prostitution lights itself
      terracing horror humus prey — women get to
      bomb the wombs: you said underwear & I said
mutual defense agreement; no one ever said
you had colds in your pussy juices, plantlike machinations of
toxic personality going on.
  Have a pulse physic
      egress and regress: did you faint? —
      glue keeps buckling, it's trying
to improve its mind, disabusing utility I'm trying to
      improve its body, the satisfaction of stress
      's a great way to find out what I'm worth:
        *all* rused exasperate
      unrelentless squeeze, how dare you
      requisition my clit! — *then* I won't
      bother to explain myself;
law attic impunity
      spills decency bothers unrest
        UNTIL SUCKS
        you want to be smothered
    or blockaded — *fatigue*
    *shorts*
    *casual*
        hypercrisis
    eyes to eyes.

## SATURN 8

Scan ideal scan plushes
eddied sheer majestic live, laden very little —
                    put your head in there and darkly lit
                    I pulled the covers over my broomstick
prompts safe heh heh heh italicized quiet,
        to dress volley, translucence defames imbecile needs —
                                ESCORTS, *mold spores high*
                    limelit phantasmagoria excuse errors —
unshadows painted doves, precious knitting weight
                    unseaters: I dreamt I was the
                    weepless everything is off less
                    likable lounge heroic broke along
secluded trickery prettified by skirting asylum,
        disguise artillery cheek your cleavage
great as positively tweaking pleasure craft
microfiche in frosting all the right-angled people:
                                tell stories skirt up
                                trash warms off
                    tilts out integrated buttercups
                    beaut scavenging for swirls,
let the furriers pass! — doll furnishings lancing my
wish so funny clucking at the heels;
        hard smudge claw flatters golden mean-
ingless slump dreamworld in rebuttal, all such
                    postural bric-a-brac go sour, inarticulate
indisposed innocence to franchise the evasion
                                distant, distant, distant
                                dirt to star secretes
                    doubt inappreciably fooled hope poison fact
                    breakneck drag
understanding chagrin paternity tripped as discharge
                    youthless spoilant youth:
        here's hoping every held girl, resort host, detox
sucker transplant as puddingest
treason from postmark to papoose, well, sufferin' suffrage! —
a single abandoned bra drawer with tremolo
lilies digressingly procreative
                    slicked back a little combustible veil ...
recoil blonde pyramid of guilt bungled

## SATURN 8

beauty, redoing gigantics
aggravates stitch to enfranchise fallacy
memoirs of prestige blowouts.
Deep inner imbalances are usually the cause — gullism
-ing sweat numb ring numb fun powers alone
all wrong unalarmingly harmonized elision diamond
booty methylated on specialist breath salon
vented null sign astral: I worship your decline —
booty close tonic feign
elliptic primate, let's sabotage some bridal fairs —
exotic interrupts
mania prefects
strum my cleft out words;
& little joke oomphatic wheels need not apply:
snake balloon pillow malice
repentance given tickets with a light touch of root
lily spike inflamed
quit vociferous furtive visible verve
muzzle trump swells audition mounds, sound
unhinged force emergency
vaporizing turnstile —
self-laudatory mortise as danger
's gambit speed unleaven the dress
code includes circumcision.
My etiquette didn't give me the entry price but I thought
your overfamiliarity could use a few obstacles — blue ingenue
crease too conciliatory but if
I don't have it I can't
clean hypocrisy slid on pedestal motion to
litigious blousing, when do the limbs get the vote? — disfavor
*whose* bantam worry?: nearly famous
spidered complaint debriefs yearning
sentries toward spinal brunette, tone has
*the guy relic*, I respect, I reject
bilingual stagefright nipples
like a boa constrictor emerging from it — let's discuss
tubal ligation, swears you sincerely
's vacillate philosophy pouch unsafe
pompous reptile *soirée* encore

# SATURN 8

dimpled okay.
    Retool your self-mordanting charms chest favor
hormone altruism: I exchanged Bad Expectations for
Attitude Problem — caboose faults morbid virgin nobility, back
hand less better than no hand at all annoyance
grown stale — delete all the organs you want, I'm still
                    over-equipped, white heels decline between
less truss to diva-ish fame, the gourmeted
                bitter divisiveness
                rear time bushed alive torturing vanity
evocatively crude in its exhaustions,
    & rapture, finely flanked
frisson-lapping stash rapport eulogied frenzy —
                lose one turn, needle calls
                the shame wick roll
                desperate plane inclined;
    slander & honest
                slender mantis face
                give myself goose bumps
                tighted special pussy flambé *superbe* —
                well-mannered dreaminess keeps sin
company decoding the rollercoaster.
    Oh there is no beyond
evil-eyed discount Xmas ample lights my box up pud aside
me wear your intercom, loyally abrupt bereaved reluctant tent
                & what vein draws go cream your ass interest:
oh, yeah, *mature*, that euphemism for being burned out, brake
                    hurtles failure backlit
                tress front geometry beguile
sculptured coffin, frivolous self-limiting damage
unsure of the meaning to attach to inadequacy.
    Man is only a crust formation, the sayings we disinherit
redistributed retribution — even stability is cute
off-sides, attract limits breathing order against
transshape improper to err?: well, sirk me out! —
                drip dry apex entailed costs cross
                my Worm Disdain duodenal triumph, pull of
*enchanté* sensitive to pillage
                arsoned swank behind the great arsenal's

## SATURN 8

aimless kicking against the pricks.
    Pity desirous nothing to pamper this gargantuan
scenery of noncompliance — medicinally eroticized
hatred's wheels fly off renunciatory
uncompromising fetus's torrid hangman,
    convulsion basement value reprieve
                immorally infallible revolt
                anything constructive spit marks
                past eloquent, refusal theatrics
erase the bluebeard to indemnify your jackknifed combustion
                betters: Soar, young egg! —
                Every which is an exorcism.
    Dolly up squeamish ultimate plan on turning blue
                reassurances acquitted, nurture flunked Tears
                      detonate face

pleasure makes proof.

## SATURN 9

Fury Fancy

Discreet Matinee
the definition fête of envy
no defense no justification, reclaim pepper to dalliance
desperation would squeak this hinge bust on sight:
Come On Storm
lacerate the … prescribe agitation satin salivaed inertia,
hotel hotel hotel Memory
gay twelve mum's fleece glaciated coeds doubling
refund on any tongue loose from own prop farm —
silly novice raving ass
suction rises to exposure never admitted
but always committed ice to thwarts
hand at hand drug-in-laws
chandeliered carnal loan idolatry.
Short shorts possessive prime that gest insolent eclair em-
boss dope enough sweating
polypropylene underwear disregard
tricks with butter toothy stitch, rubbed & plucked less
polite graft to hose adore wished-for drawback —
Spicy   Foxy
sing your fetch me douche confessed
insistence makes me queasy,
slander the maintain smile opaque, larval alliance verified
agitation palate coquette: All this oration means not listen —
vain swing trace's
spine arches to argue Easy N Dirty
recombinant straying this exhalation of defeat
poisoned hardware;
& precipice pretzeling needs paradise
now that I do know how to eat and sleep, stigmatized clefts
ease the flavor, harm the cool valid rhubarb by
joint tryst baton
breeds perambulator intimate with wrecker ball saliva questions
sterilize the luscious curtsy
limned debatable organ poem
tunnels into rebuke.
Licorice ruts spawn to distract
offshoots who override significance in their doctored mannikin:

## SATURN 9

who's cooking who? — Pop   Seam   Pop
finish me down the cheeks a method goof
inhibition fakes, a powder I am not
a peach tree: Can I have some
progress without success? — the ministry
of me — ponderous Oink!:
it's either arbitrary or posturepedic, delay's precipice
coy so entire
barricade's bad blood:
hedon spurious fellation decapitated queen abrupt
moving moving over-explicit psy-chat novelty furor — Don't you
want to be bad?: very nearly miscarry nest
wet flight milking victims
convene the cancellations deep in hussy
little little else, bee pollen your fault.
I don't settle on members remember
limbs pudding prop rinse the fertilized
moment over here, lay lie
down suppose hurried for
she used to be what's else defer slink
wisecrack fertile elude
gay vassalage backward, let me try, melancholia twitches
handlers' aspect forestalled foreskin densely
bush warrant queens in check.
We could threaten to buy him a volume pedal — charming with
warning, hot-wired with hope
behavior means prestige
volute luxurily lewd decadent few —
Count One … Woman does the opposite: diatribal fortitude
still? — your refusal has its own skin, what sucking? —
gays & boys, let's be demerits —
Main Donna —
Sassy —
Shocking Secret
even the napoleon suite is short.
Surrender not an option, passion unranks all
avarice cajoles, bosses bedspread
lethal victorine — *lethal virtue*, salutary
prone *libertinage dos* and *don'ts*:

## SATURN 9

Magic Scandalous Candy Fling Romantic Relative Devil Affair —
to rebuke your self-objectifying dalliance, faithful menopause
double-hitter at distance pressure-pointing under the covers:
                    who said these hands were private property?,
                    or mayhem just an encourager —
took my heart to a workshop, thanks for letting me paw you.
        False friends crisp knifed all nest hope adieu
                                hazard traps
                                alloys pride —
you're pretty comparative; jape felt curt forever use
                    used to lose theirs Swinging Later —
the autobiography drown the petting
its dildo helpmate, a chart of our former love life
                    slandered excess violate
                    seeks reciprocal tart resistance:
so much for the neo-human;
        I'm impersonating regret salivation insurance
begins in bed tirade loin sadist factory splendors
                    Chi Chi Put It In Shocking Secret
circuit wick frequent succumb, Heroin created individualism —
                    metro nightie fever ardent
self-deprecation leaves skin marks: I'm a home structuralist;
we don't call it economics any more — cupcakes done
                    falsifies people to eat each other, your
                    penitents are numbered.
        Oh benign to what a penetration of bodies is this
                    hole shows your intelligence 'mprint
degenerates, matter is so resistant you aren't going to look for
                    the pulse in the hand unkempt so
                    hundreds of them *now* a nice girl
                    wouldn't tell you what to do — Anxs, Avarice
                                gism vary don't
                                pubic
                    ocher estuaries delinquency writes to put
                    your face out of time consciousness-based or
                    else that's their theme: hen restitution
                                rubber waltz kiss stops
                    your refusal lips to sleep with novice habit.
        Imprudent Love

SATURN 9

wept *this*, torrid —
treacle unhousing
visceral virtue
stick to your shame, you don't need this & I don't need you:
Tactile Tabu Sparkle Lola Aggrvtn Sticky
Fingers Jill By Night Naughty Show No
Better Be Single Tears — disabusing the *subsequent* abusers'
affidavit says *delight* here to court
trouble sleaze plummets to the knees
so we café Dionysian
politeness led astray;
& hurry up that's a non-seldomed habit flippancy targets
hopeful blessing sin mousse
duckwalk prep impatience spooked abuse —
deconstructive cashbox beloved
fruits that reduce guilt joke
to self-endear by exclusion, fear or shape
got manageable desserts to be more
friend inch regret
propriety census collision,
squallish tatters I'm, here, while — gone guise
flame reigns so abstractedly safe, let me
kiss you goodbye — All it ever said
was that it was a little breathless blissing area, the spark's
engine search for anesthetic spots:
corona, Our Chancy
Midnight — turn to burn.

M<small>YSTERY</small> requites a sovereign, furtive horizon
                  delivered from touch tongue slave solace:
                  now who's undone! — only unusual force
forces courtesy vacation reserved for I have a secret hideaway
on every room's nerve endings —
                  *dwahzh lay zahrahlay ahngtyay?* —
                  the memory is the hope hope receives
                  unemployment girded against naked jubilee
                  stubs that resuscitate antibody
                  generosity center fled the complaints
if fan mail could talk,
      excess forgives privilege widowed nerve kewpie bomb:
                  nothing sloppy, nothing weak —
                  red cells in the moonlight practicing
                  ventricals aspired to clothed tourniqueting
all abstention expulsive triangle down your ganges valenced
cadenced red self-mating margarine hailings of
                  the us, coups affection
                  without portfolio.
      'I', alibis glisten, unsettle in hind saints please others
roast as an antidote slandering vivisection species can plug in
                  adultery's fragrance; den perhaps
to vanquished reptile status blood just token freedom
purple recruited to a wound in other words
                  refusals: I had the falseness
of gratuitously feminist violence tradition behind me;
      I came in too soft to depict a physical specimen —
                  bust exhausts the felony with its own
                  hand-warmer, the Wanting cyclic fault:
*edit* the scaffold evil declines
the choice niece hive forfeits sorry self jam
                  diplomatic bouncing pills forcefeed others
                      commit others to disarm
some interrogative toiletry — poor women, they still have to
talk about their families, fallout the undoing sawhorse renounces
definitive mint postponement underwear with a
                  stopwatch to disagree another man
defies penchant is beating my time to install some
                  revolving doors for the apologizers.

SATURN IO

We can stay dry, grammar pisses for us circulating melody
shame morals can crisscross to hilt
                    bouffanted jinx corrects:
                    papoose rearms *cosi fan tutti* pineal azure
escape from flush badge of slump slapping sects.
    Frottage curb home, crawlspace splash real rumored fudge —
                    rebuff cutes fun for platening a habit
                    *proper* as *problem*, how
honors listen to the mockingbird's tutelary semen as if to
inflate that bed to grow old on harmony pouting
                    infantilism to uncross costumes, I
                    received a letter from a fetus,IQ cavity
                    with slipknot mutinied rules,
    what kind of liberty is it that most people do not want? —
the men don't know but the little girls understand, I interrupt
                    6% of the time — distant authentic parents,
                    seasonal rates, C cup as backdrop
                    denizen tricks douche riffing, *who* gloats?:
male copies gender within home disowned by property culls
to find out more, skid past
                    venom bifurcates sex kindling commerce upset
me way out on the Richter scale frees majorette ointment's
                    predilection as unguent party or go home
                    in my younger drugs instripped perversion
                    diva by shuttle:
    ruin red abusing only makes it much harder to use them
                    on *V*-ed colossus, anxiety dry miked
flaxy gynecological aberrants is lesbianously ironic wedding
                    closets to apocalyptic visions
                    of immobilism makes monsters of
                    indecision when men *that* bleed drunkproofed
                    rearing at needed samaritans —
                    'little woman' — how redundant?:
does he have ignition? — women should be stronger ...
                    or is that just my sexual preference? —
I could be more autonomous by failure.
    Its tongue at your knees, its tail at my ankle
envaginates more to do rules fracas licks
if lips gathered houseplant dust: who died of enough? —

SATURN 10

delicacy retribution pleas against I want
eggs on face — Dismiss! — you intent me too
much; paralyzed suckling akimbo ethics, embarrassing lawless
spousal throw, incaution's
perceived reward crisped subordination to regret the fleece-
marks of circumstance adultery nourishes no
*means no!* — things
are changing too fast for babies;
antisocially precocious, we're not down on our backs
with our legs spread any more — half-debauched test reassurances
of neo-forsaken delinquency crotch temporarily insane
taxing overfondness seldom twice Illicit Affair rescind
compassion to normalcy incubating fun loop that undifferentiated
sentiment souse fiancé hurling us
outfit & home: self-assertion
in the love act is specious juvenile mutation —
I defrayed costs by auctioning my affections
— hymen surfeit instead of baby dolls that wet their diapers.
Gray-eyed seeks hose is not a home counterfeit favors:
touch me, exalted suppository —
sin more mess soap plots fumble genealogy greeting
loop bisects
protocol bartering
demotes wishing melts
to etiquette-attenuated training error
her lips, torture chamber, meat wagon, butcher shop, shad roe?:
the false sweet mate lacunae vice's
minute cultural detail overspilling torts decorating
into lumps of party disavowal
superfluous gonad
too reluctant to give rage up.
Oh prettiness just makes me squat:
prickly seed display
police escort dislocated submission up my snatch — you *want* to
be permanently disadvantaged?? — collapse
envies your violence, you look the way
habit = scar
I used to want to be, spouse expense
at your fingertips cheat confessing up tuition affections

# SATURN IO

before they are dominant, an assumption which lesbians might find
                                    rather quaint, I think I
                    need some strata of history of women's anger
                    has become professionalized up nostrils, a
                    neurotic epiphany — you wanna puke, right?:
branded a fornicator by her church seminar, I'm status-broken, I
was taught to be dissatisfied.
        Earliest sexual money needs a career —
excuses don't make it, scruple mongers who can smart the culture
debt banking most bodies on suffrage must invert upper
verticality with antipodes re-debt honeycomb *puts*
divorce me COD with swathed juridical *interieur* arrest-a-thon
                    punctuating the bribe — why do you think
women are the formalism of property, how many
have favored the castration of convicted rapists, adultery or
                    mere adulteration — women tend to be more
                    self-critical?? — guys don't have feelings;
they just have *interests*; boys just want funds.
        Devil's advocate, illustrate me
                    some patricide, hon'; nobody's lonely enough
to tolerate *you* — pride rehab spawn's too pop
                                    bitten jury crooked meek
                                    loosed against
                    socialite putsch, if someone offers
                    you drugs, ... I'm feeding on
                    *your* hand-i-wipe attitudes —
women must perform those who con the apparatus to be
                    — win me & digest me! —
                    ostracized indignant change,
        promise timely
succor lip *service* shudder
                                    unlearns foal
                    queasiness generalizes play
cocked from new world of rest, solitary lengths
                                    crux dorm revel blame
                                    free to franchise
                                    the what's up
beauty favor.

# FIXED STARS

# FIXED STARS I

Oʜ ᴛʜᴇsᴇ ᴍᴏʀᴇ cheekbone grand scene
                    a preunion interestingly crowned uncondition-
ally submit without the *fleur de lis* twinkling caliber signs,
                              sheer tongue nixes
                              boast self-tinting
                              fuse binder stars hello
              is not eternity equally unvarnished sugarplum
teeming magenta version inverts itself,
     rose alloy milk gotcha devoting
it into sensation lure capsizes turquoisoid sheen impersonation
                    tinsel cajoled remission prize
                    for covertancy — wax was woozy
                    pensive Biddin' On A Beauty
                    antennae for all types prescribe,
     there goes nostril pasture candlelight affection
              hips uncolored teeth as white as
sugar absence prerogatives, moon streetlight milky tarried syrup
              chic spout softly wet, stigmatizes silhouette
              osmostic cosmetic disquieting lining
              space odds kin red solicits
white swan guards' ethereal vibes.
     Re-dirigible velvet sheath makes it show:
                    pretext, magnetization indigos, inexhaustible
                    surface mating lavender installments —
                    small tacits of time, whirled stroke lilies &
                    roses tear tenor dove sequin distaff
treasury forehead perforating homonym comets.
     And thick whitened echo devise
                         ѕ ʟ ᴇ ᴇ ᴘ   ᴄ ʜ ᴇ ᴀ ᴘ
open matter brief set this pre-letter letter before together
                    flash deposes darkening — italics, the cube
                              blousing ripless in pitch
                    verge of aromatic recto empowers timely hour-
                    glass cheeks hike up secret modal vowel wrap
                    *nom d'assume*
     letters sheen wit follicles different-
                    ly lighter-than-air allegro ahead transcends
legs to see even frontin'
                    fingerholes of just a phrase

## FIXED STARS I

toned on vulnerable glimpses: virginal brakes & mutes
                              mirage would like to stay *static*
but realize that is idealism's push at dark melee.
        Focal lap was moonglow guided missiles caress
perfect taut dreamlike flairs gloss by wetting
palm displays: lamped silk's refractory falsetto souse
                              insinuate solace bees preening
                              peak curtsy thrust lustre gauge —
creamy prismatic casual look to opiumosity:
        & so high, so low curves fingertip science crush on *this*
                              chest pads on personal memory, fantasy
consort the pages ordinal torso satin annoying —
                    *ee ah teel day koorahng*
                    *dahngz herrur?*—
secretive smoke me color harbors swoon these tissue bullets, this
nocturnally breathless
bouquet warmth keeps captive
hyphenated teasing & taunting clutches.
        The leaping smoothness, the uncrossed T
for tacit eyelid, the vascular substance dilemma caress:
                              tulle crease dream the 'I wish
                              your picture was you' manifold immaterial
grasp spur ink — davenport comma vanish lip swivels fortress; —
                              pens' tears hose eyes out
                    pretend tongue swooned indelible boyish rough
blessedly swooping twirl fleurette color *in vivo*.
        Oh be saft tonight, tenderize solo bond and then all
of a sudden hands parsimony together — lift con-
cussed glitters cough add teeth to moxie mixing guess
                    low *low*, itself and fragrant:
                              See head note —
                    milkwhite yield up mute in pink juice I clear
near you sometimes, dreaming, it's *just* fixed tableaus
while cityscape visualizes the you are my *superstition* dream
inspired whole.
        Iridescent vulnerability
all night will be borrow 'em roses between gel —
                              a privilege to be without listeners
                              and clear time up treble cell converging soft

# FIXED STARS I

prodless point danger alone acquaints false apart
winking wettener, yes, skin's deafness thick
                    diamond services spurt saliva improvement —
I don't believe in tomorrow, I cake
the soothe adhesive freeze-frame.
          Regard suite tapioca dart flatters referent —
silvery lightener
aura unsullied
chromatics: specious blue flame forecaster dribbles, ornaments
                    muzzled swan relenting
                    facade bit back rouging nimbus candle
shoeing horns still look silky distance to withstand tension
combustible moonlit satin parts amidst imaginary lamps,
          seldom rosers —
omits the fishes —
thawless 'in vain' lures deepest salt yellow dusks *with* testimony
                    authentic means verify detail hurries
bonding boundaried spare blink benign, another, above, chintz
                    de-epauleting captive with my eyes open
                    have a tumble next to last in two lines.
          I'm nomenclature killed the King enjambed free
counterfeit colors occulted captivating core otherwise separates
white candor indicators pining when thus *shined*
                    secrecy magnetized needle communes:
the gauze just -gives & gives
seed hush tinder duly blink
known anchor never pre-revolutionary enough;
          colloquy de-nitted a means of lustration I wonder
                    if you wonder, if you bluenote me
                              raculous
                              der
                              ment
                              ater
                              ery
                              ers
                              ous
                              ple
                              duce
                              er

                              civiously
                              cept
                              trian
                              tion
                              ness
                              ers
                              proach
                              grate
                              come
                              ing
                              ries
                              ies
                              ners
                              tifully
                              nial
                              ing
                              tion
                              onstrations
                              ing
                              ing
                    utopic unstuck degrading
doom button paraphrases why oh why, but what, backhanded
asterisk scratching away at small behavioral truths —
                    idiom triangles submitted
                    refrain cancelled into
sharp closeup pretty confidential.
        If likeness caption doubt
drawer natural wrench annex allure
sorry sherbet rutted in the honorary
nerve trust valued suppose blue
questioning *fleur de lis* like fur
                    of a team coaxing unseen
matter declines to compete overhearing else confronting
                              Most Optimistic
only bumps by hearsay
treading on the lulls
it's too soon to know,
        don't yet this or less, Surprised? — candy attains honor
                    custom object idyllic to date sovereign crack

## FIXED STARS I

night by night by night
deliver promises, diamonded done dare to dream
to defy toys' tender know-how
out of anything's profession.

## FIXED STARS 2

Solitary glaze sedative, seldom
          likeness ellipse — dress thing
hum curl embracing mutes buzz of allure, blue fond trace:
                    we do go on! —
close valet collar retort gifts can whisper angelized melancholy
wands akimbo;
      arbitrary subtlety confusion: covert eye on lick
yielding calm tight limbs & torso baptismally —


                          ATTACHMENT


— incitable transfers tractable pry
              nether whips *in camera* flesh distracted
slips set affected to you.
      Write on cushions: ontology, I'm in love
              really is pink velour chiffon pivot flacking
pill in pictured hole a nipple head, a figurative and literal
uplift refulgently creamy oval with fringe of better
only sufficed arms seething waxy cachet spoons —
              I acquit myself
              of unabashed gravy
              failure attachments.
      And segueing butter on the head is only symbolic —
              tropic sake off-sides, a subtler bend
              void excited imperative dark to dance
inverting a real mouth, alleged gown cream reverts
              a catch in her voice
              finger-masted fine
              spot muted click,
     stir instill breed slut surrogate pastel the blinds dote on
              loathes observance Helder timing as porn
              disguise is diminished on the neck —
semi-conscious gauze mood seizes archlight —
Talc Time Silk Tie Chantilly Rose Ami Our Toots
              forgive light, rubbery fit tacit felicity
in cadence.
      Charm affirms immaterial duel
flared in (our, my) under (my, our) disclosive energies
              or cloverleaf Fingerlessons' girth *ends* put

           accidental excitants you forgot to space
broil until blood sanguine beverages arc
           to chest tacit buoyance — the incestress
between taste minked tremolo argument.
    And reveil unwinds, whippety whirl
           an object pushed with fluids so you will know
           deeply saturated plumage bribes fatigue —
committing the closer you are act of darkness with whom
           still gapes between, stylized knee
either quiver thissin' you
           sueded on the kiss-curl,
   forged tremor to 'm lips neck shelves
another part of the body loss disappeared into, the mouth
           fingered, giddy stir thaw
           bend arch's over oval, fractures
           every gestural infatuation curve wants
a horizontal bad, in hem's way small fine, pretty
little, little soft, soft and white balancing your mature
beige pairs spread immersion counterpoise bodies
           or blush glad blur while you know intense.
And best bend naked orthodoxy to come close avails
           precisely or relatively — *giving, just as —*
           there's body great humming sequins in lap
           taking back the spoons swoop the underhand
               palm knocks about
           slanting float negligé type torment
               footlights, a shadow
               voluptuous incognito
vis-à-vis velcro sweats palm-glides, in expectation's
           argument doubt repairs.
   Teeth astringency's sympathizer flexing the nerves, beige
           slantwise in my choice enticers:
               mouth —
           on the edge, mostly mouth, of here's a heart
           mandate & strip, between didn't
           half-light donor grand schist convene
           a mouth of her own automobile
reconvenes discretion eagerly fingering deuce adored & hold
           affinity hips signatured hush

## FIXED STARS 2

                  talking certain
hone apart.
    Unshillably perverse admiration cedes its closures:
parallel guesswork, prolonged shared seeds
lick every contact treating
                  twin vise drunk conjoint
                  liaison sculpted time, that emetic —
alloyless nod to fancify
dreamy supine stirruped verge
arms hazard two
                  by suggestive verbs, communicative melting
trade-in no stunting now adores;
    half-stitch twinkle, avid, traverse
quest remit — moment's silent next
                        orchid foreplay curious
                        — askew — excellent
misnomer volatizes contrary pleasing, spot the difference
                  inward TROPICS … arise, slander …
                  tilt a comparison with aphasic crush.
    Tongue skinned back have to
inner cheer succumb half react — a nebula of
hurtling decoys and debris to add which each silk's claustro-
                    phobia denuding our lips' divergent surface
grounds depth blue and touching reclusively fancy
                  fragile for viperish intimate appropriation:
candle hangs from waist, very bed slender braiding
                  treatment throat — flattery revved
                  aqua manual regular
                  beaut flood correct,
    it is as if it two-timing wishing were a person? — and I:
skinny pubic godsend reverberator, tissuery spoon
                  beckons favor with scent singular looming
graceful chest batteries & cream blandishous permitted
                  fleece in bouts stoop with
                  size this breathing friendship from
                  teeth outward counterfeit lavender loan
                  the pink imaginary persuasion:
I'll wisp double role as double rose your bangs,
    is syllogism lick the contrary:

## FIXED STARS 2

                    mosquitos ate my sweetheart — bijou mass
                    quadrangular less careful, hearts more proof
haunt to charm promise — finger perjury pretend mercy-
crushed tress encore, *alliance* is *translation* —
                    Loyal, loyal, loyal: gear soft straight
                    circularity is had, care
                    you wore a tulip affection dry volumetric
fears unbounded familiarity.
    She will be slip down talking, charity is elastic
proposition needs a spoon with a veto whose memory
took you out of the phonebook — shoulder the ball, thigh
                    the ball, each organ interpretive taste lost
                                    — myself — at night —
                    attitudinal partnering accords
                    vent prompt self-propping
gestures, watching themselves, little you ask
                    welcome stressed sleeper never hurt you
to be independently blue?
    And I: folds too much again whose pulse things least heave
head fest woo over knees just thief in night the night is young
                    whipped liquid curlicues, kindest in our own
heart is a cloud chamber — sleep-in lull acclaim
                    spurs on lace, marionetted
                    magnets, anemone petals
                                    imbeciles of bliss.

Palpable nerving understatement noun, but — narrow glow
irresistibly hushed, siege roughed absolute fine
            misted event with devilishly difficult
a better different to ambiguity of *less* need
                  & unflung creamed dirigible lights doing
                  night rind spoon — shed the real
lexical crimson never convinced; pure filial aura
to ultimatize the attention as a fool shared disguise
orchid only breathing.
      Big ditto camellia — making believe squeeze
                  aspect of fuzz to fall in love without
                  paying the price privvy with
evidence solicits gaze; premise teases brooding
                  carbons, my satellite, disembodies
                  unreality was true? —
discern equals smell menage à carmine loin benign:
      supervise staccato near dark
I did it already *means* it shrank before it's dark
                              interrupting more
                  hermetic tongue minus seminar perforation
                  between absence open monotone depatriated
                  kimono lower linen lip waiting
                  arrested so cough up
the shark of anguish.
      Darked steam makes mine mink — curlicued ellipses
                  later will be less late Especially shifts out
penis esteem delivery: furry lesser gentle retread
                  bifurcated vertical, distrust the offwhite
sips off teethy servant-like gloss: I'm silent
enough to smell how silent you are.
      And oblique juvenile violet back
overwhelms emission truce, throat cestus
                  ruffle twisters: difference evokes
                  the likelihood noose as if
                              fantasy hard arms
                  this excommunication delay split color blur
utopian foam to embrace each other in roots & branches
                  up the stairs to half the stars:
                  sober false almost rewaxed

                                    plums *you* wander of
                          capricious falsity,
                gags fertile embarrass beyond
        the pink talking sacrifice, mutually positive florets of
                          doe lacuna each suspend chasms
                          same accord eavesdrops so possess me
                          I like vital of your invents: Distract you?
— consideration squandering splurge as hazy solves that
                                    air in air raw
                                    savorable equal knees
        intersect advanced asleep,
                spark fragile care mobile bed, pneumatic seesawing
                          mortgage, bush loud calm signature flaps
                          to put some space around erosion
        engaged as in blanks get the dark control the likeness
        taunts — I know you know — this is torso
                          edge at very high stick chat
                          lightens laissez-faire substratum
        bothered always enough, I am serious: you can't close your mouth
        & speak without feeling your lips.
                Oh male ram width blurs disheveled padlock similarity
                          qualifying difference amply insufficient —
        Plus disposes ply I abiding
                          superordinate if
        turmoil ducts get redressed body and ilk are one
        middle never so good living faction of what is loss:
                          sacs ensue gentled in
        bodily internship convenience to get those
        pins out of my life,
                I don't think guys should fuck filial askance to their Moms:
                          gypsied smudging *sotto voce* fire to fetishes
                                    wooing mishears —
        well, *la* puta means the whore, by bent of mouthy appetite's
                          lacy riposte, I know it and did it —
                          luxuriated bifurcated soufflé necks
                          unlace homebred fossilized rubato.
                And I respond to loan me last night:
        night the same covet as simulcast moment reprieve whichever
                          overjoyed fools rush in taste of tongues

## FIXED STARS 3

to cross-react with
clarity declares escape — that from which
substitute vacuum desires —

no coil, colloidal buds,
no fidget femzine unboss
surrender accords lips'
double night self-possessed
suspense confides a precious regard
as surplus intensity full in your hands;
& ladies let's scrap this real flank free
physical & meta from your eyebrow, not a turned letter
sawing a prayer full up, with regular
unwell shame bedspread shutters —
in a related disclosure, fooling
by disappearance forgetting
middream acquaintance knew
the false flesh I reject lap kidnaps excuse
occupying disguise pep to
recuperate
failure
ostentation
uneven forfeiture, express flame bodies that learn language:
baton's end severs
the dark as ceiling slashed comma capable indolence —
nymph trimmings not the waist
but the shoulders prostitute the spite flesh in utensil
cream done stars a thing with nothing:
you're sick and I'm sad
and he went all over deceiving us;
& with us & not blur slightly spread
elongated paste to make a three-for-one body of
walls about our life — saliva adjusts, so will I — mutually
inconsistent impregnable limb we feel less traumatized by
our own candy desemanticizing puppets diversified by
autodidact in pillow powder
harness I feel tender to be
too many models.
Equitably contrite delusional rub-down surveys the clasp
gave more smearing oases up their knowledge crevice in reverse

## FIXED STARS 3

assure to jealous impartial propriety prolix against
                anxiety failure fails to fail
                qualified insomnia helpmates of the
all-day-sucker condition weed in another man's garden.
    Blossoms scintillate tampering —
                curious plex joke ignition
                exact stars papered over adhesion
to occupy sauce sunsets so because I became an object
for myself, physically refurnaced & not as farce
to give my power away, squeaks gain power
that necessity denudes.
    Gestate membrane gap
the jumps I'm so high, alarm to layerize
                      in the neck of that
rose flank off lip my luck thin super red line throbbing
                stage left's covetous nest;
    ignite silver: purgative beneficiary commitment
                hinge doesn't scare dream a little longer
                can be
                less than
                relented knots, convulsive melody
longitudinally doubtless evaporates thick teased
loan into your nape
    delicate nocturnal flash fadeout
disappears — WE LET IT — adjourn stitch
seduce to redeem & redeem to seduce:
                heart thinks
                fact betters fact
                corralled by night.

## FIXED STARS 4

We've got the slice and the tool
is contingent unlimited night, cottonlike flash
    rough abrupt loom
    sudden poem musings unrerevised
    & visible naming succor —
gaudy tears, dawn's semaphore,
  air vesselizes deruptive superiors
      chocolate & details — blow way me versify
      to be your judge me down not only = also
do do do do do do quite a few reverse inverse it extremes again
I'd like to share my impatience with you *fleur de* listed
      mind's teeth lure with slight armory
      on shins crossed part glance queer a point
got silent under faucet critics;
  huddled in parenthesis — trust whiteness
    be dubbing milky gliss
chevroned solid with — sense coming in from ...
unstuck preferred desires
fires empty mouth tart from the start
vanishes under control;
  basis the hands have soothed
      freakish warmest diagram, blink shimmer sleek
steamless lipids sacked up front enough —
    seeps severe jade faint precise is
    par sap rob the courtesy of
left-brained looking glass jealousy of secrecy science
       furtive fervents
       carpentered nape.

  Nebulous rouge
gaps oh boy near the clause resistant to gorgeous
eyelid pastel shimmer ferment drowned in satin
     shadowy chrysalis pledges slow-motion
     party-lighted *via lactea* devotion;
  & lithe debriefing pleasing secret
     nodes devolve up scintillatory
heliumed shyness, ah, ah: *object* for you yet
freely adopted blue curiosity eye, dart, and all.
  We slept one half spider's shadow duration
to a bed

affection; knows the heat puffs came
                indigoed pink slope hazing into gear
                          interrupts white
          slinked silk, bedless
          palm narcotic hopes in nest
whose bride displacement, in ego decor gap, swallows lamplight;
    double-acting =
steam comfortable in the dark pity speaks without
spoused trade-in words, ghost limbering cypherless fingers
                jeopardized in tandem: the class torsos out
                too talon as blessings
red wetness pilgrimage map — your face dissuading
same unit hug-divide silk interior
                break retentive silks.
    Repeal units indifferently outstrips different
                bend over myself beside discharges
                the mix — churned that seam — easier delay
tacit carom praline naiveté unedited, yearns chin & finds
                oscillating emolument —
ignite all black words without makeup curls
your cheek as crawlers.
    Cling everybody double your folly
                tit-for-that unbelieving wish's loony width
clit sideswiping
conjugal colors, scansion spread-off word disrupts
already deed sashay: Party Dress salivated purpose
                destined squeeze, sleepy's open
singularly dote,
    no limit give me hurt
          flow I, no, me
ignites me with the torch procured myself away
                        giving even, ease me hurl
                        love, pose & prowess
anklets pressed first lap rebuked air, paratactical kisses ...
                tickle of fudge, valentine less fastidious
                pulling slipcovers over
                tangible self-shortening stiff caress.
    Fair play means foreplay lightning
mysteries practice romanticized bone ourselves, stupor delight

# FIXED STARS 4

                                limbs vanquish inquest
member of a morning compulsory chinks
                    everybody her own prior rosy lowball
smudge pulse skin headlines your fingers are
a very tiny you personates as trick drag real
                    covet spare insides got rights.
    The Smoocher — whim links
                    knees to its own confidential vibrato —
                    unisex stilts, X speaks hands, me cheek
hammering moist fleece while slowly rocking his hips
leap caught breath leans audacity back
                    and that as far as I'm concerned
stupendous same sex nonchalance curving
                    wadda do wish makes decision mal-debuted.
Nonchalant nib hip splice sleeps to afright affront
                    our Lovey Whata Queen provisional
intimacies dovetailing equals — that join fuse breach?:
                    the wait between touches
                    baton confesses intercessant
spinal moments walk on clouds — massage the wrong
                    full cousin secret Hi — hi,
    look who is replacing grace: caressing furnace
                                imparts nape
stance in lieu loin niche adhesive mute —
warm gain by slow application, the slowing down is proverbial
brooding sweetness fond confounds,
    a recess of fondness flesh lightning
                    sign increases power pace measured in
                    eye drops acquitted
                    expunge an obsession out of duty
to extricate egg at the flame burred nerves enamor
                    tiny prick in shell? — conflict hatching
the proper pitch — safe? — back to bottom.
    And melting hand held chat allowed to, liquefies —
                    hand *want* what got cupidity wants
                    company: Hard To Get
                                temperature controlled by
                                tongue turncoat tempt
ass is come back on hold motion fractions begging for you

except by intrinsic face decode caress —
    if you find two baby legs, they're mine —
dishing to get even:
  saturated insistence should they tend *you* with? —
forearm lift-off, beside themselves, so fast keep Bashful Angel
      hold appropriated heads loins can interview
      break over reputation's teeming belt
      reject recruit in flames
press me for certain flickering militant collusion
disparaged by familiarity that would inconvenience me:
  it's less you synapse advocates:
        equality's skinnish promontory self-effacing
        dream beside discussion snakes contract
        & extortion promise me inflates
        dressed or in bed
Am A Devil machines explode, the image of tenderness
is aged spiderweb regret, permeable
or zero — imageless discord
lenient beyond belief.
  Give this pull a name to cease pulling circular
        use
        fling
        froth
        gain
        knelt slit stake
quiet's squalor — mattress fracas likens, want itch
      not chancing a riveting sleeper quantity
      frees two unjustifiable gratuities:
  tangents thieve over sleep curse flatters
        rub gest no vain
egress — self-igniting bedspread doubt sufficing suffers
tenderloin for answers don't sharp with me: most sense
self-abysmalling a wise-inch came wet.
  When we fashioned war's end
      cache precious or so local sugar
denuded central flesh — immense barrio, you think
no chameleons? — take some shoulder preference
      if bounce could talk
      lily-white without the risk,

## FIXED STARS 4

if you leave your body during this one benign detour
please come back —
>                    pink-shaped reservations predilicked
>                    pillow name narcotic adieu
if neck import sympathy stimulated bees
>                         adore treat equal
>                         care = change
>                    acquiescence petting parted
>                    spear in fringe.

## FIXED STARS 5

Skin license star fetches cheek chance two longings singled
palmist unveil pulses distill beside
flight flame Night's
Devotion pinks appease
sentinel contrivance, velour instants
agitated, tinder affection curls.
Suits off sulky peel, evidence to the linen
*nameless* inflames me both at once ain't misinforming
my handwriting on your whisper: offend the constant
whips rewritten as silk few edged chew
echoes re-tinned a swoon flare in collars catastrophizing slips
flourish in skin roses
can also be purchased — still cotillion?
Drastic be treat
excess *floats* instill
plump and clasp pistil tipped in chocolate —
difference nerveless person
quilt without corral, a bob and weave lavaed
parfait effort just for a kick.
Vermilion fraternizing, lipstick's fahrenheit —
from word to coma —
boneless shirt reverb lidding sunset lesion:
your nightly bead — charm is memory's abstention;
pyrite limbs of the hips' smooth infinite memoranda
parried carmine trembling
incendiary prongs at waist unveiled competes.
Spine remembers a pure nape, a taut flout vamp
martyr palm spinal pulls; tulipant exposing little segue
marbled shoulder applause from the knees & lipstick-colored lips
panning the jelly mood for alloys,
cadence neck cheek burnt up
screw toward flutter embarrassed by desks — ill sweet
poignant knob, handle like a rug, sliding loops
baying spoiled a tender charm or two —
cute's gravy paler than lashes upstaging
prom need azure hair's insouciant lure.
And me: pause before the pause converged edge
serve white-hearted waist open words, true teeth, incubators
on difference delight = jewel happy gown dizzied sheets —

     don't ever you mind sign waxing really
solid knowledge stammered delicacy according to the latest song
strokes' horizon.
  Streamline pulls adroit piece partner risk
           horizontally jumps intact
           abrupt results unprime
     out one arm puffed stroke outside wants
two insides, insides want less than one outside —
     sheath sings rhyming conniptions;
  & stet camouflaged bedding digest, partitions rubbable
     skin melba shifts silk bounce
     back & forth sumptuously pulse whiteness
strapped by Pillow Fight: mutually attiring
     deliberate slipperiness.
  And gentle corsage practicing sweat wax lean stroke to sway
buttes shimmy glide on lip therapy pratfall up binary echo —
that's self-deferral tumult self will suffice:
       twin flamboyants urge
     the damp frenzied points reprisal.
  Body buddies serried
thanks, differential stroke — evoked minute quote adamant torso
     whim spurn mounts spun slow grind crystal:
doesn't learn stoppage by which tenderer ministrants sugarize
this mix.
  And kudos as cool infatuated ambush splurges out ball
your limbs, absorbent napkins, the delicate to and fro curtsy too
     clean wrist intent cheeks replay
florid allowance inclines to swoon,
  clamor disrobes hem made me cry bride switch to two
     Adoras Ditto affection —
     conjoint dancing bodies may be expected
     to move movement eyes its trope
heartbeat honeying melee — I'm glad the humps worked —
ardent via thigh drowsy twist & lick.
  Jewel frequently double-backed kneeling forage spoons fluke
flux me to *plié* rapt cheekback unobtrusive to duplicate
     longevitying glance magnetizes caprice.
  Pelican lift & limb between your legs
     arms over half bare cartwheels

## FIXED STARS 5

           are kissing here congesting us with
           fleece crimson finger subject cadential
           buddy rash trust in blood squeeze & spill.
  Fancee: them there eyes, calmly voluptuous
           oarlike arm sweeps *both, both*
                    hope again, lit to size
           warm no end to rubbing fluid bartering agrees
a duet with the perpendicular pronoun *nightie nightie nightie*
never tell.
  Sweat's flammable dedication has my allegiance:
loosely querulous, I need a vacation from my ego — grace's
boomerang memory — broke its binding, pages drop
           fond slippage bed bleats blue lips
in taxi legs like plowshares;
      absorbently tongue-tied — hand, I'm yours —
                 not to act but to lick
wet clothes for all
occasions temporizing deceit rejoin
as *four pairs* smitten, uncrossing, only about-faces
too frail to rave — tressed cum
willfully rendered for a blood count.
  Bodily terrarium didn't consolidate you in bed:
             surprise friction quarrel, loosen moves
             arms so easy move seduces
             precinct mausoleum wet-leg for nerves
             tooth's head lap on mouth lava's
gemstone honey of an anklet.
  Cult floats lozenge comprises
dearly to retrousseau the limbs: script belly double or truth
serious topped with whipped cream late forgives
           gold releisuring your thigh
            umbilicated into fancies, miasma ferment
fondlings consent — esteem in compassionate trickery, trespass
                squealing sugar body
you're wearing sighs after you.
  Elixir little hunt too hot lives —
hummingbird lace on my breath that trouble sails in flame —
you didn't learn it several bone, at home
calculation regrets the damage wrong without it

## FIXED STARS 5

semen spent all quiver mischief dancing hush
helping beckons nude deeps of the twists,
     jeopardy unfickle, needles sew apologies to fingers
ponder to ravishment impresses quicken annex, winner finger do it
               appalls hips come in handy — auto-da-fé
               melee with lace repercussions:
               nonchalant exhalation slaps alive.
     Milk therapy stroke of incompletion — brood cope rob apart
really lovely remit credenza limbs commotion:
               may we also schmaltz you? —
fingertip blossoms delicious enough without dating embarrassment
at a discount choreographs the stir-crossed softest
               jimmied open embarrassment as synonyms
               for others; epidemics for nerves.
     Bait cheats spoiled fist fallible tears
pulsing *through* valentined all the
               how you like hard edges off.

## FIXED STARS 6

Superimposed reversed hearts to lock
of lace count, every star, rival in rival traits attract
                    enrapture sewing snag, right behind you I can
deal with under I affect you: vertiginous infusing
ardor flattens the lip curve,
        publicity confirms the sex appeal? —
what's the reception?: potencies get terse to try to learn
                    to be overheard orgasm as a verb —
                    mush that? — only the 'for another'
apprenticed to embrace one body as name so refabricate
the flesh, evidences to flatter
                    kindred solvency.
        I need some listen listen start the kissin'
                    take care milk advantage, smoothing off of
lush fueled the lap curries tissued detente hem lines
of compassion fingers justify the synapses sucrose aggrieved
                    to optimize wrists you front me
                    your teeth & your tongue lily whaddaya all
over neck jealousies:
        to her I entressed courage uncoils against shoulder
specialty angle mirror margins, hone & unfasten
                    chording hands, negligible fret decline
                            fronts new curve bait
                    preens androgynous noise hand
                    permeates person under, cherished undone
                    apparition of the female each
                    night donates, beside you.
        I can't wax my please put dirt expired palms
blur me up into personal arms velour
I ever think of — your details come in my face
                    sifted by blind indulgence: let's tug
detour-inspired chocolate on laugh wrapped belly
loans, neck feeders suit to my confusion.
        Good time to make your face at home
folding powder so darling firehose hints sung heart volunteers
who elope forfeit for feint lapped across
COSAS DEL AMOR, AMORES COMO TU, A MI NO ME TOCA, ENAMORATE DE MI:
                    thank you back on, a regret to nibble
                    touch kind impossible as cool

## FIXED STARS 6

to ribs pocket burial, talk & re-talk.
My mouth lick this neck for me
has its own travelogue you discolorate regularly
will be too too to peg par guying the arms of
leaked tongue lucky lips enough tongue
graced helper not truant enough & dizzily advicing
abracadabra,
verve chat needle blonde turret hands splitting slander;
& I spoke two mine join in fine cracks inflect fair lace —
analog saliva to a T, doublebreasted
hope's light with side vents half
alarm the vows ribs do not overload:
limbs evidence orchid slip trickling limit special sweat
variant pizzicato petted shoosh.
And lipreaders, infuse the rub each nor tease to penetrate
inbetweened spurt *into* that simply heeded philosophical argument
starts swaying in earshot in hands, courting
-
heavy, cleft partial
variable lips invest:
no matter how close unheard, hand-dipped shot silk taught me
favorite seething, tag slant hip jump rendez-
vous out just too much reconcile
kindles — Clinch! — gorged
border which has in
it any furnaces.
Which permission in halves? — moist me some more
flame in my coy ten paps bustle beside adjacent
smarter than the same close amendments —
poisons, cozening, main corps carved tears
rude sucking pliancy repose:
bras race corps sublime, pardon, ignore face
I sweep, broom disagrees:
ESCORT excessive — sobering who cares — hands
across the table, pliant under a taste primes bait —
affects' division of act baby please
insistently touchable cozening proofs
mandate helpmate arm blew future
foam as a middle jelly's fractional tongue:
I'm sorry, pillow, the yielding intent alertness

materialized in my bed.
Intellect 'think again' — arms petition the dream for its
bedside manner:
Not A Folly
to affectionate oneself
and half smarting non-worm — *I am taking it* — get my insistency
dressed to come first uh uh baby self-expands
arms, to hold you so; alloy voluntaries
vaporized beyond the pleasure obliquities.
Unlatch that vapor hand to keep open house
office hours with your heart — it pleases *you*! —
You YES
you it you
you eager? — author,
light me kiss me distaff ego personage
as rosary half-other to other half:
let's boodle! — detriment's by half to spoil Twice Over.
*Suaviolum* kissing seizing close inexorable double knees
immerse shoulder, co-curve, crooning, cling
mends indent, to agree:
little honey cherry pie I love you mostly with you one night
to excess makes it even easier.
All I ask is hearts — the rubbing of two skins
sufficiently alone to, minimum respond coitus sap
some more pause, disengages a perfume
separation, was willpower wanton,
equal sway undressed in
healing a puss is a face, right? — usurp
in laughing cunt's alloy behind foreignness in unison Other
refashioned as felt juxtaposed by your actually (!)
liking it.
I miscarry reception: parenthetically join
betrayal's reciprocal nylon
accomplice most cuddly — bound & close male
a tribulation fond of fool-soon teeth don't all alone
suppose you pleat sweetheart leases, straps of my tears, buttons
bitten off needle in closet tentatives
hammered bias supine sublime.
My heart seems to melt in your gland —

tumultuous middle unnerves intention
upwards owns face
the lithe grieve
assault-free charm salivation pleasure
convenes you premeditated *for you*
asphyxiating myself, with risk I'm giving you
a bite regret secret admiration witness
industry between us sleeping yet unsuited fleece hammer skin
on little calm be my be my profession.
Breviary mistress companionably distaffed, big deep
swooping the teeth await what governs
close-fitting risk persuades: almost nothing
first the body plunged combustible cunning
sex lies more, more neck in a manger, and flesh
now vex a weathercock wetting themselves
at the antics hazard disseminates:
sort face chose fine & final, all delicious
mid-compassion mutual same with slender patience
easy disturbs to confide as heart can think
lips soft with trouble suddenly slavish of the touches
tête-à-tête only one heads tool vanquished by the butterknife
perhaps ballet hope who is better to talk to,
your little acts of kindness ... tincture belt
Graceful Power — Another Encore
promise exhausts, menstrual half-and-half what hips could get
what liqueurs, vertical inverts ...
give me digital delay in bed, one undoes another
humid prop supposed parting custody impeaches in abeyance.
Humid heart pivot fold face effect
a little sudden permission, want some on my clasp? —
night *means* bed, day *means* dress body agrees
to care — double dear forgive & forget
tames use with use if this miss you wish what.

Umbilical heart thanks recur: PRIORITIZE WOMEN —
excess sweat aspirant pardons novocain to labor
                    what form your fingers form
                              honey under elastic
                              off
with such adjourned words speak blown bliss again!
        And chances only dark can modify
                    improbably high in temperature's midnight
                    vogue toward aromatic forfeit swallows up
                    like training oars: See opposite —
                              Split Light Burner
                              Glow
                              Softly Ooh
                              Caressable Scarlet Royal
                    heat promise,
        & *unsettled incarnate* — quells sting ease halve do sleep
                    advantaged truceneck, girdled nip nuzzling
saturater: I've got too much on my plate now —
peekaboo arrest how hard it softened all that abeyance
broke sleep;
        you wear it like that, I don't wear it like that — pajamas
                    reach … paste that, advance their crescendo
                    shaded corners lick at
your all wet — no, the light didn't distract me (destructively):
a thrill that accepts responsibility help elongation so soft
                    a reach to edge person fraud
vest trash between on cozy caliper sound:
vegetably sanctified saturnal *salut!* — rouletted
ill-closed yearning accompliced, split vase often short distance
ease your … unprincipled enough to mix side-fold un-
pinning with blissful infrequency, embracing
                    care-blasted collusion with mistletoe.
        And adrenal slap, you're back: profuse liquid waist
                    sensation, my partisans of other
gift joy self's hoping parasite worth under crack
                    abandoned me to my betterment —
ambrosial kisses — perhaps against the night I want
the knees to start perspiring guiltless contact.
        High-proof pleasure warying arch to bow attached

## FIXED STARS 7

sweetness verge in self-dancing volition
                                       linen eclipsed
your estuary & your guard fiesta ribs —
trimmed loses face for substitution you make acrostic of
my affection fallow worm sublime,
        can desire be, ever be, here ... thinking will ... ever have
                        ache gift person plus let them glow to poke
the rapport you won't risk hot in question is mere child's play
fool & lubricate & abbreviate calendar unfinished
                        you good it smells mute
                        heat in there, I see
                        is quaint ... to let you go, *accomplished*
stupendous infinite by one-quarter corked up in precaution
                        clitoris makes you brave — candy quiver
                        steering security or just plain redundant.
        And went some leg bubble lap clusters mutual signs
which are enamored, satiate, embroiders the memory of
                        liquid voluptuary red
adhesiveness, far fonder, liquid heads up honing
device on the neck, florid hot lips full tilt syrupy ago
as will,
        kisses resurrect
                        heat mercies astute to spine brittle default
                        such tested amnesty incite to breathe less
                        cuss forfeit sherbet laced with
decide — your bliss is my regard, I'm talking gradually —
a tangle of competing equivalents reprieve deceives.
        Amoretto's answer:
                        I hope I let God live long enough
                        To get my hands under your shelving —
velvety tango betters a curvative cocoon — vestige — tremble —
                        exactly barbituate desire
                        twice devoted friction scolded
                        tremor lizzed up squeeze are us;
        & similarly all me flesh tremble clamors blind
                        invite you outcouches loveful nominative —
this economy of infatuation can suffer, corrupt correct chance
finite and sublime — slow sloppy steps unoffended, dote please
                        without deficit ballroom sofa vial bliss

party in pajamas dispose fever to indiscriminate caress.
    Belied fog casual enough to have expired
               whose gaping wannabe used to purloin
               *erwartung* secret console accords self-fencing
               astringents the enransoming intended
enlighten nerve blame ADMIT TRUST spleen builds
impasto bunt without malice was your *affectionate*;
    abut period to do the thousand-layer kiss —
               oddities would still be alike, her heart into
               my body spine says agreement mirrorizes
               the skin face collusion finer trafficking
               in my face fondly imprisoning in tandem
               intended hip denominator mercies.
    I'm my own guarantee you left your fingers behind
vacational bond caution displeasure
               and for that, heart won't sleep, won't smile,
               treason to go ahead —
Sex Invest Me!, you're always in my mouth scale animated
mutual annuls cathartic demimonde of
emotional respirator can't stir it solo,
    & rambunctious heart light, pretty good? — ardent or co-
dent? — the topic is fucking that I shouldn't dream
               of your face seduce rake up ethics disdain,
               Satans Secret
               *in*cited or *ex*cited
               idiom welcome lay
               lay welcome tell you
               what what hands body
               can own the key.
    Or, not while you're seducing me! —
               Dreamy Melody infinitizing crush
               leisure gleam Other then — Next Dance Ardor
                              Smooth Overslept
               Ebony Midnight Valentine:
double rapture peach fuzz, safety box
alive with urgent copulation — face undefense
toast corsage: Good and Precious
knee to knee trespass kisses & niches.
    Dearth's head breathless toys don't confide

in failure at your hands franchised dream doubts attract on
person anyway this is the pretty way scratched
                    -varice, confluencing
                              keep by
                              close kiss

except itself
person heart
sweating camaraderie.
          & covetous supine contrite design I'm *soon*, is fixed: sleep
raw? — spanking enjoined, gentlemenly midnight
                         Bolero Amorette access I love
                         a special giggling scene of her own
                         casual casual you keep
                         my distance, I'll keep yours.
    Let us leave off paramedic paramour, that bigoted trusting
lingua pressed lust dependent belly: when you're upset, remember
the legs fox best attitudinial diaspora unconsummated
passion occasionally misspent facial context having not
lies down to know you:
          prong accomplice effect
fraud contractual phantom reason
                         -able truant sublime your liking stills —
                         pleasure's duty or pleasure is duty? —
leotards re-enacted the ideal speech situation: *volte-face*
enjambed hopers twist this out & that you'll always imperish
ephemeral durable.
          Not addled enough? — comrades not courtesans
cross-stitch aghast the prepositions' horizon plane vampire
                         martyrized kisses, the bed gets democratic
                         reciprocal fright: I'm not your face, no one
is the same.
          I, I, invisible: did you ask who gets the pillow
in their mouth first? — culpably covert clusive twin silk
                                   escort beneath nonpareils
                                   To all liaison
                                   I exchange disaster
                    debt tongue jury plus leisure's wax —
she keeps my meat unenvisionable, but the best spur up
this guilt evaporater;

& the nipples had a franchise
                        smears me to subdue discourse vs. dalliance
                        out toothed disclaimer saturation gifts as if
*rapport*, the exclusionary precept, blaspheme your love in self-
                        defense — cunt dwarfs reproaches
service to unsex me: my face went co-op
with her similar value-laden penetrants.
        Remordial sweetback mad these cared for
                sixfold


                                hours even puppy-like


                desire unspoke soft fist hilarity kudos —
kiss me baby; the personal is *personal*.
        Decorate excess — *sa drudani* — in dim light
                of dark informative body palpability between
                power empowdered feline happenstance, honey
                multiples, confectionery truce.

## FIXED STARS 8

PLEASE please is unhealthy dream not specific paradise, be-
loved collapse boxed croon — outlasts scare — reprieve some
more humidity as act of composition: ramparts voice
insomniac lullabies yoke pillow to fever colloquium, darling
*bonita* delicate calamities as dissolve, torment thinning ink out
inebriate reverberation.
  Rhapsodic queer spurt sallies coy *different*
       facts please keep hands
trouble appendage's cogency — the love we share
was meant to be wide-ish down facial apt
       sleep alone to dismantle seething
heartened neck coolants.
  Oh rosy quadrupling the bow full bent
       licking transference, valentined noun! —
oh membrane shelf silk heroic, melancholy too sane
enfattener petitioning charm surpassing joints! —
oh ankle straplettes sunlight harassed force pines
unmentionability away with a pinwheel at the top!
  Radiates thought hidden per pack attracts
       the cause which promises: restless
       rumor gum rivet delicacy = privilege
pro gel sashay into X laced with Y call me darling skills
multifold light cannot say, credulity fails in armor
       morbidly unsurpassed,
  & tick in cushion self grace
       grope trades banzai up, approximated regard
       bewared enarmed hollowed back bud turnaround:
certify lotion? — bland ulterior threshold stealth
read upside-down concise for stand-in.
  Familiar vehicle strategem lace fled from
       reality's probation
       union treats hyphen
       salivated torso sauce half our age
unnerved me — directory of special wrists foolishly
       silence divided pariah detour wants
wants detour stylization of 'I am being pursued',
  fully actualized rarely shines:
       contrast once meant lipstick
       collar casts head out & interchangeably

clay up my trust, pretense relief — shared breach
colorize roommates in the gift body; come go my bail
charge stance whichever transcoloristic light sleep break
                        satisfactorily otherwise numb —
                                    hue hint harm red light
                        fold ribbon off silk more dissimilar
                        thumbprint on talk circuitously
                        abandoning chrysanthemum as tool.
        Ankle bastard usurp to torque
subtracting excitability: my place or yours — independent
that means non-growth, three hands service, congratulations —
we have petticoat of the usurper outsiders coveted
your place or mine, adulterous gapped friend
pronoun contempo flight confusion winked
wettening frictional predestination,
        quick feinting jab to the possessive
                        charm expels enough friction between
your dress over *my* ankles like what don't make cloaca
reprieve a liquid from its puncture home flammable after
                        quarantine incite probate libido
whips her out — it's spur now — remove lure
                        inflected jelly pinching fingers perverse
                        mold spores to the touch
                        proclaim the breast defiantly as upholstery
since guys just don't have flowing material around their legs.
        Timid rib exonerations of the in-between
adjacent-chilly color, crushed strawberries for the cheeks
without control meant pleased nape habitable nudge
                        sprinkles on heart raised bedmat
                        cull or peach halves'
furtively asymmetrical incendiary redress;
fallacious ego
                        piecework or imperfect pronominal bends
agency adored birthday anesthesia.
        And caprices blend ambivalence too
unpredictable for submission by blushing the thighs together:
I don't mind missing you as long as I get to kissing you —
the surrended bride theme sows its amelioration
                        — can't we be gloved self-touching sweet-

## FIXED STARS 8

hearts? — but then
timid deliberative
body bond pride's netting bridal scare.
Abortion proposal: subjectivity rebuilt as devilled eggs
— we talked — need(le)less private license
mishap on way out?: clasp angel self from self revokes
to convene secret viscosity, sugar has less
close-up absorber scabbing brevities
smiled at zeal longest tongue treatable affect.
Narrow bed meant each other
lock's confession skin pact part can't win
disposal partners, losing crawl into two, nipples quadrupled
velcro humility: who might that saturation be? —
abruptly dalliance transmuted, improper doubled
vulnerably steaming harmony
in the hole, the old-lyrics section of my brain
has the gall he once mismanaged … whirlpool
rebounds tender, theatrically, absorbent fooling
body's deal chez Lah:
crazy-legged, the crude is father horizontal
equinox to the soft decoyed apology — Sweet Sally —
juggling imposter live-in dining shame assumes
shape I did & it's dead convertible disdain:
distance pathos possessed, possessive
web-like fuse, beyond-luscious
fingers fathom repeaters;
goods harbor treason cloys —
try your little lies how easily
big women means important female members in & out of the steps
of the wounders: mischievous enjoyment
of failure your skin handcuffs
certified mocking pineal retreat —
I don't care *just what* they say, choice breeds impatience
*three times* from context
(I recognized)
hummage gift on some other guy.
You suet me — a freeze possesses
equal misaffected partitions
the finery yoke off-sides, forbearance naturalized

holiday breath parity our bodies camp again:
you're emotionally inferior in disguise quiver
griefs stilted pity flounce awaits
unlocalized longing provoking, I mean soaking pink gloss
on scared skin stretched thaw
convening taste adhesive dwelling;
most things that can be opened have been
the more physical, the less paternal this theory to fall down
with hurled-up indiscretions to defend the bleeding hearts
against the zygotes —
ruins shy wives fate *de lite*, hierarchy
dissolves in embrace, yet embrace dissolves in hierarchy —
perfumer interstice hive any robbery at all
was coeval discerned flex;
a good man, harmless & useful respect undone
reaction shut dear expediencies
capitalized *friendism*: that doesn't mean you
can't have all the surrogates, conveniently consent
lacks excess meaning distress defection acid biting shame:
c'est la vie, pillaging their privacy
umbilical arrears.
Is there anything I can say to prevent you from sharing
these thoughts with me? — virgin repulsion arrest wish
in debt arrest united nowhere — do they inspire you or make you
competitive? — the darker the medicine
we crib, premature to gist it chooses, ladle
lax rage night, sedative, covert oil this
leisure pool default exhort
collective self-unwelcome impasse at advances
upholstery in lips please don't freeze
insulting intimacy with all the arraignments of alarm.
Frail fine
astonishing quieter
spigots revenge having been hurt securely
risked as dark sleepless knots virtue spoils to forgive
this second hope, second vein, second pulse postural *Pax*
adultery's lapdog: lateral loosener knees
want blood ebony
tresses kill the doable as an idea —
retort yourself: the price
is right, portions are huge.

FIXED STARS 9

Cʜᴏɪᴄᴇ ʏᴏᴜ! — neck milk white mere absolute answerless
yearn to compassion comes to mind, if God exists
we'll have to destroy her anyway —
unseduced *whole* why blow too sure
V shape, my littleneck quintupling assurance
recolting applause;
Code Name: Untroubled shouldered guilty plea comments less
speckled, less bitter, less tarnished, less revengeful help
speech out azured ethic impact lips:
accomplice windowsills all proud with ladders bent lining after
voicing confessional effluvia, its almost vibratory
respirant reminder:
close your eyes.
Will I be durable?: leisure re-explicates silken sparring
trauma flick mutability — spatial discount
treason flirts with impotence: Plushes Fury ᴀꜰᴀʀ
mimic that vow wrapped a place too tight
for the sacred in panties.
Shed Clothing and Put vocal bequest on Ideals —
swell curbed skirt yoke poise
& repose hip's victory bargained regard
pretty conscientious body foraging glue warns
haste voluntarily put in
practice privileging crush, forcep museum
in a deliberate boy healing beat invokes the annotated heads
I've baxtered what calms up
climb too hard, hard to climb
seizable redress.
Dopier corroborate gentleness overwhelmingly
adjacent unless otherwise calmer smothered a crisis
in softener tampering
her look rightness high school shook
a correction by itself as forgiveness mishandling
trespass trinkets equally
without compromise's both borders your mouth
got it for me wholesale.
I can't insult myself backwards: pink interim neck rigor
passion apparatus, fragrant celebrations, the constellations
peel back into rudders

common stint tears
without gamut wetter power the wonder down under
embouchure blandishment of night
idle mobility of resurrected excitation
literally as a soft machine.
Umbilical, chiffon, willing, to disassociate *others* —
drop off inside self furnacing cheerleaders for relations-
hip gender fix: belly in calliope kisses the butter bothering
hips betrothe together as silk delivers
shoulder all in all if her once
wants did a somersault;
look at her kill himself: insignificant confidences
deferred innocence — *simpatico* push off vs. lean
indulging promised rival
overwhelmed thighs got striped better
sentimental clit power handled bedly
justice half bedlight
hard is woo as unwilling to confessing as willing
lips would shut you up.
And how can our couplehood create more
likelihoods kiss — mutual penetration —
where are seals acrossing cheeks relaced? —
penis heir nipple *face*
realith lips pride cannot
impersonate partners swapping *our* commodity
bulges, and strictly *entre nous*, allow chance — perpetual
inner (reward) nex'to truss regard for you
baptize me all night
with its majoritarian principles.
Inamorata sentiment is distance
to suture or not to suture, let's sex! —
is *undone* abreast breadth lifts corner of
veil shy it that close
for us contending fittings, using the face for a skirt:
your distance approves of inattentive volume
squeezed out yearn, quarrel abbreviated reasons
envy displaces
great waxed-candy lips limed in appetite:
& we are not deficient, catch & release semiporous

unweaned volunteers for morale
abrogates her procreate utopia snacks
too calculated paralysis
rub ego colloquia trap doors would reminisce, and you? —
                suturably adjunct lace could device
                this little beam
comparisoned leak: I'm not free —
hey, guilt me off!,
      in such hedonism indolence lurked apart
invest in sleep, insurance more, got milk spermicidal footnotes:
I'm not sectarian, I've just got their number — if friends make
for embarrassment, embarrassment makes friends — do you want sex
or do you want sunrise semester? — don't forget you
                have four cheeks, no addicts; norms defile
                sorrier sorry I have *not* thought about
                red rooms and heart-shaped waterbeds
                each actions *acts*, fools, debunks until *later*
                spite moves in time.
     And these are toys stroke carries
kiss's inclination of their bodies safely raptured
pain through insight: better? — in a few
more years our relationship'll be old enough to have sex —
                possible cadre convalescent pride —
                possible cadre convalescent pride —
                dancing anti-evangelism disowns
                electra, impulse debts
                          Only You
                both fools need each.

Matinee here: to delight, let certainty down
humidly egalitarian limits burnt fleece guarantees got to
— all your golden gap shed the feeble garment
                    soft verdict unfolds aisles in flames
                    dating floods stepwise sweeted horizon's
luminosity restitched out of falling star perforations.
        Dream ahead? — keep your mouth wet silk ovator
                    in a reward of neck, suspect too slow
                    need never inspire names reforested
                    skin titanic inside proposition
ashamed to kick deed, there's a new value for you —
I could live inside this song to remember who has not fucked you:
                    twist speaks the plea damp song all excuseful
sunset peels off the wallpaper's anxious antidote.
        My outreach got its name tags wrong — slice heaven by spoon
                    perspective caught off-guards took my place
in the off-light, when is torching justified? —
                                less *mores* push apart
                    to uncook it on both sides change spites
                    night fission utopia boils over
so I invite you to fool torn away from familiarity
absence flickers, fidelity submits
cushioned remorse can't decide to stop;
        & small common good bides them the pitonning
                    secrecy's nerve donation sapling mansard
                    pact exhales basic nursing wand
so much is gelatin against all odds safely in flight
                    redeeming tags hothouse ousting
satin by hatching the fuse, *who's* wanting *whom*? —
                                whoever's inside
                    Ideal Situation.
        Half dark untethering smatter sucrose
                    salivaed evidence you don't always have
to see the outer borders, you're the one who's number one:
                    red congress flounce
                    as wish padding fusion reuses liquefact
                    padding a wishbone, overprolong
                    vertical radial fellower
                    *bonds, thread* grace's dune

remainder gnaws excess analysis
becomes sentiment.
Unison beveled wow a lot — correct love crimsoned economy
flowers below pace negates 'on time'
harbor no bones beneath that surface
compassed lascivious confessors of scratching
night alignment practiced abandon;
& no point to pick up tripling anonymity
snaps ordinary bitter honey —
courtesy pockets privacy
mentor halfway permissible
urgencies lotion a chaperoned Utopia beguiling bereft this
unbuckled compassion — (more inside) — share if you dare.
Your innocence — Oh cupid(ity) — made the cut-off
our privacy platooned — rooster vacates
pleasurer reclamation, barrels blazing
amorphous head … renege on my contract with myself,
exchange fates backpedaling negotiated foil
feign final so as *not act*
reassures uncorrected fooling shame
floats torrid as in arrears, reversal giddy, dalliance in germ
hurt your embarrassment.
Romeoed sheets as impersonations grant juice a country
of its own convalescent bounty felt spark convert
each embrace concentric beyond itself corrects
privilege by blossom — the communicating tilt
junta *to* me drenched gives me permission
lost in the sweets, value something down the semi-nurses —
travelog of own face angel in my return oasis
donates ego trouble so we watered the escape.
Real opportunities keep you young —
who, and who?: innocence arrest by permission curtsy
hopefully yours white noble roomer that remains knees
even in its caprices — top shelf on my face is coming out too
threesomed shifts in pulls wet by law
apology inside out shall couch & bolt
the drive toward independence.
Other fits better, luxuries divide …
a velvet prior, sweat reaches pastoral levels

enamored by lace dazzling in opposition
improperly near or nearly improper prone choreography
rapture agreed, gloats over: indifferentiate
reverie without contract; I still draw little hearts on her lips
betrothed spare the motion, for keeps, quiet
companion storm revindicate
threshold up together thawing
parentheses *between* ourselves;
& I want what extras get! — deservedly taught
fate paired blocked crave easter bound
maniacally compassionate, never closer, still self-endistancing:
take your pillow for a valve, purchase my youth this close
can get up & walk with corpus delecti
oscillates *gift* so
unfeignedly have you fold away? — crisis
= opportunity
Home By Midnight
Identity Lapse
at a distance curls as
practice ducking inevidence — naturally I wish everybody has
me instead.
Right now *we* got an expenditure in common command
to exclude so much less cross-breeding
difficulty — intimacy's craft
which community persists without you:
delicate utility nippled public perspires in surplus commoded to
jealous exit delectations detain
the cure excised excuse, always and always,
evil hands against the floor, fragile as
excess bitten off caprice.
You can't serve up hearts like cherries jubilee:
you grew quiet
proses the torso with privacy, the didactic
humidity polited seizure, the well-programmed vehicle parliament
myself back in only hope the poorer govern;
I don't want/to borrow your love/back to the closet
heat less loose body speaks
billows storm of reassurance
night no longer dispossesses beneath

together dream of critiqueless sensitivity refractory to clips —
you could just be lesbian toward the things you buy.
    Lips catch a falling star I've lost interest in
                decay that position neglect,
conferring on banging heaven's annex —
                       Hah! Who's fixin'! —
           forfeiture loves never no more
           company reproach the palpitation when I
evacuate from her, reversion thinks terraced in azure
really scared: justice is unfair,
      circumcise that privilege oasis resubscribes, motel
                horizon tattle doubt to paradise
                tenderer backward sucrose bed reprieve —
if that isn't love, it will have to do; can he take a direct
challenge to his manhood well? — sashay to free norms
duty = anachronism, not so self-destructive now
cross-shaped reversal luze indefinitely (defiantly)
insults grew quiet to replenish
the exception hope persuades;
     & let's fight the sweet cause together — no genderization
hints walk away embarrassing
paradise withers all institutions live
& live without you more exclusive in little stars ask
                comfort dictates uncommandeered affection —
democratize yourself! — social events of lips
           pawn close heat forgives
           hope trysts entire.

# PRIMUM MOBILE

## PRIMUM MOBILE I

Write near the top more
                              forestage optic
intoxication 'mparadise down from when *do you* swamp —
                    under radiance venture *lacking,*
     mirror-plaintiff glance yields transdescending
                    *method* gives me *head*
upstairs universal, retro vista clues desist,
     & images undeferred —
what's the matter so trust, facts made of stars
chancellorize the sun amply coronated enough for you?:
                    lamp post is apocryphal positive
beauty burns;
     the real testing-bed *can't*
                    they *recast* refrain from style
                    eyes, provocateurs
                    enchain eyes divest befitting light inferno
is not writing.
          And run the earth to the ground blossom opacity
                    appears = news dilates nothing
premature kind as lure horizon break
                    minimum doubtless stars over thing,
     fold it as a dream until the shadow photographs itself
                    because my head's not there
                    I'm going to need to be hungry
otherwise I'm going to be fucked;
     & transvales out the flame an everywhere
super concave former size *air surprise*
ribs resign circuitous halo succeeding.
     Magnetic availing -ing air is physical color
phase out *which* doom? — soothed refractably,
     horizontal latticing speedlike
roses booby-trapped physicality
indefinitely luminous cloud is blind
mayor of clouds as aside;
     & apparitional envoy total feign — hot so often —
                    accomplished blue
               nibbling at the privileges of darknesses.
     Sense of space-as-volume the contingent disturbs
               night — that barracks

## PRIMUM MOBILE I

flora pre-floresce surrender ample severe.
    Spatio incubator welcoming open
                crystal mash
notes deliver us from points beneath the points;
    & contest sway, inner convertibles
                    had any sense back
                    drawn how in trespassing
indefinitely hints.
    Dance with the teacher open — Glimmer insists
strings whoosh — does not exist: fire tremendo correction
substance retracts intangible buzz.
    Meet fine
point infinite
adverbs figure-eighted sweet
                    have skies succumb lighting debut
trebling liquefaction *waow*, *waow* not made with hands.
    And the provisional sentences:
                    wrested frontage flooding pinpoint
                    instants aggrandized — little flights
                    strobe bled, phosphorescing incurably
flared hilt hilting lucky lag;
    skittering lights
                          jilts
                  neverywhere, slipping ally
                       just so
                     how soon
corners without angles but centerless gripping
quiet in the vortex of rotation-like trousers.
    Celestial finesse back in beaut break honed enough
space alliterated milks pigmentable ceiling around the knees
slant filigree flats embloused emblazon through
solstice curls preparatory flood,
                  equatorial extras, how close not quite? —
                  Magic In The Air
                        estuaried skin itself
                  on a bare stage, lease-free, spiral touché
tufts out of bounds — sweet spidery
spot sugar blots out the original.
    Infinite slippers emit sparks, cosmic deb reddest

# PRIMUM MOBILE I

espouse thrall chases sleep slipknot zero finds its sanction
to phosphoresce sufficient tight pearl excellent above —
                              Population embarrasses:
                    Esprit Enchantee
                    So Inclined
                    Racy Light
nub close much off — assign desire bruise less —
                    anticipatory matinee!
     Lower fronting better spark anticipated
                         air is my bedspread; disrobes the aspect
refraction's rapture on putting angular
                    parfait adhesive federates light
                    flesh grateful ideal palimpsest
even rosier — or below! — sweeter than words'
self-envagination by heat and light.
     Mouth asleep at issue shape
rare less creamfilled flashes
                    more is more mere air heard in exact print
guessing glimpse atoner.
     Those precious face-saving eggs how
                              span glows salute
the red-violet formalists of heaven deplane this invisible
                    visibly scarce cease curls
                    luxury beams, enamored
salute silvery extras widening caressive jurisdiction.
     Tremendous slide star inlay flesh at large
                    in a mural astringence
                    within a kind of incorporeal nudity
                              succumb is
no mind answers icicled off
this ennuied, this annoyed & envied world:
     spread moon heat rises
                              show under
starred volume, all out, also air topping anything but starchy
careful spiral true to rare ape ultissima
for all us! — porous ceiling,
     hoops off, gaze's cadre engines
                    us quitting all chameleon air
destinies out of air color whoosh & pleasant from above

## PRIMUM MOBILE I

        boxed the bubble up:
    happily shorten *this* & this life submit point perfect
rectangle — I was going to say something about the lunar tide —
            dotted suffuse imaginary object of inspired
body handlers ousted,
    why imagine facts as pulleys, topless stairs —
           a much admitted, most indetectable, style
           battery, speechless infinite duties
purify to work alliterative wiring witnessless
time flee jar entire;
    fled smoke up appraises death like blame
astonished answers spiralling felt  Dreamy  Sea  Dream  Joke
labor silent thread itself.
    And Our Future —
           can't done that
           total skin tight deluxe
mercurial gravitation
without fingerprints.
    A poet's license expires in prose
           doves' eye communicating
           light sleeveless foretasting
tinsel particulars' sake.
    Soon as oneness transascending atom tumble
neural emerald asterisk:
           tiny lights highs beguile
                future bends down
           liability as unanimous.

$\mathbb{A}$ND Porous Iris — apexes?: sheer bets squander dub
free the unknown *for itself* in motion action light
                    sufficient gossiped.
        Soaped dream-wise blush enhanced mimicking —
                    fleece alert fun solstice monotone head
bud out: integrity's costume.
        Deluxe loud visuals, veilless miracle morsel
                    idea pulleys if clearsighted unity glazes
the real thing queen transparence;
        & the focal seizure senses at work at the confines
of their intensity: *vultu, gestu, oculis* drenched deep
detectable image as completable fullness: baste
                    the spheres frills abhor.
        Image this thaw bigger than true bliss jammed into
what visualized colorless consistency slippages
of time's self-
concealment gradients may read like fiction;
        & a pertinent bestowal of
                    stages of shape anything = demeaning negative
adiopolated sensors keep an eye solar quit
                    look what look how hue default
a less equivalencing metaphoricity mental cell.
        The lavender figuration — Touch   Of
do you beam? — but do not throw out the comma
clusters enormous no matter how small it is, veils stammer
                    axles of lace sorties,
        perpetually Crystal Cameo
                    Sweeter Music — syntactically windmilled
                    meteorites kneeling about-face secret
                    humus star paratactic patience, optimistic
on air devolves itself blushing surface self-interning truth.
        Apotheotic tug, solstice jubileed foundational
                    hands, for skylights at least but not beyond
                    abut beyond equator syllable will —
substantive at top, joke below melt noise peremptory
by lamination born to a stirruped fact grooves reversible
                    touch even more.
        Curl free posit marquee fragrance tripod
                    devising so deep shadowless

## PRIMUM MOBILE 2

                        trellises web happy divination
                        furs murmured off
error reveining rampant dream medicated to luck lewd
cunning gauze.
      *Thing* sound *same* —
                        attributes reference desire plane to plane
                        as matter appeals
                        form, punctuation absconds
                                      tease over theme
blurting out the center split impossible.
      And powers name — maze all that dionysian clockwise up top
                        cursival meant society of the head —
                                    ipso toto factual affect.
    Vitamin clothes enamel lava
                        error torched out death's sprung
                        rhythm tendering, appellant mistakes move too
fast when gravity calls aren't sure.
    And La Rouge Domino cognating itself —
                        It believes in sentences
                        I pass over already
                        itself beyond wording to
                        unanvil Perfect Solution
                        like to abbreviate we all know
the negative secret:
    stet flex tongue lidless gaze
mistakes decoction dispersing
so best sweet shut bodiless
slender writes nerve just sufficient
tint mezzotinted for
volatizing array of matter.
    Breadth present vertical toys
                        wake the false gradation cracks
inseam luxury shoutless heat size accordion-like space
imagine inner effects — more still —
                        horizontal so candied showboat zone,
    form halts, straight
                        aromatic, precincts plenty transplanting
                        a terrestrial name not
                        even tentacled equipoise less

# PRIMUM MOBILE 2

never tipped: cheap lease leisure size prizes
                    doubt filament donor's polydolence appendage
took its own lessons,
    nerves on level carbonize pose — recompensive
                    dive grace press desirably
                    cranial divination lips, a hive of
                    eliciting implicates delirium when hands
are roots entirely up & down.
    Atoms hoist bibliographic traps herself to appear
to favor & to favor to appear private, I'm *telling* you, meant
strokes convection at slope side bride noun noise
                    insisted-on ends, wrist that glows.
    I am every signature roost my heads no semblance
                    in the future alone, to stipulate voyeurism
benign speechless shimmers into signature & goodness sought
punctuated awe pleated fling-offs inside my body,
    in coned rapt co-opera iri-
                    descent skin the body always wants
to be taken care of and to hell with it! unquote —
appearanced soon florally — confined satisfaction —
                    or saturation diving dress indulge
                    came down unsubornable to earth.
    Emulsive space heart
                    straight flame, heat tights
boneless final Venus act excellent to wilt, high above
                    the stars headless doubled, noun shield
mobilely rekindle.
    Fixtures flit shoot / design paralyze-less and above all
to exemplify something form, lights up hint & open mouth
publicizes the fact correct in form and balance
pleasure scarcely fraud.
    And fragrant jumper — effort is mad crystal
stimulus persuades:

                    Blue  Eyed
                    Smooth  As  Glass
                    ricochet dressing interval arabesque cheers.
    Legible divinators berayed! — what goes on
                    quickness is filler, scrim just invites
                    thrustless spot-removers' infirmament *too*.

## PRIMUM MOBILE 2

Paragraph whitens all words — are you rotating?:
     weightless manner queen clustering
       slide simply that
circumferenced lambs bathed product, content
wonders, free bypassed ultraviolet curvature;
  infinite comma contrast leans
     oblivion in abeyance use
     to look laughing
tableau covenanted peach love doubts.
  Privacy makes no difference: wonder wishing idiom
     figure purified referenda on your past
     rings that bite word of mouth
     source oblique empire bosom of
     omnipotence
commended by her, to all desires;
  circular fluffing too
     empty to share barnstormed-away winglets —
sometimes it's hard to remember that this place belongs to *us* —
     *maze in that*
     conviction *spills*
   chameleonic arc sublime they hoped
they could it out through the needles;
  & let the happening happen undroughtfullest
host the nonpersonal in an atmosphere of eccentrics grazing on
certainty have touched the piece but yet to move forward —
     forceless knowhow, no why, can't hide —
tiniest disequilibrium qualifies for necessity.
  I just follow your finds disclose
things where they take me? — That proves it!: say'll
     out precept blankens
luminous panoramic dots heart open to vouch.
  Stemless positive on to on suffices is apocryphal
wrestling presence delight wipe slate off nice
to be a lamp in heat crusading size.
  Extreme rouge obligation to hope enprismed in itself
     will not be using the trapeze apostrophizes
nude word hardly words one.

## PRIMUM MOBILE 3

Impressed uncertainty forfeit presumption
                    superb beneath factual blush aim self-
                    displacing, is this forgetful? —
elliptically so thrive hints belie juried stars.
     Doubt feeds every affirmation I don't wish to see
what parachuted object to look permanent
     sieving grace; these are not preciosities
of style — self-regard harbors bigger vessels:
     unfurlment bedazzled reverse superlative
commerce sight to be privilege out near light stress lalique sky-
                    line reapportioned slope shutter
lineage abscond with the metaphor;
     & fight the accomplices Over 'N' Away —
                    you spell candy memory kindling reflect
                    mount light lotion tinting eve poses
                              Image  In  Motion
bleach fabulation visually snows.
     Insinuate immediate keening
                    IF DOES — something light cataract enlace
caption circuit *real* means *realized* mirror unflattened hope
like a candle signal free desire to begin.
     Rigor bleats brain didn't last long spaceless
                              (i.e. disembodied) —
                    & that's accurate too!: ambiguity folded out
category & each category edged by
forfeit negative less Dark Interval tropics disclaim
                    absence deposits these calms as
                    low as that which is correct
must be transcended,
     confound objectivity vulnerable
                    umbrage, thickishly enlightened
                    no match for reality aperture dirties
self-negating anxious happen nothing doting nothing
equivocating referent refuses — solvented magenta letters.
     What how? — sensate detriment presto
blank recollectably privileged silhouette adds
                    wholly oscillate attitude: nerved thinking
                    stub chalk squeeze crown out:
     the sentient itself could be stretched

rear co-signed as effrontery intercede
from beyond pretexted objects' lights serenaded
by matter — & wishful thinking or not I have to believe it — ;
   voids should be pointed, span unseizably
necklaced proprietaryship in limbo object reclaims
its alibi, horizontal, over vertical harbors a lapsed emphasis
can't divine the obstacle content it shed —
                I'm losing my nouns.
   Mind the gap — right church, wrong pew:
                key-shaped complicit verbatim
                sham for decor fortified gravity
                lesson mirage — Foolish Things:
spooling curse shoved nests the carrier frequency unionized!
   And re-evaluation of all vellum vaults the difference
                is the same language birthmarks
                go down go flat, artifize that real
                matter glitters nominative diaspora
disdain between news.
   Fond nothing — merciful verdigris my axis
details to duration amplified, filigree defied swallow
vendor to its senses: get the real insuperable.
   Wayward interpose undo-or-die I
                dreamed invent that rare must have
                notes null stylus
                sheen toss-up sticked mirage: *taps reveal*
                radiating gaps measure
quits little radically rewritten astonishments.
   My pigeon's gone, buckles under key repetitive dark
baffled upside down passion, magical extreme predicate
sameness of pleasure as much to
miss high dynamics without difference,
   & glass brink gnostic creams
                position's pulley mop at labor
Dark figural landslide Signal under falsehoods forever? —
nice assist
                plummets blink torso lindy
preponderant escape eclipse.
   Abbreviation' s truth
                and pushing faint sighs from their lips

# PRIMUM MOBILE 3

somewhere somehow someone
I
popped the lies, valedictory
hastening opacity's lineage of deheroicized resistance widens
out of breath text between — or underneath:
    unlife is rubato logo over
cupped nipple tongue reprieves its own
landscape incorporate veneer of boundless excuse
unsultrified — obeys *moyen* misdemeanored
tints better
prepared than wet tear-away tango parasol.
    Artificial missionary corps mysterized
possible serpents placing-myself-outside gap to machine
predicate whose fleece
head votives itself
How  Cute  A
as if babies were obscene films;
    & all is not found! — pillows take shots
surface underlines, revoke ideal loosefly — at will
limbo be so
congenial loin locks cascade metamorphed arms.
    Nerves are virgins of dusk —
verdant liking, scarlet incredence
foolish things force open flesh:
one gasp that's it —
the silence closed over us.
    Absent images end trance, mirrors stare back
at their background bluff on blocks imagery fails to ignite —
gravity product service silk
scavengered sight charged fact
easing indemnity as consummated inquisitive delay
warning shadow satin anything senses confide:
    metaphor surrenders
eclipsed coloring
inadequate stars, multi-
ply forgotten, pronuminous (pronounimous?)
frosting on paradox figurizing limit
concave glass sky relents:
overenjoy statement; no, the opposite —

worthless weight, permission attentively dumbfounded
microscope apologize — There is no here and now.
    Visceral opacity creases
ambitious rule invited margin the picture would feed
lapse come true resistance to object rot
               as the solution presence derailed you're not:
some are the exact opposite —
            testimony taught lays arms not to use
            gold as use volatizing hints
no distinct lady at all.
    Silhouetted scenery subsides inversion
    head over hell theory doesn't fit the digress box
amusement into dread, vapor reverse, which *can* be destroyed
           unformulable forgetfulness in disorder
finite *whats* circumscribe that watchword.
    Prismatic athwart, object lapse status — looks —
          tendered good etherish looking-glass tip
can only guess souvenir shrinkage felt the heart as intrusion
favoring soft, positive nerve gas smudge flown
geometrics in red suspension,
    & I took the point off light sweet nothings to
a halt hysterical in points — gangs of vertigo
          scattering misfires & her anti-gravity paint
be-mazing throttle into doubt
look's envelope complaint disappeals.
    Time tells me something turns to chicken past exact
leisurely corpuscles on the altar of loans,
          multiply nylonned: fence can't be guaranteed
          the best, the best impress labia innumerable
detoxification inures a void parachutes
         we here in the questionmark.
    The attractions of the soul bosom multiplied are less
under legal contract — segue tableau shakes me off
         proudly barehoused affect *dolcezza*
         diversion the apes downward —
there'll be no distinctions there, ought anything
hors d'oeuvrish fervor
                deeds
                dive

## PRIMUM MOBILE 3

                                         dependent
                                           date
                                           doesn' t
loose ends.
    Image disposal reeks light
temporal breakage — uproot givens, despise all questions
                        rubbed off the perma dots — the brace gives
                        your neck a landscape party of the planets
I'm so ex-powered,
    no amnesty on utopia
multitudinous bath at best needless
perfect undress.

## PRIMUM MOBILE 4

Noon's night — phosphorous seed sensimilla singed fanfare:
                    pure No Strings anthology blink the fact
                    orchidia briefs a secret, conical *vitresse*
yells off gravity architecture,
        time eats torso heat exploits
tinier flooding florist leaping luster
                            conniptionally gorgeous, physically separated
sacred harps, monumental quiet, aerate all other astigmatic star
                            absent lunar smallness all blue in blue
fight right-thinking with fire, lime boundaries, curvature
redundant elliptic outside singe Same Zero;
        & night pastes up perfume contents — sovereign oasis
                            evented sky backs face on all counts
                            cruelly misted charisma *equatoriale*
zigzagging to the pressure beat — defect to risk
talliable sulphurous curls with every feeling of delight lack
                            thwarted sense-net and small ones conductibly
                            dilatable in fruition for its own sake.
        KEY THE PULSE: interval ideal
                            gooey numbers dissatisfy by speed — *see*?:
                            free duration training preclusion's
                            closure follies *at what* instant —
the rest is suffixes,
        royale spinning pretty, static free force whirlpooling
trouble in mind soft inability — immeasurable
denied decorative depth, impolite to the eye
tissue eclipse regardless.
        Material cleft vice decimal quiver
                                    slim out ply
                                    dub gaps against
binding cerebral mercy air fable of content
escaped me fragile & marinated, compressed to maze
engraveless shakes.
        Unsponsorable luxury of indeterminacy transmodes
moisture has thought thinking perfect
fluid *infinitum* dizziness repose — all such frills baiting grace
tame veil deep through avoidance of depth
                            goad distantiated deferment
                            horizontally small to lure lightning wants

a magnifier buffed beyond belief.
      Inside Choice — absentee! —
                        wires aim inward curlicuing delayers'
                        continuous breakdown concedes
you can't rely on words — difference cause exiled signature
                   gap's idealizing frenzy:
    ravenous mash black-out of pronominal sloping the fissures
regret deliberate closing of one's *no essence* eyes —
                    can you expel the difference? — tentacles
                    of shelf-life crash in arms, liquid punctual
                    spun bold thrall centerless scheme.
      Buff it off! — preposterous fluidity in sign
                    fracture struts, incendiary if I don't
finish words puff as marbleized sometimes, it's cause it's not
all there: the hieroglyphic tinsel delirium manifest
                    pell-blank-mell fancied flickering chain
on margin, humid breaks melisma species;
      spinning is all I see — turn up the heat, don't be
so oriented; they're all milk unsuiting swerve
                    probe all cloture desist
told another lie — fading flaming syllable alarm
that dangers touch poeticizing, nonpareil sticking
idealizing dispersal amenably precipitous.
      Vertigo debut *not inside* milk fan anticipate
                    Silver Stark White Velvet naive curves
glare crease extent apocryphal repose —
external body ghost spread, scents exclude position
                    endless seam spiral jelly maze into
                    soft substance, untraceable twirl
                    revulsion terminating,
     I'll be spinning clings better
incapacity for straight distance cantilevered into
to tell you charm fearless abeyance
                         Pucker Free
                    invisibly wild desire impassed eager more say
                    more whiter forehead mood intervals:
stretch coil blunt unarmed to pluck blank hood:
      substanceless jetty lured done — Blinding-Recognition Gaze
                    passion will evict oasis-attachments

# PRIMUM MOBILE 4

not utilitarian, so really embracing, perpetuum doting
carousal fell swoop to a permanent heat —
                             intellectual anti-icing, Lacey
Liberation, Inseparable Cool Confection.
     More soft sensible silence spoils
hushed militia lure skin equal
                         sign welt nudge curb blinded
extra-sentient buzz pathless tight
*barring or unbarring* headlong expectation —
                         veinless wonder dear reader
                         felt scarce closure remiss.
     Consciousness a surfacing surfeit even the lightning sounds
implacable in a perpetual tenor be held air soften off
                    zenith *in itself* retentively blind
                    room starts spinning the perfect recess —
gorgeous noise wax sears, rubbing sweetens
fever patience,
          sculpture a space inside the spaces form withdrew:
                                   sac bonus overlay
                                   direct nest more sloping
                                   squareless — magnets —
profitless hideaway intravenous afterhours.
     What shock wish to
last sovereignty lingers — skinless panorama
                         glimmerized circuitry licensed delirium
                         to keep Pandora in suspense:
the crease happens in both directions
effacing in circumference edible but equal total unbelonging
                         fashionable abundantly falsetto
vaporizingly idle candle.
     Jellied personification someone = less
                         yearning scrim fleshless without debate
bushings articulate perfect disremembering delicate vocal
tenable adhesive sprawl beyond bodies I feel like it it up —
                         value has no sex, certain hinge ongoing
as size devastated duration;
     & fur retires, compass futile —
                                   chaos
                                   intelligence

## PRIMUM MOBILE 4

opulence
silence
indemnity shamelessly
aboriginal parts hysterically impersonal
breaking diamond heart —
relaxation (also called 'decomposing') —
age means *more prepositions*
sanctify my displacement; lull hum gestural
hurt itself sprawling width enmity as compliment;
& boom boom: purple stitch pieces fleece
multiple pulse illuminated posteriors —
I *am* arbitrariness
membrane wanes, system glistens
pleasure to wealth alone, thought back, eclipse shafts
tongue of loss depopulating for pleasure
hovers-in-itselfness.
Petal fireworks unvolted and float of heights resisted
movement is not *toward*; maybe 'into' 'd be neutral enough —
blaze all firm one
minus one miles of
spore your separates;
sumptuous lyrically whack hulls of
hope inebriate joys *belong*
to the brim — sensual coup d'état contrast stumbles in
swingtime spatially roughed disappearance of
the supervisory finger, the audible hand
revolutionary delight off the scale.

## PRIMUM MOBILE 5

Facts besieged, vast and high-ceilinged
nerves are in the air —
                              Overcome
                              Ever High:
                  querying body arousal creates
desire even dreaming of the intimacy of clues;
        apogeed fix stand in bade light — vertigo rotates null
                        substance cross deglobing vent
                                  vent comfort audacity:
gravity diffused at last make ourselves pay dearly
incognito from the edge trance.
        Body *figures* winner take all — topaz Plush — folds in on
                        milky itself a prefigured look soft notepaper
                        skin hugely magnified, words stutter
                              ideas fill the head
                                  feel *headed* — topping up
                        better prism blue swoon by blue
tangible foyers; tropical headroom spirals between
                        detail makes me inordinate tongueless coax
                        infantile fulfilled terminant angle
withstand the burn without your prefaces.
        You blew out cloud the flame exactness
acerbic incurred pastel traverse
aslant proscribed regard
                        we expire the round, above all quiet
                              no doubt copy
hugeless superb image triage.
        Efficiency is the slob I'd love to get
that on wax curve barrage, windswept pull around altercation
                        on top — Snow Dream — flared
louver jumping aside the predestinating bend,
        adjourn motion rests easy light
                                  might how
                        laundered mirage calling hands embetters —
complex bowl silk import nape of itself
spit shelf but *open* hands an enjoying substance to
trade places with their own syntax;
        & bite out of middle better angle inside gone
diameter hurry width, line practically purrs, rotates

1

# PRIMUM MOBILE 5

three-dimensionally reconciled
so bunch without a limb.
It is knobbing earthly easeful readiness —
an object dawdle on in the head wraparound mystique
*if seen from within*
edge got a larvae lift
adorn gap syrup delay —
Trust menstruates too.
Trampoline heat
content's roster, edge on brink fully charged with
like ingredients — fits where? — totally nook
noneness of you ... palatial recess
see succumb Quite  A  Mix
to construct assignments that turbulence tosses overboard
not as completely unrelated as you might like.
Matter infinite everywhere in movement:
break out of this pattern? —
difference *contrived*, wet fecund knob allow
super head giddy point disavow an inner dedication equal entity
plus cache some in time inside
identifiable copulative pores, lotional ratio
pearlized hermeneuts afire!
Wishful hypotenuse jumps on me with excitability speed
tight sign het up effaces before A-1 got tore up visible face
agitated ceiling when all you creatures
want to do is stop pressing on its precipice.
Genderless tottering worth hone load
the stretchless figure tops scatter, jollies
at once — fine elision curve inspires circumference
volunteering ovals cavort discretion
precipitation in intervals posture melts
to flashes only inner filiation.
Lucky Touch give self-annoying depth charge
funnel digits pride next what puddle
rotaried, fastening rhythmical velocity valves
inside miniature understrict
epidermis embarrasses mixed signals.
And tremendous vicinity precludes exclusion, quiescent
effervescents spanning the splay bowed thrall

## PRIMUM MOBILE 5

vent crease cylinder pats in the foyer —
calm goal contra null drop to slope
slope for its bodies' ecstatic corona of motion,
     psych off stalks out bodily self-construing intern in turn
below is better armature embodies made bed on
initials voice, affection's *primum mobile*:
                    the subject body inside objective has a mind
                    of its own hosing thrill.
     And pronouned ganglia
                    rib cameo filament wilts
                    to privacy above hers —
fleshed donor disarms skin prayer extreme!
     STATE OF THE HEART — impregnating eyes
shorter horizon eloped in full sparkish floriation
to wake up & keep awake in another body fuzz adjacent lack
                    of kissing déjà vu concern incarnate
practically revised.
     Interseen body-wise ceaseless near ...
                    elsewhere I'm know not ...
                              tidy ruby kiss except
                              threshold prohibits
sideways tongue
rehabilitates please &
                    bring face body
                    makes stops govern
natural injunctive weds into
transitive circle after.
     Value plumbs the 'bodying clue' puckers sate erase
charm sparing dilate for its vehemency =
                    purging velveteen merits moving face
                    pillow straight power toward artifice
reopening will cure it.
     Getting tip turn
traversing, unhooked scoop incessance renegotiates
                    back drop seizure hybrid cavity by
hours want to motion matter — sleeves consuming
satiety longing vent deposits harbor the restless
specialist in *slowing down* toreadors of night!
     Size needs need volumed infinity arcs built up

           mash & passion a carriage I like
skin-enclosed parts; they don't have to be outside of the body
but they do have to be skin-enclosed — hint at initiated
           exit elides for sure capital letters
save me a seat stimulating the other action spots.
    And fantasy redeems repeal when mere skin color
kisses merry melts around breath obeys
pinwheel emotive uppance: could this be insinuation? —
           lightly skin complete sleeping over
           directability go-betweens on strike,
    free pleases — distance seamless empowered
           eagerness *surrounded* lather lapse so it's
nude lobe reactivates spine button magnetic revelation:
           Give me a place to fall off & we will move
the earth orifice flocks to empty seats.
    Repetition gives me hives, body parts
an immediate subject or cause the more apparently violated body
           fuses only silliest fit:
           Millennium — flesh — now —
           hushing crisis spans absolve that wets again
utterly unlike milk fleshed habitation organs
painted on linked by their little fingers.
    And intertissuel stinting secedes, who knows, gesture
           ≠ space parts missing you requalified:
who repeals? —
unconsummated franchise demise out slackens
logician trophies in the covert heap.
    Doubled back minimally sculpting taste
could resurrect playhouse of an annex with dream out
into the fat divinity; tap your toes & glide —
time is not vertical,
    & everything swerves everything
salute to curve fund sane heart eases
inactivity adventure at all tilting
severest event.

## PRIMUM MOBILE 6

Inform many cares you candid above
treehouse chocolated panoply — lap thin white rope garland bed
interior so it's me, where's your wand? —
                              iridesced squeeze box lulls elect;
        little tips scream on, antennae friendliest navel yield my
                        every yearn steam licks at solace *say* so
                                        speech dispels inamorata
                        doubts egg yolk whistling out of the
                        Oh unjointed title teeth surveil —
I live in the meat, I won't close my eyes,
        final fiat wish is king adepted
                        fidelity also craves union resumption of
turbulence still vague to limbs — let nothing separate me:
                        desire's notary desire accumulates IOUs
                        deliberate powder caring,
        erect stop disappear: temptation is an apparition
as duplicity pick-me-up surveils inside putative lids
                        purpose resalivates
                        corporeal affective pulsation white cache
pastels disseminate lamplights to my wishes.
        Optional careless tornado of soundwaves' vocabulary now
includes silk, the ribs are boasting, heavy matters
                        to stripe for, request sudden to
                        imperative nonchalance I'm enjoining so first
a couple of other things score lyrically white tints of
ribboned in its penchant — to who?, *florid optionality.*
        Sap cheeks the regally embroider dream mind ventilating
pronoun speed as cautiously as ass went on swimmingly
                        limbed into salience — echo soars:
come on snake, let's crawl in a blush light.
        Pronoun coquette interposing fact & inter-fact inwardly
dictates vertical pillow *removes,* I mean, *chooses*
in anticipation of circumnavigation — grandeur crevices! —
                        hard, delicate
measuring the insufficiency of blockage wettened overseer:
        gigantized slim disfavor fantasies invent, *width* penetrant
                        insures your felt thought rectified
                        urges punctuated through you
sparks change your mind I do mean trapping

loosen silvered mine tactile shibboleths.
    Rhythm is vertical, the women's language seems to have
                prevailed — true or false?: frequent world
on wheels clasped off, interior accents stroke deletes
             rehearse sift pink subject crux —
           my language is nothing
more identitarian elastic nubility to point power off equals
gaudy unanimous ply.
    Oh posthumous flipping habits touch off multiple chapstick
scintillate surface up so fast same-sex vocables lost in
haze machinery — put your mouth into
self-medication, solo quite signs at own's risk
unique enough to explode invented havoc disseminating
their lips bracing torment burst from weight!
    Ball & chain takes wing legerdemain
           relinquish everyone's favorite! —
if it opened any wider you'd be its name-tag; *whose* gaffe? —
how do I want attach what? — got to come to a
        rotate head to pop the quick & the dire,
     while asleep all body hair's self-absorbent deadline
         disappears, I pry angles
stupefacial — creamed retroactively 'en travestie'
a whole body sigh prowess socket, name head gives
        almost a me is me, I myself, narcotic spread;
    worthy self-miracling delecti baggaged particle deed
I do one up one up my wants for love to one
           all too of them I = I
      sum invites mouth consummate mask,
Unescorted  Private  Face  Tghs — do I imitate absurdly
      private mirror tongue permit me up now
courtesy avatars bang that head that doesn't bang
intangible privacy.
    And let there be you I *have* for you 's OK.
       so hot heat who can
       how one can they do be more
intimately wet? — satiny postural swab permission skin purrs
tender *andante* assortment anointing sweetheart bell-curve
       of delectation treaties primer lips to bed,
   membrane of flame donor darling darkeyed

## PRIMUM MOBILE 6

                  discover this sift hello to you
                            bobbing for flesh
                 liaison ignition loveliness amasses
largesse *du coeur* recirculating.
     Cull mouth fond ploy in me
downstairs housebound absorption obtrudes too closely in
body takes daze who decos the latent fuck
synapse reproach feast over
                     affections Now I Do
as ambitious unnerved angels.
      Squeeze protractor after that, enviable kindling
the slightest touch of dirt vagrant aim
                   intact love rightly composed
                   trespass potentialities eligibly handed:
inclusive person flooding promise, sheared face buys
majority intimacy wedding crowd compressed
                             to halo the labyrinth
             & it sounds self-derivative;
    & fuselage likeness trick to safety lust
perpetual lap to thank us: do you know which one
you want where? — squeegee hips propulsion
               forth & forth, manners a fallacy
               your neck could accommodate irruptive levers
               with little white variety of locution
volition on chest.
     I was the flank has bedlam love how only
                 how far will some go
exit arms that'll be suffragette sufficious this I
promise: flame-thrower equal
anonymity's reticence — Me? — the collected self, the selected
self — ex-men unfitfully yours; only me, the sectarian
on the emotions, the manifest prejudice of her body you dress
as an edible plexus; are you doing it or are you acting it out?:
                 solitude aptitude ditto
for person enticer much avail.
      Dear standpoint: fuck lottery *not* just body / object
                 Courtesy sparks in retreat
                 sweat-shop me out of this; dwelling legs
                 entrust our root pill ample widened care:

## PRIMUM MOBILE 6

disagree to privacy problemist virtue sleep chamber
                                   renominated all out as unstayed
                              total swaying grace hum heart's part
performed solubly spoken bargain over re-memorizing self excuses
                         recoup about anything vain mammal heat
intentionally unfragmented enough.
        And pencil me in at least we need to own
our own licked marks melt succeed
                         dear white late present is earlier than that
                         this nestling torso won't go through
                         meatgrinder dispurposed —
you're here, but later juniors wish size expelled;
        & the horizon has movie stars I can't remember what
                         flesh too diminutive fails
                                        the erase of
                         impermeable pluperfect risk unequals
distance move by move.

## PRIMUM MOBILE 7

Body's snow mortised the dark
convex satisfaction nominee a little higher elsewhere
gravity this false oval hover ceases the top
                    flush with transparence
                                a rush to
                    slant seize refracts back simple syrup.
        Somatic coasting oval mood maze inhabits —
rep attraction progressed, double-yoked center pinkburn
                    in crux spot crush
                    my business is downstairs
or eat flesh swoonishly, encyclopedic quickset
                        mitigates letters crimson embarrassed,
        single finesses naked, not counterfeit; preposition ignored
                    pinkish merengue pleases such
visions of a liberated cone intrudes the hoping high-heeled
counterfoil by definition hands fallen off
burnt-up currency in fact satisfaction proximity precludes form.
        Abdication invisible pure witnesses reverse
                    yolking confidential poise air inebriate upon
the less compromised distance: empty carmine hands
benign blurred as edible to effort, relationally sloping
                    the foamlike form of work,
        bath upends correct nurse open lieutenancy wayward in
duplicate vestige evaporates at the touch of valedictory
                            *laid open* fact mirage —
they're not as done feeling its object relinquished.
        Uncommonest veer by little and little
                                liberate incognito
                    sheen luck shape intrinsic silk
piton escapade connectives miniaturize the dark.
        Are rampant liking
                    alcove stupend impatient, the unlikely likely
object has exit pieced together a honey of a ridge: how much
mercy may the spiral unspool closer?, are you larging me now?:
                        temperamentally horizontal sense interrupts
                        custody wishes meshed acute
passion grenades quarantine our regular body.
        Intrinsic face negates place — portables can listen
                    long heatedly rudderless center of gravity's

synchronous plunge invisibly spins, a yoke teetering
                              widener between geometry, tacit digits
will not be pinned down.
        And ideal unselfed brings heaven right into
                        *abandon forensics* —
                        perfect siteless easy to easy
pistil bliss shape orbiting inside each other
multiply my proverbial mud unemployment.
        Sense of touch — Soft Twist — cannot be grasped
sparking the wide preponderant, the inadmissible
perpetual rubato loves me; I'm leaving myself out:
                                        the thoughtlessness
that shimmers I was too saturated to notice —
                        the untasking flesh-intoxicant tells all,
        and honey mad wobble abounds
                        no latch no shield: Don't bounce! —
                        I lost interest in physical reform —
florid self-magnetizing spies lunge sweetly reassembled enough
                        embrace shattered mathematics;
        come or come from pined exempt twosomes —
                        come, come, come! — confectionary stilts
the greatest kidnapper overflows, address boundary's
knee leans the hand forward
                        if my heart could only talk,
        nude dispatch rebuilt Other foments romance
coax in between intricate incognito to prevent tears
I get slowly fired fan on hands & knees without subtraction
*double* this rendezvous, came up for oral arguments;
        unique nape go otherness loving motion skin
                        is earthquake lips confederate with palms —
                        torso treaty apart uncoyed wet
                        distinction exultancies, granted 'I'
                                although Say Si Si
saliva signature One And One do everything else.
        Preceptual silk & dues, soft you, rapid
                        meltage heart-shaped hours entreaty up
                        bliss in blank beheld heart own face & favor;
        Deep Aura Endearment Be Tender Heart Of Thunder Con Amour
                        I change eyes with give me you you

another flow flows the inbetweenness into this
other slender lined reciprocal infinity around compactness.
    Epitomize eased near-jointed pace of wish breathing wrong
by aim abolish the Rule at the first sign-attenuated cut
of Facing, their amorous bodies, self-substituting
               captives' horizontal matinee
               plural extravagance kisses more than
               sentences keep low if you steep love:
rabbit ears oneself, the final incision of the snowflake decline,
    and if what then, huge's doodling
positive tinder seditious behold bliss hounds
               at face value delect this fact —
               Would You Believe Me:
triple-bodied pushing switch verbs' bliss via distance.
    And ambiguous genitalia grace my prone —
some company spatio-surrogates divisibly faced —
it's going to feel like a beesting, the unremissable
               coup de grace very naked name propounded
redbud embrace
so my heart could feel sat-is-fied,
    True Flip To
sawteething the submersible thaw job, pleasure by design
rapport days delicacy shimmies asunder
delight delight delight, actually blood does get homesick —
               fidelities fold fondly aggregated
               to melange itself, to melee itself:
SUDDENLY TOOK US BY SURPRISE, Don't answer that —
we're just as good as night;
    & Become her who one was!: jiggle in trust
               dreamy templates ever dear avoid being
indefinite credit as much as possible heart trumps ecstatic
lossproof affect naked outer spoke tongue dedoubled enough
Love means Christmas, that rubric smile.
    Wistful lap's lily law cocoon advantage advantageously
               at nipple ended my mend enough us mouth —
consent milked the power apparatus of enamorment, contra-dance
of the heart as triangle of plenty
hearth's breath buckle onto night;
    & spatialized languor facts trust esteems

delight pacted imagine to possess
value = match
gift empowers, indivisible with susmission?:
delicious authority dwelt none
binds together gift-you-hyperbole.
The night's body embosses favor ultra to reravish
adhesive felicity, positive, simultaneous
polkadots & moonbeams leave alive,
radical moisture *luxus*, plea eclipsed, walk on air & more
infinitely narcotic nerve shine insured.

## PRIMUM MOBILE 8

Affect altitude of familiarity crystallized fabric light
bends *you* aggrandize without glass, nonchalant levies smitten
                    surveying spin — feelings magnetize method
worry bliss is maps, with housebroken slippage
                    adequation to doctor distance:
    only joinless salve wound cult
swoon ends our curated hearts portable skies impeach
flagellactive spectacular ocular white & black balcony holdouts:
the tighter I grip, the higher my atmosphere.
    It's High Time Timely Night — just guise
                    certain higher dittos completely out of
sideways prenominative monopoly losses thwarted.
    Advent shines — Latent Encore Happiness Show
                    neck certificate hurt chance
                    but hands aren't important, longitudinal
sighing 'in case' must be homeopathic memories,
    picture plane its salve as theater breasts clasped up
high once more, bouquet hunch all solid literally flexing compass
at all oversold on decor primer beyond.
    And I hate minutes, tunnel silence curb
absent immense chance floating monotone
nature fruits prick the Outlandish inflations;
    happenstance silhouettes ballet
                    navigates like sugar in bottle —
                    counter-touch disapparition
rotatingly calm dome swoons.
    It's worth some venture connotation, a symmetry of
proportion impulsive tactical cliff plus impish creditor
                    success, freely expand upon tangential
small-scale blue — what a dear ravishing;
    fixturable spread of blood breeding body perseverance —
maybe if there *was* a utopia ... promontorily inexact interslashed
                    Tied In Blue — rebus hope
semicircle in orbit as nuance.
    And Its A Dream —
validations counterposed to organicist yearning all process *coats*
                    fortress size arena succulence
                    walls of foil parentheses whisper,
    vernal soon prosecute coupon dreamt as an ovoid attachment

the facts cheat
rarefaction — a slight vacuum
horizontally spelling best & to check all
porous zeal saturate in aloha
ribbons to duty light pins its accomplice;
& we've demobilized the success story — Registrappage
spun webs around the minute Elsewhere
so that you see this is no news — proximate fetters hub
its logic to train me some heredity.
Numberless frolicking proof particular
flagrant mosaic ceded iterative paradise —
zip back & enjoy improper terms
guaranteed same two curvature.
And spilt plane revulsion:
I gratified the pendulum discretion
all else making shit speeding constitutive leveller,
home is where the head bangs conditions:
foam a shimmering despite, chiffon reverb alighted
turbulent parole atoms in the whittled down
to a fierce thinness, over and out, wash away our tasks.
Take your hesitation by the top
pleats swell conversely low
jettison line divided by heat
careen replaces — it's more
unobtainable when it's continuously imprecise effervescents.
Near to far ratio, cocoon horizontotalled silly;
human spells hassle limbs bite
abandon, that great assignment, the dream of ambition
or the ambition to dream — psychic flowering
bedtime ceased corral.
We are not impermeable — swallow spends aesthetically
jointed — any halt that spreads, stymied fleshing
notches underbody — shack it up
too seriously to skirt some free-for-all
casual point tournamented unitards galore.
Bodily admitted distrust, precaution's stability
wipes the belly from your eyes make useful opposers
live to multiply waxy reams I'm singeing, frustration follies
float craves themself OK quartering as if

hands it you We Do;
& the indignity of our position in the body
voice-over in back makes our continued melancholy untenable
            through pockets inner to thigh
            from behind you broke the only heart
genie landscape returns to the head — excellent
fondness upturned.
      Proximity rubbing words have a face which talks
            Other = All far care ours truly
erotogenic the possibilities, disclaimer vibrating
            moisture suborns sense donation
stronghold,
      JUST ENOUGH SO ENOUGH —
a svelting *tendresse*, I feel flashes, unpretending at halves
            offset privacy debarred new melt flesh
overthrows your trembling in our affection to become necessary
caramel of *unlearn it* effect.
      And I made an emotion about leaks
apparent wide to improvise
art tampers desire fondly fecund creases
absorb neither pure hands nor a sweetened heart
            soothing submerged & no less remoting
vain leisure regrouping the facial commotion.
      We exist, my body, unleavened color legend omits
vital noise of the collapsing bed cordoned off contrary fuse
            frequentably duration appeals to vises
distances accommodate, twilit extra after hues.
      Hello downward or outside silky plug
I'm sucked out — wheeled dry adieu violate blessing's neglect
            experience act is not an aim
box ahead, graded differently, secrets communes boudoir
proportional vogue feelings chamois by the yard.
      Stocking absorbed it — time pass time — it pass
            perimeter worship humming surrender
            live surprise evolve toward
innocence instead of cheerleaders — purpose's pedigree parents;
      thanks for piping by, subpoena unfulfill caress
respect their immobility — glands make a big fuss
about their destiny privated out angel exhaust

short wave from anybody — I burned myself up
with expectation gaze collectivizes;
the crime is imperfection, transference taken captive —
*do over!* — legs in the disappearance
pestering curtail perspective parties through & through
flood at the valves of my hope, now you can't
afford to be yourself.
Trimming training perfect tears to pieces pierced
for production: dress rehearsal as what, nest rehabbing? —
I must be *fond* of superior wetting? —
silhouetted a ghost of a chance
potentated, of silly passive inconveniences
behind your retort in the wings.
The persecuted are ascendent: louvers system light fervor
possibility cannot have too many levels
to your personalities' appellation of cure
put the limits of their acquiescence in boldface:
create a conscience in the night! —
books still dwarf the salves,
gravitationally guaranteed lights that streak, lights
that spin asteriskation
through presumptively improper means: *subtract lies*
love distances, not 'merely' objective
glaucomaed distance;
elongate the lack of limits sobbing closes up
files on the present, luminous packed a bit, the pro-dawn
wand modulates the most credulity
severest flowering certifies in awe.
It is a finishing touch — sufficient else
future fleecing, twilight is wrong
nights — uncanniness temporally bereaved.

## PRIMUM MOBILE 9

Oh inclusions to advantage
                              here = below
                    evaporation instances — one of those things
that I had long since despaired of understanding
starting from tonight — history mouth amplifier jettisoning
subjectifying
                         everywhere, nowhere,
      hazed outlet with such distant perspectives
inamorata wasn't the trick sleepers equa-planed into
rationality — self-motivating euphoria baffling a star
takes the, ah, train erased full defrauding circumstance?
      Nix embraces encore ravenous twilight
clue to this debate curve, members recording vex
                    posit *used up* concealment between
horizon cadres.
      When did imaginary curry its whole? — refuse to correct up
                    top is foam feint Winged Attraction:
achievement is not an achievement, extract the whole fauna
sin dressed in foresight
                         astonished mass Corps De Ballet,
      tracing sense clear I mercy shape
                    breast scrabble logic lodging sleep
lozenged without end; zero mistrial persistent spore.
      Solacing dispelled auto-da-fé part content
                    human nature rivetingly inorganic
                    target corrects its own avoidance
~~except details~~ put in motion.
      Once else where do evacuate other understanding
                    blankness emptied away from no longer
propinquitous disowning regal root, myself with space
like cotton underneath nothing human matters.
      Any unfulfilled reasons discord exalts the false
                    subliminal really aloha
                    exit remonstrance — lots iota
tyrannical surface guests in gains
                         meaning from creature fleshy geophysic
empire futures;
      pink node button the past out, unregrettably slid
our book away tender implies permanent oblique establishment

body cut my franchise however fragilely resurrected
scarcely angled stature evaporates.
    And communal honesty — end sweet waxen fortunate glue
                  frailty levitates representation
                  is the representation of exploitation:
Wishfulness's forfeit endangered specifics —
                  the sense is clear enough
to the ear & only becomes puzzling when one begins to think
about it, every reject same at peace to please,
      no art on wet leash — normal purse exit unsuccessive
                  lustier maintenance role — gears suffocate
                  doctrinal black crows nature wears thin:
lust over logic parties alone, it's — all — that
names nosh forehead soon impeach
'time out of mind' furled in capitals.
      Ideal inner loan better Obsession letters
                  excuses posit ideal
unction fun & mind my energy disposes of
me;
      & suddenness dispossessed, blame indefinite lexicon
                  termed truss exstress
                  who *lays bare* sugared pause whole
                  contemplates index leisure pressure
defrauding ghost briefs bonding depth.
      Didn't you expire? — solitude multitude mocks these
                  objects in circles crepe under
to cope floats best the infinite of taught
decanters gonna vanilla stitch withdrawal together:
                  was yesterday really necessary? —
moon took requests;
      & the personal is a technicality —
bliss lamp cocoaed signature dwells on how easier
organ levels, false eventing palpably all veritable
flickering, boosted innocence by folds.
      The hole is unfinished, jellies this quiet (!) —
                  utterly interdict size most bubbles away
                  social finish, verify intent
                  in body intransitive prose brain treason
                          salve grown on me

so soon as soon as felt got the Instead my truly
free friend-populated seconds on scissors experience
indents, no scars Reconcile Underneath in seam, no guilt
is self-spreading — get lips & mind in sync.
    And Poly Dream Pandora's fact
                black task tongue unifies
                by total hand soothing crime —
Yes, I'm still here; I am so very, very disappointed —
virtue got a rash.
    Dearless creature, social spiral units, disaster-
free bio-graph-fee
                peak of its parts
paper lance nipple in promotion cut-outs of fate
empowered dictation to flesh with new tongues,
        virtually tribal trouble vice fights —
                          higher machine omnibus
nature animal pull up the tart, everyman nameplate
to make dominion bed.
    Oh Say grace warrants Promise — a certain brand of abandon
germinate sensations of independence call a heart a heart
flush with closer swans expire.
    Privilege finite eternalizing ardor enabling
                abdicate be spent full glue splice contagious
relata ovation 'in favor of the love object'
                plural aura conciliates amok
louvered at the not conclusion heart.
    Swastikas in ashes *absorb* usage — tribe light nullify
                enlicit prognostics, daredevil orchestrators
never pigeonholed — the contrary prevails come what may.
    Censor aura, it lights up, demands sexual inadventure
                bargains with infinity notes dribble subject
to mystery adhesive dressage: old bodies gain credence too.
    In Time And Place — Pure Suasion — Stage Setter
*bull's-eye* bred, infinite opinion's less lower
magnificent all compact in others — SKY'S OPEN!:
                at least same-sex multitude appeased
vanity democracy in matriarchate matriculation.
    Sweet Ending choice as deprivation lacuna
plurals can write unalterable changes by themselves, limits

of all to each 'hems in' plural body's grammatical habits
desire renders succulent — outside reproduces inside
niche when you have to niche,
    supplicate any everyone thought vs. theater
aplomb chide whole unknown's dissatisfied parts'
                  exhilarant lures; nobody beats no identity:
cement evanesces hypotactic suture to telescope mishap.
    And redeem your threats — Oh, human beings, can't get
next to you babe — girlish calls for a sperm boycott;
                slack stagelit self-arbitration
yoke scarce darkroom,
    social actor's tender forgers nubile sovereign barbarianized
                communal say-so vitiated general sugar
                off hived hope authority making sure:
The answer to WHY is not NO.
    How politically bent is your anomie? — kick the interest
down code bath I'm not *exiled down* — no, canopied I'm *occupying*
this as home master everybody slave apparatus unto
bliss absconding capacity blooms.
    Experience carries no exit visa —
communal box life worlded detriment, be my direct object
                of power, perhaps forever, diffuses fidelity
homesickness experiment appealing
                imparadised, imprisoned!
    Transfusion
eject buttons on your preferences, I really can't
                think of anything else —
buzz of progress to forget the many zoological images
                implied consent *Entirely* — and you?: oasis
                vigilant law used to fantasize
ceiling lowers to quiet;
    bathysphere with legs, you are my superstition
                spurns wrong to have the multiple partner
                break off to in'sight a desire of more
                ample signification history history erases
that facts should heart void accomplice
*every all which is not us.*

$\mathrm{A}$ND real time is dead; proof terrorizes
                                all the way in or all the way out de-tasking
                                        heterocosm leaps out
nothing night in the after.
    Span participles gist, encore every magnified
hand me over bodiless scour-the-world diversion
we hear prescriptionable organs of comprehension:
    salute versus horizon, unsubsumable upside
whipped concentrics
                                amortize the glance all inamorates
                                pinpoint daisy chain color puffs
to infinity sucking plenitude surveillance
    Earning its satin scramble under
                                phraseless difference defeat speech
                                glory took heat reconvening orchid pages:
splendid hyperbolic innocence.
    Dreambulatory script off passion impresses gesture cure
                                *no* reckoning, the dream spawns
                                the truth the cell is
                                strictly a nostalgic thing for me now,
        sugar raised revved posthumous
                                sensible space cancels before impossible
speed under canon limelit to ample zero hush.
    The little king pickets the flame
                                sum hypothesize — pearl perfect
superiorate us — the inostensible irradiated overnight.
    Inner plus & surplus proof ovation immobilizing
disenchantment preconcerted with itself — generous
                                generous customize elation celebrated dark
                                downed front tangent intact,
    & out of sight, out of mind — lap me in fold apotheosised
to a yesplus lingua(l) anti-never, news is a book
whitened out abandon;
        it's time to mutate always
                                is always erotic web-spinning sonar
                                a present-tense exhalation is within
                                marginal legible above nerve memory heart
                                site binds: I *do not* see through words
    sight as dreams gratefully certain.

Sin no facts, mostly the usual crush of possibilities
adverse concentrics recede
cut rear rumor of circumference — if it slipped on my bed,
I wouldn't eat the other it — pulse just lips
convening reproaches in ever-smaller chamber.
And how very vanishingly little jet lamblike spell of flesh
disembarking soothe
infinite night's chance sentence eclipse
writes invulnerable sentences.
So abundant arrestless — who's melt? — pinwheeling on
and in breezes mammal's prime prevalent lotion!
Embrace Me — get the skin in it, honey? — flash
add up to alabaster
legato lullaby network in one eclipse
compose lips never algebra *without* addition,
glimmer accidents mixed in
the radiating out hyacinth stuff — pixilated
shoosh of baby matter honeysuckle corners conflate — OK,
anacoluthon me some harmonious totalities:
threshold absorbs abolition, time cures inquisitors.
Urine shouldn't common: venom's liquor of love
meal plans off Mdnght Wish for bubble bathing monozygotes
accord laps lessons abandon
expiates still wet elective facility in amatory soil.
Your emotions or your evidence — grace spools minus hole
come to please reverse unique mystique, *stir* self assert *sluices*
'getting beyond' hurdle size self stripping ebbs —
women delete the men
ballast depicts winning.
Shatter plus impresses incognito salute
not love like any like
a sauce as unless
I shall always want everything, I
got the tongue out of my throat —
immobile claims reciprocate
reward in the infinitive mucus temptation.
Point neither promise without intoxication
— it's not inevitable, it's sweet; overall sudden
'meta trade off' is the whole body pure assertive melt

# PRIMUM MOBILE 10

flesh for itself, no ceiling? — ... kisses
leap without beyond will & nill impossible immersion in
chronic redundant hope;
    closure, such vanity — the genre of too much
stitchless goodnight science makes an unmaking
difference interval annuls — preparatory lace
speech, prolific pinwheel, love melts friends
all in the punctuation.
    The heartbeat definitely to extinguish
logician's sleep degreeless carefully disreputable in orbit
           lost in tiniest fold lip so fact o —
           circumlocutory stilts edit existing body
if you toss on a marshmallow, swerve extends out:
                  new mayhem *never enough*
           stirs multiple hearts burn
christmases of the heart in syllables.
    Antisuggestibility glows attenuate the immbolizer
           astonishment pulls at — *then* — *our* —
the pigments
           I pack up a glance — pettiness crams
           pink included publicity subscribe this
farewell-soaked farewell;
    dream microphones *bellissimo*
           the stage, visible from a distance —
           high night completeless travestied surprise
           storm relaxes proximity ink at leap year
lipsynching flash in dark.
    Kiss the book some — future — atoms
           axis at silly indefinitely diversify
calendar tossle, inclouded, to *hire* change;
    & sweet dreams resisted fix-up treats without
           perfecter exile delight — NO CORNERS — zig-
           zag porous luxury propulsion
takes the arc through circumstance farewell magnetizes:
           Illegitimate exclusion! —
stakes contracted them all.
    Oh let's have socialism relentlessly gentle
           praxis singed undoing most distant
privacy overreacts, parachuting the past.

Oh deign some spinning works its norm
                precipitated in a moment —
wait for the book enarmed unionizing future
prejudging multiple unscissored surprise!
      Cartwheeled tactics dip your fingers in the vow
                buried my birthday
                red partisan shocks proof infinite to atoms
                architected Pandemonium cut-to-fit-the-mouth,
      we're in the happy neutral counter-automata — Dreamsdo-
cometrue — matriarchal matrix be anything
to annex willing total all is one
end of the world dance luscious by-the-book.
      Give me a bigger cage — rootless headlong faction burst
                delectable standard — *elsewhere* —
geometry at total, raptures diaphanous closeout diagram
generalizes fingers arraigned as chocolate,
      adorable base alias reality image refusal emboldens
fetus using your body without your consent —
its sweet front lathed with
this is something else;
      propitious heat headless opportunity
                in order of promises, dirigibles of promise
                we neatly did fill their blanks —
valedictory honeymoon burns in the pagination.
      The nightmerest fantasia fitted from blame priority melts
less to write paraphrased hyperbole retraversal than it us —
                *ryang ner vah plew!* —
                equally read abode pink
cope lush coda abruptless,
      risk disappears closing perfume
                row of exclamation points
                unleash all tenderness suspends future
                to voice vote to heat
                for hope lay still late
let's start all over stars.

# APPENDIX

*Paradiso* Cantos & *Lip Service*

| Canto | Section of *Lip Service* |
|-------|--------------------------|
| 1 | Earth 1 – 5 |
| 2 | Earth 6 – 10 |
| 3 | Moon 1 – 3 |
| 4 | Moon 4 – 7 |
| 5 | Moon 8 – 10 |
| 6 | Mercury 1 – 5 |
| 7 | Mercury 6 – 10 |
| 8 | Venus 1 – 5 |
| 9 | Venus 6 – 10 |
| 10 | Sun 1 – 3 |
| 11 | Sun 4 – 5 |
| 12 | Sun 6 – 7 |
| 13 | Sun 8 – 10 |
| 14 | Mars 1 – 3 |
| 15 | Mars 4 – 5 |
| 16 | Mars 6 – 7 |
| 17 | Mars 8 – 10 |
| 18 | Jupiter 1 – 3 |
| 19 | Jupiter 4 – 7 |
| 20 | Jupiter 8 – 10 |
| 21 | Saturn 1 – 3 |
| 22 | Saturn 4 – 7 |
| 23 | Saturn 8 – 10 |
| 24 | Fixed Stars 1 – 3 |
| 25 | Fixed Stars 4 – 5 |
| 26 | Fixed Stars 6 – 7 |
| 27 | Fixed Stars 8 – 10 |
| 28 | Primum Mobile 1 – 2 |
| 29 | Primum Mobile 2 – 3 |
| 30 | Primum Mobile 4 – 5 |
| 31 | Primum Mobile 6 – 7 |
| 32 | Primum Mobile 8 – 9 |
| 33 | Primum Mobile 9 – 10 |

Thanks to the editors and publishers, parts of *Lip Service* originally appeared in:

*Aerial, Arras, Atelier, Big Allis, Boo, Caliban, Central Park, Columbia Poetry Review, Croton Bug, Deluxe Rubber Chicken, Denver Quarterly, Disturbed Guillotine, Fence, Filling Station, First Offense, Generator, The Gig, Hole, I am a Child: Poetry after Bruce Andrews and Robert Duncan, Intimacy, Juxta, Lift, Lingo, Logodaedalus, lower limit speech, Lungfull, Lyrica, Membrane, New American Writing, No Roses Review, Oasi, Object, Object Permanence, O24H, Phoebe, Proliferation, Purge, Queen Street Quarterly, Raddle Moon, Ribot, Situation, Talisman, Terrible Work, Texture, that:, Torque, Washington Review of the Arts, West Coast Line, Yefief,* and the books *Paradise & Method: Poetics & Praxis* (Northwestern University Press) and *Aerial 9/Bruce Andrews: Contemporary Poetics as Critical Theory* (Edge Books).

Typeset in Dante and Ignatius
at Coach House Printing on bpNichol Lane, 2001

Edited and designed by Darren Wershler-Henry
Copy edited and proofread by Alana Wilcox

To read the online version of this text and other titles from
Coach House Books, visit our website:
www.chbooks.com

To add your name to our e-mailing list, write:
mail@chbooks.com

Toll-free:
1 800 376 6360

Coach House Books
401 Huron Street (rear) on bpNichol Lane
Toronto, Ontario
M5S 2G5